Stranger to My Self

Distributed in the United States of America by The Book Source, Inc. Carson, Virginia

Copyright © 2010 by Jeffrey Abugel

Johns Road Publishing

1290 Johns Road

PO Box 367

Carson, Virginia 23830

Abugel, Jeffrey 1952-

ISBN 978-0-615-38523-5

Library of Congress Control Number: 2010942455

Printed in the United States of America

*For single copy orders of "Stranger to My Self" visit our website: www.the-book-source.com

*For bulk orders please contact: <u>michel.lacroix@the-book-source.com</u> or call 434-246-2127

To William and Juanita,
whose love transcends time and space.

Cover image by Sean Blake (1968-1995)

STRANGER
TO MY SELF

Inside Depersonalization:
The Hidden Epidemic

Jeffrey Abugel

Johns Road Publishing

Carson, Virginia

Contents

Foreword
by the Stranger Inside

You don't know me. But chances are good that we've met before, though only briefly. I was the silent accompaniment to your car crash, the sudden tragic death of a loved one, or the relentless verbal abuse at the hands of those who supposedly loved you. You didn't know it, but I was there to help you, to distance you from that thing that was for the moment too unbearable to be experienced as a part of your real life.

If you are lucky, I spared you some suffering. I took you to a place of no time, no memories, no ego, only briefly, and allowed you to heal. Then, when my work was done, I left.

I am not always so benevolent. I can go astray, forget my purpose, stay too long. When that happens, God help you. For then you become mine and you are never the same again.

I am as old as consciousness itself, and I have appeared under many names, many guises. People once mistook me for lunacy, or demonic possession. Today they call me depression, anxiety, bi- polar disorder, even schizophrenia, and they are wrong. I am greater than any of these. And still, wise doctors, psychologists, priests, and shamans refuse to see me for what I am. There are those who even deny my existence completely, which only feeds my power.

My strength is born of the one thing unique to every human being — the individual self. I exploit its solitude and pierce its stability with impunity. I diffuse the fragile membrane that separates dreams from reality until you're not sure which is which.

In time, you may learn to live with me. As if stricken blind, or immobilized from head to toe, you may adapt to a life that is decid- edly different. You may even think that you are enlightened, having stumbled across some great truth. I don't care how you interpret my power over you, as long as I make you suffer. I am the stranger in- side you. But I will make you feel like a stranger to your self.

In the end, don't look for me in heaven, or in the void that I have revealed to you. You go there alone. For I belong among the living, the thinking. I live in minds only, as I have in yours.

Let me tell you this. I did not have to ruin your life. You let me do it. Had I been pneumonia, cancer, depression, dropsy, or any of a thousand other afflictions of mind and body, you would have learned all you could in your efforts to fight me, or embrace me. But my deceptive nature, my contradictory makeup held you at bay. Nourished by ignorance, sustained through denial, I stayed with you until your dying day. But the power to expel me or accept me was always in your hands. You are human, with all the strengths and frailties inherent to your species. Me? I am neither devil, nor saint, nor illusion. I exist within you, to serve you, change you, empower you, or ruin you. In the end, the choice is yours.

But first, you have to know me. This is my story, my gift. My reward for your long search for me, and for your self.

Introduction:
Hell Paid Forward

Some time long ago, when I was young and on the verge of adulthood, my soul departed.

It shot out suddenly, forcefully, spewing like puss from an acrid sore. Or, perhaps it was more an implosion that only killed within, forcing "me" further inward until, like a black hole, its destructive density annihilated its captive. Whether some thing attacked me from without, or within, doesn't matter. It only needed a few moments to take everything from me, everything inside of me.

In time, some shattered fragments of "me" returned, like metal shavings drawn to a toy magnet. I realized that I was not dead. I was still breathing. But I would never again think or feel the things that human beings are supposed to think or feel, simply by nature of being human.

Time passed, and I viewed my actions, my internal and external lives, as if observing from the grave. I was visible, but not present. And I could find no one, no other human who felt as I did.

I discovered a comfort in writing, literature, and the arts, which reveal the mind's hidden inner workings. I read voices and viewed images that on occasion reflected my inner world, but never completely.

I was neither depressed, nor anxious, nor happy, nor unhappy. I was not crazy because I knew that something was not right from the very moment that it became *not right*.

Things happen to people, I reasoned. Usually they happen to someone else. But this time it had happened to me, far too early in life. And it was something no one else understood. I would have opted for cancer, or war wounds, or polio if given a choice.

Instead, this thing had taken my soul but it had left me to idle here among the living, a vacuous robot with the task of still living an interminably long life before me. I wanted nothing more than to be an old, old man, with my life behind me.

For eleven years, a strange and terrifying mental state occupied my being, and I could not find one piece of information that described my condition or anything like it. Convinced that I was going insane, I eventually learned that I wasn't. But I suffered in ways that even now are near impossible to describe. At times this condition lifted enough for me to attempt to continue my life, as if I were just like anyone else. At other times it got worse, and I went to doctor after doctor looking for answers.

I visited more than a dozen doctors, several psychiatrists. Each prescribed a medication that knocked me out for a few days, and then, after weeks, brought me up to a functional level. A level wherein I resumed the lower-level suffering that allowed me to be a student, or take on a job. Happiness, well being, a functioning ego were not even secondary considerations. Maintaining the façade that convinced others I was normal, even intelligent or funny, was all that mattered.

Sometimes, my humanity returned through drinking. The ever-present viewing of my own life became a film noir, a black-and-white movie with dramatic outcomes, tears, and emotional overload, before the hammer of the hangover struck and killed the projectionist.

Decades of a lifetime passed. And after years of traveling the country, moving from job to job, relationship to relationship, apartment to apartment, in one remarkable meeting with one remarkably human and humane specialist, I learned that what I suffered from had a name.

I learned that the condition was not uncommon, but just the opposite — it was the third most common psychiatric symptom, after depression and anxiety. I learned that this strange unfathomable state of mind had been studied in Europe and in the U.S. for more than 100 years, and that there were dozens of clinical papers that had very clearly described every one of my symptoms. People suffered with it in silence for fear of being called crazy. Sometimes, they took their own lives as one final demonstration of control.

I had been robbed of more than a decade of my life, wandering like a blind man only to discover that my eyes still functioned. They were merely covered by a blindfold created by the complacency of doctors who refused to acknowledge an illness outside of their typical retinue of diagnosis and treatment. This thing, this "filth" that had blinded me is called Depersonalization Disorder. The very name described what I had been searching for all along—my self, my personhood, which had somehow been deactivated.

This is the story of a condition endured by millions of people worldwide, most of whom have no idea that it has a name. This book is, to some degree, autobiographical. But who I am, where I come from, the specific path of my life hardly matters except for its resemblance to the lives of so many others. How deeply this filth determined the course of my life will always be a source of wonder for me. Through a time-honored medicine and undiminished "capacity for insight" I was able to live a life of my own, even as others were encountering depersonalization for the first time.

*****

When information about Depersonalization as a symptom and as a chronic disorder began to appear on the Internet in the 1990s I was intrigued. Did the personal stories that people posted reflect my own experience? Who were they? Who diagnosed them? What had they learned, if anything, and had they found a cure?

In 2000, with a willing partner who also suffered from DPD, I created the website *depersonalization.com* (which later became *depersonalization.info*). Inspired by Oscar Janiger, the brilliant psychiatrist who had finally given me a diagnosis nearly two decades earlier, I began to explore depersonalization in earnest.

By this time, clinics had been established in New York and London for the purpose of studying the condition. The English clinic was actually gathering material online—one of the first uses of the Internet as a tool for clinical research. And yet, while interest in the condition began to surge, I learned that the existing literature which astutely profiled the condition in medical, psychological, and even philosophical terms went back nearly a century. More recent research showed it to be more prevalent than schizophrenia and bipolar disorders combined. Then why was the condition so obscure and so inconsequential to doctors, psychiatrists, and therapists? Why was the term not a household word?

For ten years I searched for answers to these questions while also exploring philosophy, literature, and spirituality. I casually operated my website and read hundreds of personal stories with strikingly similar descriptions of experience. I followed the ongoing new research which contributed pieces to a puzzle that had yet to be solved. I spoke with many researchers, experts, and doctors. In time Dr. Janiger and I began gathering material for a book on the subject. To date, there were none. One of the people we approached for contributions to the book was Daphne Simeon, MD, primary investigator at Mount Sinai Medical Center's Depersonalization and Dissociation Research Program. This proved to be fortuitous, for when Dr. Janiger passed away in 2001 at age 83, Dr. Simeon agreed to help me write the first book specifically focused on depersonalization disorder. Our efforts resulted in the publication of *Feeling Unreal, Depersonalization Disorder and the Loss of the Self*, published in 2006 by Oxford University Press (paperback in 2008).

Since that time, depersonalization-related websites have continued to proliferate and articles about DPD have appeared in major magazines. (Pop-up advertisements for "cures" have appeared as well, unfortunately.)

Additionally, two independent, autobiographical films made their debuts: the critically acclaimed *Tarnation* by Jonathan Caouette, and *Numb*, a touching, yet humorous autobiographical account by writer and director Harris Goldberg, previously known for comedies such as *Deuce Bigelow* and *Without a Paddle*. New medical books about Depersonalization Disorder also have appeared in the media flourish.

Still, despite all of these cultural and scientific sign posts, people who suffer from depersonalization often face their greatest obstacles in the very places they seek help—offices of doctors, psychiatrists, and psychologists. They are still met with blank looks from their friends and families and a nearly universal ignorance of the very condition for which they require understanding.

One purpose of this book is to help change that once and for all.

Stranger to My Self distills all that is known up until now about depersonalization as a symptom and as a disorder. I have enlisted the assistance of some of the leading experts in the field to assure that the psychiatric, psychological, and clinical information is current and accurate.

At the same time, *Stranger to My Self* endeavors to bring a human element to the experience of the disorder, through narratives that go beyond the typical case histories found in published medical papers. Depersonalization Disorder includes many subtleties, many nuances. While sometimes these reflect its co-morbidity with other disorders, they also present a clear picture of its complexity and variability as a syndrome in its own right, independent of all others.

Portions of this book retrace a personal path of discovery that has lasted more than three decades. It is, in part, the story of a search for truths about the nature of the individual self, and how those truths may be influenced by brain chemistry, spiritual beliefs, and culture. *Stranger to My Self* is, in a sense, being told by an embedded reporter. Liberated from the bonds and affiliations that may arguably inhibit medical professionals, it attempts to explore all aspects of the depersonalization experience from the inside, through the eyes of those who live it. As such, subjective opinions based on life experience and observation will inevitably emerge, but they will be duly noted as such.

The stories told herein are neither patient profiles nor clinical "composites" taken out of context. They are true accounts from people representing various stations in life, as well as varied depersonalization experiences. Some of us have traveled parallel roads of discovery.

Chapter One of this book is an expanded version of a broad overview article that has served as *depersonalization.info*'s introduction to the topic for nearly a decade. Through the years I have been humbled by expressions of gratitude from scores of people who happened to stumble across the website while trying to determine the source of their misery. On the strength of the comments it has received through the years, *Stranger to My Self* begins with this broad overview, with considerable expansion of each topic presented in succeeding chapters.

1 Through the Looking Glass

I wonder if I've been changed in the night? Let me think. Was I the same when I got up this morning? I almost think I can remember feeling a little different. But if I'm not the same, the next question is 'Who in the world am I?' Ah, that's the great puzzle!

—Alice, in Wonderland

It may happen when you first wake up, or while flying on an airplane or driving in your car. You may link it to years of ongoing, low-level stresses, or to nothing at all. Sometimes it happens after smoking pot or taking Ecstasy. Suddenly, inexplicably, something changes. Common objects and familiar situations seem strange, foreign, like you've just arrived on the planet but don't know from where. It may pass quickly or it may linger. You close your eyes and turn inward, but the very thoughts running through your head seem different. The act of thinking itself, the stream of invisible words running through the hollow chamber of your mind, seems strange and unreal. It's as if you have no self, no ego, no remnant of that inner strength which quietly and automatically enabled you to deal with the world around you, and the world inside you. It challenges the simple being you took for granted. It may follow an acute panic attack, or the fear of it may blossom into a series of panic attacks. In time, it will likely settle into a feeling of "nothingness," as if you were without emotions, dead. But when it hits for the first time, you're convinced that you're going insane, and wait in a cold sweat to see when and if you finally do go over the edge.

What you don't know at the moment is that this troubling experience is distinctly human, experienced briefly at some time or another by as much as 70 percent of college students,[1] and an undetermined number of people of all ages. In its chronic form, popular culture once offered little explanation other than it being part of a nervous breakdown. Some have called it "Alice in Wonderland disease." Philosopher Jean Paul Sartre called it "the filth," psychologist William James dubbed it "the sick soul." It's been linked philosophically to existentialism, and Vedantic Buddhism. Yet to those experiencing it for the first time, it is anything but an enlightened state of mind. This is the world of Depersonalization Disorder.

The term "depersonalization" used in this context has been around for a long time. Back in 1898, a psychologist named Ludovic Dugas coined it as a unique medical condition, having borrowed it from Frederic Amiel, a Swiss diarist who described his own feelings of unreality and detachment by stating in one entry: "I am *depersonalized.*" While the word "depersonalization" is often linked to dehumanizing situations such as life in prison or brainwashing scenarios, chronic depersonalization is an insidious mental condition that often begins on its own, seemingly from nowhere. The individual's perceptions of the self and the self's place in the world somehow shifts into a mindset that is different from the norm, becoming hellish, or sometimes unbearable.

Depersonalization can be a symptom that appears concurrently with many conditions, including depression, anxiety, panic disorder, even schizophrenia. Fleeting depersonalization is what the majority of us experience at some point in our lives—after a life-threatening car crash or the death of a loved one. Psychiatry considers it the mind's way of distancing itself from an unbearable reality. It occurs briefly, with no lasting effect. Depersonalization Disorder, however, is a chronic psychiatric condition that can take a dreadful and long-lasting course. It is the mind's defense against trauma-gone berserk, resulting in a slew of symptoms that do anything but protect the human being from harm.

Despite its seeming obscurity, Depersonalization Disorder has been clearly defined for years (though somewhat buried under the Dissociative Disorders heading) in the *Psychiatric Diagnostic and Statistical Manual* (DSM-IV), the bible of psychiatric diagnoses.

According to DSM-IV, Depersonalization Disorder, in part, constitutes the following:

...a feeling of estrangement from one's self. The individual may

feel like an automaton or as if he or she is living in a dream or a movie. There may be a sensation of being an outside observer of one's mental processes, one's body, or parts of one's body.

...Various types of sensory anesthesia, lack of affective response, and a sensation of lacking control of one's actions, including speech, are often present. The individual with Depersonalization Disorder maintains intact reality testing (e.g., awareness that it is only a feeling and that he or she is not really an automaton.) Depersonalization is a common experience, and this diagnosis should be made only if the symptoms are sufficiently severe to cause marked distress or impairment in functioning.

Depersonalization is also clearly defined in the diagnostic manual used outside of the United States, the World Health Organization's International Classification of Diseases (ICD). Interestingly, the ICD places the disorder under the category of "Other Neurotic Disorders" and defines it as follows:

A rare disorder in which the patient complains spontaneously that his or her mental activity, body, and surroundings are changed in their quality, so as to be unreal, remote, or automatized. Among the varied phenomena of the syndrome, patients complain most frequently of loss of emotions and feelings of estrangement or detachment from their thinking, their body, or the real world. In spite of the dramatic nature of the experience, the patient is aware of the unreality of the change. The sensorium is normal and the capacity for emotional expression intact. Depersonalization-derealization symptoms may occur as part of a diagnosable schizophrenic, depressive, phobic, or obsessive-compulsive disorder. In such cases the diagnosis should be that of the main disorder.

These diagnostic manuals are regularly revised, and new research fuels the debate as to which category is best suited to include something as unique and confounding as DPD. Certainly the disorder is dissociative in that it manifests itself through a perceived separation of the mind and body, and/or prior-self versus changed-self. But it has little in common with other dissociative disorders such as Out-of-Body Experiences (OBEs), dissociative fugues, or Dissociative

Identity Disorder (formerly Multiple Personality Disorder). On the other hand, while panic and anxiety are commonly linked to DPD, there are many people whose DPD experience remains free of those symptoms.

Ultimately, the categorization of Depersonalization means little to those suffering with it other than the degree to which it provides some guideposts for doctors or psychologists seeking clues to the best path of treatment. In later chapters we'll explore the paths of observation and discovery that have led to the current clinical definitions.

Depersonalization as a symptom or a full-blown disorder is nothing new. Yet strangely, in addition to a broad spectrum of common symptoms, DP sufferers share another experience—a pattern of going to doctor after doctor with little or no relief other than the standard trial-and-error treatments for depression and anxiety. Even more surprising is the fact that finding a health professional who is familiar with depersonalization, or who even acknowledges its existence can be extremely difficult and demoralizing.

While depersonalization may appear within the context of other illnesses such as schizophrenia, it is not a psychotic condition. The individual knows that something is *not right* at best and frighteningly wrong at worst, and grapples with trying to figure out exactly what the problem is.

The late Oscar Janiger M.D., the Los Angeles psychiatrist known for his groundbreaking research into LSD and creativity, often called depersonalization the *opposite* of insanity.

"It's like being too sane," he once said. "You become hypervigilant of existence and things around you." And through all of this, reality testing remains intact—you know something is wrong and spend endless hours trying to get to the bottom of it all. No one understands what you are trying to explain except perhaps others who are feeling the same thing.

Excessive rumination is often a symptom of DPD. It also can include the unsettling sensation of over-consciousness alluded to above, wherein each thought seems too apparent, or too loud, like the volume of a low-playing radio suddenly turned up to its maximum. Even when rumination, the endless thinking about thinking itself, is not predominant, a foggy-headed sensation can emerge with the effect of a radio stuck between stations. Everything is hazed with static or somehow off in the distance, a mind somehow detached from the body that once contained it so comfortably and naturally.

Signs of depersonalization can occur with many illnesses; however, it isn't clear why the condition persists for years, even decades for some people and not others. This distinction likely lies in a genetic predisposition to the disorder, which is ultimately kicked off by triggers such as early low-level trauma or specific substances like marijuana or Ecstasy.

Chronically depersonalized people (who we will call D-people) have traditionally been viewed as highly intelligent and prone to intellectual rumination, although there is little clinical research to support this widely held view. Onset of depersonalization is most often seen at an early age, from around puberty to the late twenties. There is evidence of direct links in some cases to early childhood mistreatment, such as verbal abuse, as well as Temporal Lobe Epilepsy (TLE), and migraines. But it is the widespread use of marijuana, Ecstasy, LSD, and to a lesser degree, Ketamine (Special K) that appears to have thrown the condition into the spotlight, in near epidemic proportions.

In time, some people manage to accommodate the condition, especially if they find it possible to rethink their overall philosophy of life and pre-conceived notions about existence, or if the experience of "no-self" or emotional numbness predominates over anxiety or endless intellectual rumination. Most people eventually realize that DPD will neither kill them nor make them insane, nor is it a progressive illness. Adjusting to chronic DPD is somewhat like adjusting to a pair of glasses that makes everything appear upside down. Eventually one may find ways of adapting or dealing with different aspects of the disorder that may express themselves at different times. Still, it is difficult, if not impossible to find someone who would not want to get back to where they were before it all began.

In light of their altered internal world, people with DPD become masters at maintaining a front, appearing quite normal to friends, family, and co-workers. The sense of being an automaton, as described in DSM-IV is consistent with going through the familiar routines of a lifetime.

"You do what you're expected to, and say what others expect you to say, all the while feeling as if your acting out of habit," says John, a 32-year-old computer technician who has experienced DPD for six years. "Your mind is always a million miles away. All natural spontaneity and joy of living is gone. You know something is wrong, and you're constantly battling with what it might be, and evaluating how you feel."

Interestingly, depersonalization manifests itself in ways that are true to its clinical definition no matter what the trigger may have been. The evidence strongly suggests that the condition is the same, whether it was trauma, life-experience, or drugs that ultimately set it off. The underlying predisposition towards DPD lies at the heart of it. We will examine these triggers more closely in later chapters.

DPD is often linked to panic and anxiety. One young person's stream of consciousness account is typical of the feelings of unreality laced with intermittent panic that often besets sufferers in the earliest stages, whether drug induced or not:

"Three times after I've smoked pot I've had disabling depersonalization as a result. Again, it's the same numbness, then far away, unable to control my body. Time feels like it's flashing like movie stills. I cannot tell what is happening, even when I am thinking. Sound is far away. I cannot speak. It is as near death as one can get. The terror can be inexplicable. In between attacks I experience feelings of unreality, sometimes lasting days. I deal with agoraphobia and panic. Dread of dying. Sometimes I just feel it is hard to move around. Like I will become disoriented and fall over (which really happens during my serious attacks). I avoid people since they make me feel strange, especially if they are too close. Being in a store with fluorescent lights worsens it all too."

A Google Trend?

Depersonalization has received a lot of attention in the last decade. Why delve into it at length when it has been clearly defined as a disorder, an offshoot of other illnesses in the medical literature? There are several reasons. First, there is considerable evidence that more people are experiencing depersonalization and Depersonalization Disorder, and making it known than ever before. Research from New York's Mount Sinai Medical Center's Depersonalization Research Unit has placed the number of D-People at somewhere between 1.6 and 2.4 percent of the population in the United States alone. That means as many as seven million people in this country are experiencing the disorder, which outnumbers the people with schizophrenia or bi-polar disorders combined, not taking into account the thousands who are misdiagnosed. As words like neurotransmitter, panic disorder, and obsessive-compulsive disorder (OCD) worked their way into the popular lexicon, depersonalization research, which had sporadically gone on for many decades, suddenly looked like a relatively unexplored avenue where researchers and psychiatrists could make a mark on their professions. The Internet did much to open channels of communication for people who had suffered in silence with this mysterious condition. It proved widespread enough to prompt the founding of numerous depersonalization websites and discussion forums including *depersonalization. info*, *DPselfhelp.com*, *dreamchild.net*, *depersonalization-home.com* and others. Since the late 1990s, thousands of people with strikingly similar experiences, personal stories, symptoms, and triggers, have congregated regularly with a hunger for information through this virtual venue.

All of this new interest prompted the formation of two medical clinics singly devoted to the study of depersonalization. These included the aforementioned clinic at Mount Sinai and the Depersonalization Research Unit at the London Institute of Psychiatry. These clinics studied Depersonalization Disorder in depth and experimented with new methods of treatment to offer relief to those who find it to be an unbearable condition.

The last decade has also marked the first books on the subject of Depersonalization Disorder, including *Feeling Unreal: Depersonalization Disorder and the Loss of the Self*, by Daphne Simeon, MD, and myself (Oxford University Press, 2006), as well as *Depersonalization A New Look at A Neglected Syndrome*, by Mauricio Sierra (Cambridge University Press, 2009).

For more than a decade, Daphne Simeon was the primary investigator at Mount Sinai's Research unit and monitored the progress of volunteer patients who were screened by questionnaires and interviews to determine that they fit the diagnosis of Depersonalization Disorder. But simply establishing DPD as its own unique and separate illness has not been easy within the medical community, Simeon says.

"For a long time, depersonalization has been thrown in with a group of other dissociative disorders, like out-of-body experiences and dissociative fugues, but I've always been convinced that it's an entity unto itself," Simeon states. Even now, the medical establishment doesn't always agree. Papers on DP alone are still being rejected by medical journals. The condition is often linked with depression and anxiety states, yet there are many people who feel depersonalized but not depressed, and not anxious, unless the DP causes them to be."

"I never felt what I would consider to be clinically depressed," says Ron, who now in his thirties has suffered with Depersonalization Disorder for 15 years. "And the anxiety isn't spontaneous for me. It's always a result of my thinking in circles over and over again about life, death, infinity, and what's wrong with me." Like many reporting into interactive websites dealing with the subject, Ron traces his DP's origins to a single marijuana cigarette. His stream of consciousness is often marked by a pondering of things that are familiar to the rest of us, or the nature of existence itself.

"Its like I fall deep within myself. I look at my mind from within and feel both trapped and puzzled about the strangeness of my existence. My thoughts swirl round and round constantly probing the strangeness of selfhood—why do I exist? Why am I me and not someone else? At these times feelings of sweaty panic develop, as if I am having a phobia about my own thoughts. At other times, I don't feel 'grounded.' I look at this body and can't understand why I am within it. I hear myself having conversations and wonder where the voice is coming from. I imagine myself seeing life as if it were played like a film in a cinema. But in that case, where am I? Who is watching the film? What is the cinema? The worst part is that this seems as if it's the truth, and the periods of my life in which I did not feel like this were the delusions."

Still, there are cases where DP comes about for no particular reason, as it did for Karen, a young Englishwoman in her twenties.

"I came from a normal family and have never been abused. I've just always been this way. It has never been a choice for me. I have never been officially diagnosed for depersonalization. But all the things match up. I've never really known who I am. I wish I did. I envy others in their secure identities. Things that are supposed to be familiar look bizarre and incomprehensible. There is a big hole in my understanding of human relations and communication. Nothing makes much sense as a whole. Often, when someone calls my name I don't feel identified with it. Nothing seems real."

A Lost Generation?

Like most DP sufferers, Ron and Karen have been involuntarily thrust into bona fide existential angst, a term that unfortunately today seems more relevant to a Woody Allen movie than an individual in crisis. Their poignant observations run deeper than simply thinking in circles about the nature of existence. They *feel* the black emptiness of existence that post-World War II philosophers endeavored to portray. It's what the French have come to call *Le Coup de Vide*, the Blow of the Void.

"Depersonalization is a very unpleasant feeling, despite the fact that it often manifests itself by a seeming lack of feeling," says German constructivist psychologist Ursula Oberst. "Stories by depersonalized people have a true flavor of existentialism about them. Philosophers wrote about it and theorized about it. But D-people *feel* it, and the feeling can be too much to bear."

One who wrote about it and very likely felt it was French philosopher Jean Paul Sartre. While he reputedly scorned the term existentialism, his first novel *Le Nausee* published in 1938 portrays true Depersonalization Disorder with bone-chilling accuracy. Existentialist or not, Sartre either knew depersonalization first hand or, under the guise of existentialism, presented us with literature's greatest coincidence:

I buy a newspaper along my way. Sensational news. Little Lucienne's body has been found. Smell of ink, the paper crumples between my fingers. The criminal has fled. The child was raped. They found her body, the fingers clawing at the mud. I roll the paper into a ball, my fingers clutching at the paper; smell of ink; my God how strongly things exist today. Little Lucienne was raped. Strangled. Her body still exists, her flesh bleeding. SHE no longer exists. She no longer exists. The houses. I walk between the houses, I am between the houses, on the pavement; the pavement under my feet exists, the houses close around me, as the water closes over me, on the paper the shape of a swan. I am. I am.. I exist, I think, therefore I am; I am because I think, why do I think. I don't want to think any more, I am because I think that I don't want to be, I think that I....because....ugh! I flee.[2]

Literary depictions of depersonalization, panic, depression, phobias, and other states of mind have threaded their way through most cultures throughout history. Poe's *Tell-tale Heart*, Camus' *The Stranger*, Borges' *The Aleph* and others come to mind. We explore some of the literature that depicts depersonalization in Chapter 11.

The word "panic" originates in ancient lore, which attributed a fearful shift in consciousness, or panic, to anyone confronting the Greek forest god Pan. Throughout antiquity, a variety of gods tempted humans with glimpses of a hidden universe, or knowledge that their brains were not equipped to handle, resulting in insanity. Cosmic consciousness, and the brain's inability to handle it, appears again and again in popular culture, from 50s science fiction stories and movies with mind-expanding machines, to Aldous Huxley's *Doors of Perception*, which suggested that mescaline could open the brain's channels to the higher knowledge promised by those very sci-fi contraptions.

An exploration of all that depersonalization involves will take you down many paths. Paths of self-exploration, or explorations of the lack of self, may ultimately lead one towards the ancient teachings of Buddhism or other eastern philosophies, or western mystic literature and contemporary Christian writers known as contemplatives. Depersonalization is also often compared to psychological states found in Transcendental Meditation, specifically as taught by the renowned Maharishi Mahesh Yogi. Numerous quotes from the 1967 book *Maharishi Mahesh Yogi on the Bhagavad-Gita: A New Translation and Commentary* directly parallel the descriptions of depersonalization in DSM-IV. One statement from the book could fall directly under the DSM-IV subcategory of detachment. "In Nitya-Samadhi, or cosmic consciousness, a man realizes that his Self is different from the mind which is engaged in thoughts and desires. He experiences the desires of the mind as lying outside himself."

Most psychiatrists and patients are convinced that Depersonalization Disorder and Samadhi, or bliss, are not the same thing. "Many people enjoy the states brought about through TM. But Depersonalization is an illness, sent straight from hell," Oz Janiger once said. "It's a psycho-physiological problem that involves the integrity of the ego and body image. Whether they're treating DP, or just social phobias, psychologists often spend years trying to build up a patient's ego with little result. There are many people who are successful in their careers and who have received plenty of laurels, awards, and food for the ego. But it doesn't do a thing toward alleviating the pain of losing one's self because of this strange and uncanny condition."

Still, the parallels are worth exploring, as we do in Chapter 11.

The search for cures of more pressing illnesses, like alcoholism, has kept funding for DP research on a back burner. (Ironically, many D-People find that alcohol is the only thing that brings temporary relief to the symptoms.) The existing clinics are a beginning and much has been learned. But the study of depersonalization disorder when compared to other disorders, remains in its infancy.

As more sufferers of the condition converge on the Internet, or present their experiences to the existing or new research centers, more common symptoms will emerge with greater clarity. For instance, D-People seem to be particularly susceptible to the condition when they spend time in fluorescent lighting. In addition, for most persons, depersonalization seems to be strongest in the mornings and progressively better as the day unfolds. If they take naps, it can re-emerge with a vengeance.

This tells us something about its relationship to sleep, Janiger once pointed out to me. "It's odd how so many people refer to it as being in a dream or a dreamlike state, but nobody seems to have looked at how it relates to REM (Rapid Eye Movement) sleep. If you visualize the brain's two distinct types of consciousness, REM sleep and wakefulness as being in their own separate airtight compartments, depersonalization might represent some kind of intrusion from one into the other." The respective compartments may not be as contained as they should be.

Whether it's linked to the sleep/wakefulness cycle, a natural part of the human condition, or part of an awakening to a heightened consciousness, Depersonalization Disorder isn't going away. And the need for more research is pressing.

The DSM is due to be revised in 2012. Daphne Simeon is part of the committee examining what needs to change. In the meantime, I have always found the concise classic description by J.C. Nemiah to be especially on target, and for the purposes of this book, an excellent point of departure:

The central characteristic of depersonalization is the quality of unreality and estrangement that is attached in connection to conscious experience. Inner mental processes and external events go on seemingly exactly as before, yet everything is different and seems no longer to have any personal relations or meaning to the person who is aware of them. The feeling of unreality affects the person's per-

ception of his physical and psychological self and the world around him. Parts of one's body or one's entire physical being may appear foreign. All of a person's mental operations and behavior may feel alien to him.

A common and particularly troublesome manifestation is a loss of the capacity to experience emotions, even though the patient may appear externally to express them. Feelings of unreality and strangeness may invade the patient's perceptions of the objects and people in the world around him. Anxiety is often found as an accompaniment of the disorder and many patients complain of distortion in their sense of time and space. Especially common is the experience of a change in the patient's body; in addition to his general sense of estrangement from his bodily self, the patient may feel that his extremities are bigger or smaller than usual. An occasional and particularly curious phenomenona is that of doubling; the patient feels that his point of conscious "I-ness" is outside of his body, even a few feet overhead, from where he actually observes himself as if he were a totally other person.

The experience of depersonalization is often accompanied by considerable secondary anxiety, and the patient frequently fears that he is going insane. It is a curious paradox that even though the patient complains of being emotionally dead and estranged, he is capable of being emotionally upset by this very sense of loss. Indeed, all the manifestations of depersonalization are acutely unpleasant and not only motivate the patient to seek medical help, but often drive him to vigorous activity, or to inducing intense sensations in himself in order to break through the prison walls of his sense of unreality.

The patient's keen and unfailing awareness of the disturbances in his sense of reality is considered one of the salient characteristics of the syndrome. There seems in depersonalization to be a heightening of the psychic energy invested in the self-observing ego, the mental function in which the capacity for insight rests.[3]

REFERENCES

1. Elliot, G.C., Rosenberg, M., Wagner, M., (1984). Transient depersonalization in youth. *Social Psychology Quarterly*, **47**, p 115-129.

2. Sartre, J.P., *Nausea*. New York: New Directions Publishing Corp. p 100.

3. Nemiah, J.C., (1984) Dissociative disorders (hysterical neurosis, dissociative type). In *Comprehensive Textbook of Psychiatry*, ed 4, Kaplan, H.,I., Sadock, B., J., editors, Williams & Wilkins, Baltimore. p 942.

2   The One-Way Trip

I sent my soul through the invisible
Some letter of that afterlife to spell;
and by and by my soul returned to me,
and answered, "I myself am Heav'n and Hell

— **Omar Khayyam**

Depersonalization attacks the one thing that you carry with you everywhere, every day—your "self." It devours the things that make you a person, while draining your ability to make things *personal.* It feeds off personhood like a cancer. Try to make it disappear and you make yourself disappear as well. All the while, it feels like that is exactly what is happening.

Many years ago, I was sitting in my bed at home, a familiar place where I had lived for years surrounded by a loving family. I trembled with real fear, the blend of anxiety and hopelessness that overtakes you when you face some truth too horrible to process; the kind of fear you might experience when accidentally hitting a child on a bicycle in your car, or killing your mother with what you assumed to be a toy gun. Something horrible has happened. You are to blame, and what has been done cannot be undone.

The anxiety had been ongoing for weeks, but intensified this night because I was trying to research the things I was feeling. Words shot into my eyes from an antiquated encyclopedia. Terminology that seemed to correlate with what I had been experiencing for months—psychosis, schizophrenia, mental illness. I had damaged myself, irreparably, and my poor parents on the floor below must never ever know.

Things happen to people. Usually they happen to someone else, especially when you are young. From your observation tower, your home, your room, you watch life unfold for others. Sheltered by a secure, predictable life affirmed by parents, friends, and a book of rules, it's normal to feel ready to make your mark on the world. Relatively minor setbacks such as a failing grade, enemies you had not anticipated, even a break up with the love of your young life give you a soft prelude to life's blows.

Then, something major may interrupt. The unexpected death of a parent, a traumatic car accident, catastrophic illness, or even the loss of a beloved pet. All of these affect, even change your life. But some built-in mechanism for adaptation and evolution assures that you can eventually move on. People are built to withstand and adapt, and in most cases they do.

But sometimes, life changes don't happen from outside circumstances. Sometimes they come from within. Heredity, trauma, or severe losses can trigger unexpected mental illness.

Today, many mental disorders have been granted a stamp of legitimacy, a reason for empathy and compassion. Depression, bipolar disorder, even schizophrenia are now part of popular culture as drug companies feed on the frenzy of new ailment acronyms. Friends and relatives no longer dismiss someone as crazy; they may be dismissed, but with the degree of understanding afforded by a "chemical imbalance."

"They're okay as long as they take their medicine," has become the mantra of choice regarding the mentally troubled.

As I sat on my bed, withdrawn from school before the semester's end, home, like an ailing prodigal son once again dependent on his parents, I began to see myself as a statistic—one of those victims of bad trips who were never heard from again. Life in a mental institution, perhaps in a strait jacket seemed inevitable. And, there was an additional factor.

To win sympathy and support, a catastrophe must be acceptably catastrophic. To have returned home from Viet Nam as a basket case would have denoted some degree of honor in the eyes of others, no matter how they felt about the war. But to wind up disabled, bedridden, and terrified from having smoked marijuana demanded a degree of knowledge and understanding not yet attained by either conservative parents or liberal friends.

"You got what you deserved for fooling around with drugs," would resound from one side. "You just couldn't handle pot because of some psychological weakness," would inevitably come from the other. The truth, if revealed to parent, friend or foe, would only lead to a no-win situation and endless, pointless discussion.

A month earlier I had been enjoying college and the freedom to create my own persona, to be what I perceived myself to be despite the delusions of youth, the naiveté of post-adolescence, the shallowness of young artists without portfolios. I was 500 miles from home, sufficiently popular because of my long hair, and romantically involved with arguably, the most beautiful girl on campus.

None of us took life very seriously. Many of us had applied for college as a last resort to avoid Viet Nam. But the war was winding down, the turbulent 60s were passé, and the mellow and open-minded environment fostered a life of new friendships, scored by massive Harman Kardan stereo systems, and celebrated with the passing of hash pipes or joints made with Bugler rolling paper,

As the snow gently fell one night in February, I said goodnight to my girlfriend who wanted to catch up on her rest. In my dorm, I proceeded to a friend's room where a group of freshmen had finished smoking some hash in a bowl. I took what was left and sucked on it with a vengeance, for no particular reason other than to impress my friends with some indefinable bravado. I left the room and went down to the lounge area to watch the communal television and eat from a large bag of potato chips.

Twenty minutes after smoking, the world changed forever. I suddenly felt a strange surge creep from my testicles, up my back and into my head along with an incredible sense of fear. Then, like a whack in the head with a two by four, I felt a complete and total sense of panic unlike anything I ever knew before or will ever know again. The words "brain damage" flashed in my head as the potato chips flew to the floor and scattered. I ran furiously up to my friend's room to see what they had put in the hash. My friend Earl, a gangly black medical student, came running after me to see what was wrong.

My other friends were all still gathered in the room where I had smoked. When they opened the door, through the haze I eyed the room's large window and immediately wanted to jump out. The absolute terror and urgency for flight made crystal clear, for a fleeting moment, how and why people may inexplicably throw themselves out of windows. I will never be able to fully explain this pure, crippling terror.

"That hash, what was in it?" I pleaded, frightened in a way none of them had ever witnessed.

"Nothing, nothing," they answered. 'It was the same shit we all smoked."

I asked the question again, more loudly, and they gave me the same response. Their reassurance did nothing to calm me down. The terror was real, and physiological. No amount of talk or rubbing my hand gently would change it.

The next thing I remember is laying down in my room in the dark. The intense anxiety that followed the panic began to subside within a few hours. I finally fell asleep listening to surreal sounds of a violent fight between two people in the room next door.

When I awoke, the sun was shining through the frosted window. I realized that I was still alive, I was awake, and felt perfectly normal. I could not believe it, considering the brain damage I had so clearly inflicted on myself the night before. I thanked God profusely for sparing me a permanent bad trip and for teaching me a valuable lesson. I had been given a second chance. I spent the day excitedly telling the story until my friends told me to shut up or we'd all get in trouble.

As the day progressed, the exhilaration of being saved, of having seen the light, of resolving never to smoke pot again diminished slightly and I began to tire. In the evening, I was alone in the art studio working on an assignment when from nowhere I felt an internal stillness, a silent mindlessness and the sense, for only an instant, that something dreadful was going to happen. The horrible panic of the night before, the feeling emanating from the groin, up my spine, and into my head then returned with same ferocity of the previous night.

I calmed myself enough to return to the dorm. But the attacks continued, every few minutes. I went into the communal bathroom and took a hot bath. I took aspirin. I stared at myself in the mirror and pulled my hair and wondered whether I would scream or smash my head against the tiled walls as cold air filtered in through a partially opened window.

Only the fear of being considered insane, or strung out on drugs, or of word somehow reaching my parents kept me from finding someone to take me to an emergency room.

I went to bed and endured these bouts of terror which came in waves like the surf, every 15 minutes or so. I pulled the covers over my head as I lay there trembling. In time, my roommate came in, drunk and stoned, as he did in the wee hours every night.

"I've got problems," I told him quietly, not so much in an effort to communicate or seek advice, but rather to prove to myself that I could indeed still communicate. I could think enough to make a sentence. I could talk. I could make reasonable statements; I was not insane.

He mumbled words that have remained somewhere in my head all these years: "Hey, unless somebody's chasing you down the street with a knife, there ain't nothing worth worrying about."

True panic is as incomprehensible to most people as it was to my pothead roommate. We reserve panic for the most serious of fight or flight situations and admire those who, with cool heads, are able to manage even the seemingly unmanageable. But panic, as the world of "normals" sees it, is quite different than what I endured that night. The panic I encountered comes from an unknown source within—a place completely foreign to strength of will, resolve, and what we call courage. Courage, I have learned, is not the ability to endure situations that might provoke panic in the weak. Courage is the ability to endure the panic that is entirely unprovoked, the things that attack you not from without, but from within. (We will look at the true nature of panic in depth, in Chapter 8.)

These unwanted assailants continued to torment me for several nights, while during the day, a completely different state of mind emerged. I had no feeling, nor any of the sense of self that had defined me for my entire life. All that existed within me was a headachy mental cloudiness devoid of ego, empty of interest or emotion. I could still think, but I couldn't feel. I knew my friends, but felt no need or desire to exhibit the wit with which I had often entertained them. I loved my girlfriend, but knew something life changing was in the works, and loved her *differently*, if what I felt could be called love at all.

I decided that I was sick. Too sick to continue the semester, too sick to be who I had been to all those around me. Sickness longs for home, and after a month or so I returned to my parents. My girlfriend cried when I left, and cried on the phone when I called her from home. She loved someone, but I held no bearing on the person she had come to love. Everything I had ever thought or expressed to her, everything I had enjoyed, dreamed of, or fantasized about no longer seemed to exist other than as meaningless illusions. Everything seemed like lies, yet no revelation of truth took its place — only emptiness and wrenching anxiety over the true source of what bothered me.

I was convinced that pot, or its concentrated counterpart hash, did not do this to people. I reminded myself that there was clearly no brain damage because I was perfectly fine the day after that first horrible attack of terror. The panic had subsided, but it seemed to have drained my soul and horribly shattered the comfortable stream of consciousness that never gives one reason to think of sanity or even the act of thinking itself.

My mind was simply *not right*. I was overly aware of every thought in my head, and spent the entire day analyzing how my thinking "felt" and what was wrong with it. I blamed these sensations on mononucleosis, low blood sugar, everything possible except the drug. For if it was indeed the hash, I had done myself irreparable harm, damaged my brain, and ruined my life. It was something I refused to face.

Then one day I was home alone. I picked up the telephone and called a suicide hotline.

I explained that I was not suicidal; I just wanted someone to hear what had happened to me and tell me if they had ever heard of such a thing before. Was I the only person on earth who had had such a reaction to pot? Was it laced with something that had somehow failed to reach the others who had smoked from the same charred bowl of hashish?

The young man on the other end of the line was particularly astute and sympathetic. He was more on target than anyone I spoke to in many years to follow.

He explained that the THC (tetrahydrocannabinol) in the hash had broken through the defenses I had carried with me all of my life. The barriers, the walls of reason and sanity I had erected were broken through, making me vulnerable and fearful. Everything that had served to make life, the things around me, and the things within me seem normal had been stripped away, leaving me like a babe in the woods with nothing to protect me.

He wished me luck and hoped that in time, these "defenses" would rebuild themselves. This young man's simplistic explanation has stuck with me all of my life because it was essentially true.

Semantics always come into play when discussing DPD or mental states in general. The word "defense" appears often in psychology. Depersonalization itself is considered a normal defense mechanism against overwhelming circumstances; DPD is often defined as a "defense" mechanism gone awry. But what the young man referred to might be viewed as my personal "constructs"—the things my mind took in and made sense of since early childhood. Time and familiarity made my inner and outer worlds normal to me. The drug had stripped away this sense of familiarity, resulting in fear, or at its worst, panic.

How can a defense mechanism gone awry cause such incredible misery? What causes it to break? And how can it be fixed?

When dissociation designed to distance you from trauma goes out of kilter it becomes something completely different than the defense mechanism it was. I think of it as a beautiful butterfly that somehow reverses its life cycle to become the ugliest of caterpillars. DPD takes on a new life of its own with a galaxy of symptoms, some of which seem to have little to do with dissociation or distancing the self from anything, except itself. What was intended to protect the self, now does everything it can to destroy it.

My symptoms were terrifying, and led me to believe that I had destroyed my brain forever, by using pot. I had never heard of anyone experiencing anything like I had, other than the horror stories of people who had never returned from bad trips on LSD. I had no idea what the future would hold, if there were to be a future at all.

Failure to Communicate

There is no language through which depersonalization can be communicated. The fact that we think in words is one of the many aspects of consciousness that can seem quite strange to the depersonalized.

In attempts to explain their sensations, people use metaphors and comparisons. And, interestingly, people with depersonalization are somehow able to communicate with each other rather clearly, as if they had developed a new language of their own.

Trying to explain it to a person who has never experienced it is like trying to describe the taste of a peach to someone who has neither seen nor eaten one. Statements like "I feel unreal," or "Everything seems strange to me" are ripe with implications that may have little or nothing to do with chronic Depersonalization Disorder.

When talking to doctors, human nature comes into play as well. As we spell out our symptoms one by one, as clearly as humanly possible, we sometimes move cautiously, like swimmers testing the water with their toes before diving in. How much should I reveal before the doctor says I'm schizophrenic? How do I prove that I'm not crazy when my symptoms sound so crazy, even to myself? Maybe I should forget trying to explain this and go home.

Concurrent with the revived interest in depersonalization, some clinicians have made efforts in recent years to clarify and understand the language of depersonalization, notably, Filip and Susanna

Radovic, writing in the Johns Hopkins University publication *Philosophy, Psychiatry, and Psychology.*[1]

The authors point out that, considering the broadness and prevalence of the word "unreal" in our culture, people often can express that things feel unreal without reflecting an underlying depersonalization experience; rather, they are talking about something way out of the ordinary. Life seems unreal to someone who is depersonalized, yet it also may seem unreal to someone who has just hit a jackpot in Vegas. The latter person may be having an intellectual experience of unreality, as in "this cannot be happening to me," because "it's too good to be true." Less likely, he may be actually experiencing an episode of genuine depersonalization, essentially for the very same reason, triggered by the overwhelming nature of the extreme event.

The vast terrain of depersonalization would benefit from a broader lexicon to help find words for the unspeakable. But to date, depersonalized people must rely on the subtle nuances of simpler words or phrases often used as metaphor to capture the experiential with language. The word "unreal" is *the* keyword for depersonalized people. To describe "unreality" they often must use metaphors for comparison to other sensations that may or may not be more understandable to everyone else.

The "as if" aspect of DPD also comes into play quite often. Words like "mechanical," "dead," and "lifeless" enter the picture, as well as the use of metaphors such as "I feel like a robot." The "as if" prefix, the Radovics note, reflects the uncertainty about the adequacy of a proposed description—it is simply the best verbalization a patient can come up with.

There is a second important aspect of the "as if" feature that shows that a patient is nondelusional—that is, he or she has intact reality testing as a required criterion for the diagnosis of depersonalization. The patient doesn't believe that he *is* a robot but feels *as if* he is functioning like one.

The word "feel" is fraught with its own mysteries. A person may suffer immensely from lack of feeling, yet the suffering itself is a feeling—a negative one. Other people describe feeling nothing at all.

The language of the *DSM-IV* itself can be subject to interpretation, despite the care that is put into the wording. Part of the manual's depersonalization description mentions "a sensation of lacking control of one's actions." Does this mean that someone is fearful that they might act on impulse and harm someone, or themselves, like a person with obsessive-compulsive disorder? Does it imply a sense that one's arms or legs will give way involuntarily, like a person with tics and twitches? Or does it mean they do things robotically, without a clear awareness of their actions? Even "normal" people can sense a lack of control from time to time, under the influence of intense emotions or new and unpredictable circumstances.

Explorations into the language of DPD have at least given physicians food for thought regarding the messages depersonalized patients are attempting to send. Decades ago, however, it was readily apparent that no doctor would understand you, nor diagnose you as anything other than neurotic at best, psychotic at worst.

The Nine Circles

During my first year of depersonalization, I struggled to explain my feelings through the "as if" metaphors. Then I stopped. No one understood, or ever would understand. Two more years passed, and the obsessive focus on my mental processes began to reveal a bit of their nature. The path of my mind's experiences were circular it seemed. With my intellect fully in tact, it occurred to me that different mind states repeated themselves at different times. Like a medical student learning to dissect a corpse, I deconstructed what was happening to me and created my own construct of consciousness.

It was *as if* my mind took me through nine concentric circles within my head, ever descending, heading toward the center of the last, deepest circle, where madness awaited. When I reached the seventh or eighth circle, I always returned to the first, and the descent began all over. As I slowly returned to a planned, linear life, through relentless self-observation, I was able to determine which circles lay closet to the center. And, as certain phases reappeared, I was able to predict with some accuracy what I could expect to go through.

I didn't know that this thing that plagued me, this "filth" actually had a name. I knew nothing of psychiatry, or biology, or mysticism. So I created an imaginary disorder and an imaginary diagnosis consisting of circles within circles inside my head. I would escape one only to find myself in a smaller circle within the one I had escaped. My interpretation was, perhaps, my answer to Dante. His Hell became *my* metaphor.

The first was the Circle of Panic. This is how it had begun, how I had entered the strange world from which I was never to return as the same individual again. While this circle gave the impression of being near madness, it was in fact, only the gate of entry. If the words "abandon hope" were posted, it would be on the gate at this outer circle.

The second was the Circle of No Mood. Emotional death, the loss of spirit, ambition, ego and personality all characterized the circle of No Mood.

A mood is a wonderful thing. Imagine thinking with all feeling removed. You become a thing that sees words passing through your head, moment by moment, like subtitles in a movie. Mood changes that. It blesses you with the luxury of living your life, doing things you *feel* like doing, thinking full and complete thoughts with attached sensations of happiness, nostalgia, well-being, even anger, within an extended period of our most precious resource—time. Even a bad mood somehow proves that you are alive. A good mood gives you reasons to try to extend it, somewhat like foregoing dinner because that third drink tastes like more. Moods make you feel human, and a part of life.

Depersonalization is life without a mood. You exist, as a rock exists, as a grain of sand exists, unless you begin ruminating about and questioning that existence. You become acutely aware of thoughts because no emotion gives them life as part of you. Thinking itself becomes strange, and not knowing where these things called thoughts, come from, you begin to fear what strange thoughts lie ahead in the moments to come, or in the months and years to come. When you no longer own your thoughts, and your mind can neither muster nor cling to memories with feelings, all that remains is fear.

The third circle was the Circle of Detachment which reinforced the current concept that depersonalization is dissociative. Time spent in this circle places your mind in a place that no longer has anything to do with your body. You feel as if your thinking, your very being, is somehow back and to the left, overhead, or generally somewhere other than within the body you are supposed to inhabit. It isn't an out-of-body experience, per se. You don't get to look down and see yourself taking a nap. But your mind feels as if it is a thing unto itself, somewhere in the vicinity of your body, but not quite locked into it.

The Circle of Detachment is marked by strangeness. With mind and body no longer in their proper alignment, the things outside your private Hell may look strange as well. I remember looking at a Quaker Oats container in my mother's kitchen. Intellectually I knew what it was, but it appeared as if I had never seen one before. I observed the Quaker mascot himself as if he were alive and going to wink at me. The kitchen momentarily became a new planet rich with colors and objects that I had never seen before. Sensing that I was at last going insane, I washed my face with cold water and went outside to look into the sun. For long periods thereafter, familiar things around me held no personal attachment. Emotions that might have normally been evoked from my car, flowers in the yard, books, pictures, or music no longer emerged. Was there no emotional attachment because things seemed strange, or did things suddenly seem strange because they no longer held any emotional attachment? The end result was the same, no matter what the cause and effect.

Because DPD's manifestations are highly variable, and different sides of it appear at different times, the ability to trust your mind, your Self, is severely compromised. While the strangeness of thinking in words was for me a constant, a rising level of mistrust arose in my consciousness as well. This mistrust did not relate to people, but rather my own mind. I sensed the power I had in simply being able to control my physical actions and speech. But how and why was I doing it? I wondered. Sensing no self to be in control of my actions, what was in charge? What kept me from committing any number of insane acts?

I remember once attending a rather boring class at N.Y.U. seated next to a sixth-story window. I heard very little that the professor was saying, because during the course of his lecture I could not stop wondering what was preventing me from hurling myself out that window. My mind focused on the fact that no one knew what I was thinking, that no one ever knows what anyone else is thinking. While this sense of isolation and entrapment in my own body would later reveal a circle of its own, on this day the emphasis was on whether or not I could actually control myself from doing something completely bizarre and inexplicable. I envisioned the next day's Daily News with a story about an N.Y.U. student's inexplicable jump from a window. "He gave no impression that anything at all was the matter," said one witness. "He wasn't depressed or anything..." This was my entry into the fourth circle, the Circle of the Fear of Losing Control.

This fear of being unable to control your actions is a common theme in depersonalization and in my case, the obsessive component to the disorder manifested itself through the inability to quickly whoosh away such absurd and unreasonable thinking in the manner most people do. Clearly it contained an element of compulsion and the need to test your sanity, much like using your tongue to feel a sore tooth. Doing so makes it worse, but you just can't help it.

The Circle of Obsession was the trickiest of the circles, I determined, because it often appeared to occupy the same space as the other circles, like a shadow or a ghost. Obsession interacted with anxiety, as well as with the feelings of loss of control, strangeness, and compulsive tendencies. Once trapped in these other circles, it became easy to obsess about them, hence the Circle of Obsession could appear concurrently with virtually any of the other circles.

When I was not focused on what was wrong with me, some individual aspect of life would become strange and foreign to me.

Usually, a single fixation surfaced at a time. Once resolved, there might be a period of relative peace only to be followed by another obsession.

For instance, I spent weeks in the strange waters of the Circle of Detachment, perplexed by the concept of wind, and the invisibility of air. I swept my hand in front of my face numerous times a day to feel something touching it. What was it? How could something invisible flow around my face, mess up my hair, make the trees bend over and the leaves scurry everywhere. Was I the only one who thought there was something odd about this? We tend not to believe in things that we cannot see. But…

Who has seen the wind?
Neither I nor you
But when the trees bow down their heads
The wind is passing through.

The trite, tired lines I had learned from my grandmother became my mantra as the existence of the invisible wind took its turn as my *obsession du jour.*

In essence, any number of the things that people never think about became the focus of my attention and analysis simply because suddenly, inexplicably they had become so intolerably strange. It was *as if* I were from another planet where everything was the same except the one aspect of reality that my mind could suddenly no longer comprehend. It might be the wind one day, human anatomy the next, or, more regularly, the simple act of thinking—invisible words seemingly from nowhere running through a human being's head at lightning speed all day long. Did this not seem strange, incomprehensible to everyone else? If not, then why me? Clearly I was headed toward the center of insanity.

Still, I always knew that something was *not right.* This "reality testing" assured me that I wasn't crazy, only intensely neurotic, insecure beyond any familiar definition of insecurity.

These episodes continued for several years, always switching direction and focus. I now know that they were manifestations of two specific aspects of DPD in certain people—derealization, the strangeness of the outer world, and obsessiveness. Different aspects of life, things "normals" rarely think about, seemed particularly strange to me and I obsessed over their strangeness.

During one period of several weeks I was intensely intrigued, and ultimately frightened by being unable to grasp the concept of infinity, in time or space. This marked entry into my Circle of Awareness.

Perhaps Joyce's mention of such things in *A Portrait of the Artist as a Young Man* triggered my own wonder and concern in a way that it never would have if I were not trapped in The Circles:

Eternity! O, dread and dire word. Eternity! What mind of man can understand it? ... You have often seen the sand on the seashore. How fine are its tiny grains! And how many of those tiny little grains go to make up the small handful which a child grasps in its play. Now imagine a mountain of that sand, a million miles high, reaching from the Earth to the farthest heavens, and a million miles broad... And if that mountain rose again after it had been all carried away and if the bird came again and carried it all away again grain by grain: and if it so rose and sank as many times as there are stars in the sky, atoms in the air, drops of water in the sea, leaves on the trees, feathers upon birds, scales upon fish, hairs upon animals, at the end of all those innumerable risings and sinkings of that immeasurably vast mountain not one single instant of eternity could be said to have ended.[2]

Every human endeavor, it seemed to me, was merely a distraction, something to keep us from staring the dark mysteries surrounding us in the face. Most people put a ceiling on infinite space, or perceived space and time as circular, always returning to where it began. But what was outside the circle? I wondered. This was not a new astronomical curiosity, however, but a genuine fear of infinity, a fear of the Void, an existential crisis.

"If you really dwelled on things like that I bet a person would go crazy," I recall my mother once saying. And I found myself dwell-

ing on the infinite with a fearful and unhealthy sense of awe. The
questions that we all know but rarely dwell on demanded answers.
At some point, we all accept the existence of the unknown as a part
of life. But changed eyes see the mysteries of life as if they are being confronted for the first time, so the need to solve them becomes
pressing.

In time, the endless rumination would somehow resolve itself.
The old *defenses* that kept me from even thinking about such things
would gradually return as if my mind was just too tired of questioning
the unknowable.

Obsession, left unchecked, led to the Circle of Anxiety. And anxiety usually led to something else. It often took anticipatory form,
as in fearing that the panic would strike again when I least expected
it. It surfaced in common ways known by people everywhere. I was
afraid to fly because I had a panic attack on an airplane. I was afraid
of being out in the country or in remote areas where hospitals and
medical treatment could not be accessed. At times, I was afraid to
leave my house or apartment because it was the only place where I
could distract myself for hours by watching innocuous, non-threatening television re-runs.

Strangely, anxiety would often leave completely when I entered
one of the other circles, but life spent in the Circle of Anxiety was
not worth living.

Still, in its way, anxiety was comprehensible. It was something a
number of other people could relate to, and something that could be
soothed with drugs, drink, or doing nothing at all. The eighth circle
was different, and perhaps the most chilling of them all. Fortunately,
my time in the eighth circle, the deepest inside the mind and the one
closest to madness lasted only two years. This I called the Circle of
The Other.

I cannot remember where or how it began. But within my stream
of consciousness, from nowhere, a distinct and separate voice
emerged in my head. It seemed at times to be a little demon head, a
small, evil entity watching everything I did and making derogatory
comments. It was as if there were two voices to indicate conscious-

ness, one that was mine and another that existed solely for the purpose of contradicting everything I thought or said, to myself or to others.

Reality testing remained intact. I knew that there was no other independent entity. I knew that it was "me" doing it to myself, that somehow I had created this other voice, this other observer, yet I was powerless to make it go away.

This entity was strikingly similar to "The Horla," the demonic presence described in the story of the same name by Guy DeMaupassant. The story was allegedly autobiographical, and while I didn't believe there was a real demon within my head, I was concerned that this other consciousness might eventually become the dominant personality and hence commit murder or other unspeakable crimes. DeMaupassant was supposedly suffering from syphilis. Could that have been any worse that what I was enduring? Time passed and I went about my life waiting to see where this alternate voice in my head would lead. I didn't go mad, though sometimes I cried in frustration over my inability to make the mocking voice go back to wherever it came from. Even then, I could hear it laughing in my head, as if it were winning the battle to overtake by body. I wondered if at some point the Other would become me, and all traces of who I once was would be forgotten and irretrievably erased. Was this how true madness began?

Strangely, the years of lonely torment spent in the Circle of the Other proved to be the most productive academically. My life moved forward simply because no other symptoms appeared during the time of the Voice. It was as if the broad range of possible symptoms had distilled themselves into this solitary method of torture. The illness invested all its destructive energy into a single weapon—the mocking inner Voice. At times, the non-stop laughter, the particularly *insightful* derisions, the piercing tone of the Voice became unbearable.

When I woke up each morning, the voice was not present. Then, after a short time awake I would *remember* it, and once again the torment began. Clearly, I reasoned, if the Voice's presence had to be *remembered*, acknowledged, before it appeared, then I was surely the one making it happen. It did not exist on its own—it was all me. But why couldn't I make it go away?

Only drinking quelled the voice, making it weaker, smaller, less determined to mock my every thought and action. Severe hangovers weakened it as well, as if the thing felt just as sick, depressed, and close to death as my normal, monotone consciousness. Writing, I was surprised to learn, silenced the voice as well, as if it went to sleep during the time I was seriously creating poetry, fiction, or magazine articles. So as my professors encouraged me, I began to write seriously, then fanatically, since the act seemed to emanate from a part of the brain that was free of the tormenting Voice.

In time, through experimentation with certain pills, specifically megadoses of niacinamide, through writing, or perhaps some psychosomatic cure, the Voice, the Other shriveled up in its corner and disappeared. The respite was momentary, however, because in its wake I came to know the opposite of having an Other in your head— an unspeakable realization of isolation, aloneness.

I had reached the deepest circle, the Circle of Realization. What was realized? The fact that my mind was alone, but with intensity and clarity human beings are not intended to realize. I was not alone in my disorder, per se, but eternally alone in the universe. Since the day I was born, until the day I would die, and likely beyond, no one, no thing, no entity, no god, nothing on earth or in the cosmos would ever share my thoughts as I thought them. Nor would anyone or anything ever know my feelings, or the nature of my existence. So what? one might ask. Everyone knows that. True. But not everyone feels it with such clarity and such truth that it is almost impossible to withstand. This is truly the circle where words fail. The Circle of Realization is marked by a sense of aloneness that normal human beings are simply not designed to experience. There is nothing to compare it to. There are no "as ifs." You simply are, existing in the moment. ALONE. And if you spend too much time in the ninth circle, surely madness or suicide await. Your realization that you exist only in the moment soon becomes the knowledge that *You* no longer exist at all.

The mind has to act quickly in the ninth circle. A choice has to be made. The Aloneness can take you somewhere else if you let it. Some call that place Nirvana. Unable to find it, invariably I escaped to the surface again, to the first Circle of Panic, only to repeat the cycle again and again.

Normal people, hot dog men, stockbrokers, teachers, house-wives, doctors, taxi drivers, anyone and everyone lived outside of the Nine Circles, I reasoned. A steel outer-circle separated them from everything inside their heads. This I called the Circle of Illu-sion. Protected by the security of this sheath, people grew up, went to school, secured jobs, married, had affairs with their secretaries and knocked around little white balls on the weekends. People lived in a linear, forward moving progression, usually as if death, as if the infinite did not exist. And if they acknowledged those things by attending a funeral and grieving or looking at the stars and praying, it was done with enough compartmentalization to keep the truth at bay. I learned through the years, to act as they did. In corporate life, a personality emerged often unrestricted by the mores or correctness of my peers, to their amusement. But often, it faltered, and I looked back at things I had done with curiosity, or remorse. Then I would find myself within the Nine Circles once again.

Many years later, I learned that other people, brilliant people, had identified and defined this thing that plagued me, in scientific and psychological terms. Through all this time, I must have passed a hundred hot dog men on city streets, and given anything to have been born one of them, and not me. After eleven years, I could put my youthful hypotheses, my imaginary disorder, and my analytical explanations for my illness away in a drawer forever.

Psychiatry had a name for my Nine Circles all along. They were simply called *symptoms*.

REFERENCES

1. Radovic, F., & Radovic, S. (2002). Feelings of unreality: a conceptual and phenomenological analysis of the language of depersonalization. *Philosophy, Pyschiatry, and Psychology*, **9**, 271–279.

2. Joyce, James (1916,1963) *A Portrait of the Artist as a Young Man*, New York: The Viking Press. p 131

3   Unraveling the Enigma

We don't see things as they are, we see them as we are."

—Anais Nin

Nin's quotation *above* actually originates from the Hebrew Talmud, written some 1,500 years ago. *We* are different, by nature of depersonalization, and most of us have opted to approach this state of mind as a disorder because of the suffering and confusion inherent to it. Things around us and within us seem to have changed, yet we know that they haven't. We have. Despite its presumed obscurity, feelings of depersonalization have been explored and documented in medical literature for nearly 200 years. Each written account provided material for others to feed off of or dispute, and in time, a consensus of ideas has formulated an accurate profile of what depersonalized individuals have to deal with. Today a specific set of criteria and a clear-cut definition of symptoms exists to guide doctors and patients towards reaching a diagnosis. Unfortunately, most of this research and speculation has rarely trickled down to the grass roots level where family doctors could use it. The time that it takes to receive a correct diagnosis of Depersonalization Disorder usually runs up to 12 years.[1] (Eleven years, in my case). But on a personal level, it was gratifying that my documentation of the Nine Circles matched the symptoms given the medical world's stamp of authenticity.

For far too long, people like myself, attempting to research their feelings on their own had no idea what they were looking for. The Internet's search engines became the first means to plug in a sensation like "feeling unreal" and actually find material about DPD, something that even library subject indexes were incapable of doing. Still, online summaries invariably lack the depth and subtleties of the disorder itself. For this reason, this chapter will take a closer look at some of the pivotal research that has, over time, distilled into a contemporary perspective on depersonalization. The terminology and interpretations of the doctors of the 19th and early 20th centuries have changed. But what their patients described is remarkably the same as what is being stated by patients today.

In the last two decades, names buried in obscurity in medical libraries for most of the 20th century have resurfaced to ride the wave of new interest in depersonalization. Psychiatric icons like Dugas, Mayer-Gross, and Sir Martin Roth, have been joined by newer researchers such as Sierra and Berrios, Daphne Simeon, and others to become familiar names in the ever-expanding depersonalization universe.

Understanding depersonalization completely has proven to be a game of inches that is now benefiting from new technologies being applied to all aspects of the brain.

Since the early 19th century, Europe, particularly France and Germany, exhibited the most progressive interest in psychological problems. Medical pioneers observing schizophrenia and depression (as well as a grab bag of maladies that usually landed you in an asylum) took note of the very unique descriptions of what we now call depersonalization.

In the 1840s Wilhem Griesinger, a German neurologist successfully touted the concept that mental illnesses could be treated, and some could actually be cured. In a time when asylum reform was already underway, this assumption resulted into a separation of incurables from curables in what had earlier been simply human warehouses. He astutely observed the complaints voiced by the "insane" and at one point took special notice of something a little out of the norm:

"We sometimes hear the insane, especially melancholics, complain of quite a different anaesthesia... I see, I hear, I feel, they say but the object does not reach me; I cannot receive the sensation; it seems to me as if there was a wall between me and the external world"[2]

Despite the broad range of symptoms exhibited by every imaginable mental illness thrown into one pot, Griesinger was savvy enough to note that this sense of detachment and unreality persisted in some patients long after signs of comorbid disorders had disappeared. Others on the continent, such as Etienne Esquirol, wrote about lypemanie or extreme sadness, and witnessed lypemaniacs who felt they were living in "a continuous dream." This, he felt, was one of many symptoms exhibited by people who suffered what would ultimately be known as clinical depression—a misdiagnosis that is too often made today.

Phrenology, the study of personality as it relates to the shape of one's skull, became enormously popular in early 19th century. While a source of amusement today, phrenology did identify the brain as the organ of the mind, with different internal compartments, or modules, serving different functions. The problem with phrenology stemmed from the false notion that the skull conformed to the size and shape of these modules. Still, the idea of complex brain regions compartmentalized according to function was a step forward from the Greco-Roman idea of the four humors.[*]

The module concepts of phrenology prompted Esquirol and others to reason that specific disorders could be attributed to problems in specific modules or mental "faculties" in the brain.

In the mid 1800s, the carnage wrought by the American Civil War took its toll on Americans. No doubt dissociative experiences served their true purpose often on the battlefield where physical damage to one's comrades or one's self was unimaginable due to the indiscriminate brutality of mini balls and shrapnel. Amputated arms and legs in fly-infested piles outside every field hospital tent certainly made a lasting impression on the psyche, but the frequency of dissociative experiences or depersonalization remains unknown. What is known, however, is that Civil War veterans who were very young at the time, or who were exposed to the deaths of their comrades, suffered a considerably higher rate of cardiac, gastrointestinal, nervous disease, and unique undiagnosable diseases over the course of their lifetimes when compared to the general

---

[*] *The human body was made up of four substances known as the four humors consisting of black bile, yellow bile, phlegm and blood. Sickness resulted when one of these was out of balance with the others.*

population according to veterans' medical records.[3]

Still, it seems that a society's level of tolerance for trauma steadily decreases in peacetime. While the Civil War left deep scars in its wake, many civilians began to develop their own observable neuroses. The term Neurasthenia soon appeared to describe a condition defined by fatigue, anxiety, headache, neuralgia and depression, attributable to "civilization." George M. Beard, the neurologist who coined the term in 1869, felt that these symptoms emerged as a result of exhaustion of the central nervous system's energy reserves, drained for having to deal with the stresses of urbanization and the increasingly competitive business environment. Psychologist William James, brother of the famous author Henry James, felt that Americans were particularly prone to Neurasthenia, which resulted in the nickname "Americanitis." (Interestingly, Neurasthenia is still listed as a diagnosis in the International Classification of Diseases, but not the American Psychiatric Association's Diagnostic and Statistical Manual.)

While Americans healed and looked toward westward expansion, Europeans had few options as to what to explore, other than themselves. With its rich traditions of philosophy and literature as a point of departure, new and more sophisticated evaluations of the diverse anomalies that plagued the minds of individuals began to emerge from the continent.

Several Europeans, including Emil Kraepelin, considered the father of psychobiology, made serious contributions that influence psychiatric thinking to this day. Kraepelin believed that all mental illness was based in internal biochemistry and that essentially each illness could be defined, isolated and tracked along a predictable course, based on observations of the same illness in other patients.

While his conclusions about depression were, in retrospect, a combination of truth and some incorrect assumptions, Kraepelin also described depersonalization specifically in what seems to be the recollection of his own experience:

"The impressions from the surroundings do not convey the familiar picture of everyday reality, instead they become dream-like

or shadowy as if seen through a veil. During the episode there can be 'a feeling of complete thought emptiness.'"[4]

Reports of persistent "feelings of unreality" continued to be accumulated piecemeal until the 1870s when Maurice Krishaber, a Hungarian eye, ear, nose, and throat specialist, formally reported on 38 patients showing a mixture of anxiety, fatigue, and depression. More than one-third of these patients complained of baffling and unpleasant mental experiences consisting of the loss of feeling of reality.[5] Krishaber theorized that these feelings were the result of pathological changes in the body's sensory apparatus. Multiple sensory distortions would therefore lead to experiences of "self-strangeness."

"One patient tells us that he feels that he is no longer himself, another that he has lost awareness of his self," Krishaber wrote. Although the term "depersonalization" was not used until 26 years later by Dugas, Krishaber's 1873 case histories marked the first true scientific study of the experience of depersonalization.

Krishaber's conclusions about these symptoms had a problem, however. They were based on a literal interpretation of the patient's complaints, and he was, after all, an eye, ear, and nose man. Hence he thought that feelings of unreality stemmed from problems with the sense organs. Others with more expertise in mental disorders, such as Ludovic Dugas and Pierre Janet, a major figure in nineteenth-century psychology, pointed out that many patients with obvious sensory problems, such as double vision (diplopia) or the loss of joint sense caused by neurosyphilis, did not complain of any sensations of unreality. Many patients suffering from depersonalization were in fact completely normal when it came to the five senses.[6] This put an end to the so-called sensory theories about the origins of depersonalization.

Mention of how the term "depersonalization" came into use appears to be *de rigueur* for many papers discussing DPD. The names Ludovic Dugas and Frederic Amiel are essential to the history of the disorder's research and these two may, in time, gain considerably more fame in death than they enjoyed in life.

Amiel was a Swiss professor whose extensive 17,000-entry personal diary, *(Journal Intime)* written between 1848 and 1881, bore testimony to a life of philosophic meandering, thought without action, and ultimately a lifelong sensation of being detached and "depersonalized" from what he thought to be real life. Dugas, a psychologist, noticed the term and began to use it in 1898 to describe types of patients that had been observed earlier and often, with no specific diagnosis.

Dugas was particularly interested in memory disorders, specifically "false memories," one of the hot topics of the day. He is sometimes credited as the first psychologist to use the term *déjà vu*, in a clinical sense. It was during his exploration of false memories that he first encountered depersonalization.

"Not realizing its novelty, I missed [the phenomenon] when I first met it," he recalled. Dugas wrote of a patient whose own voice sounded foreign to him:

"Although he *knows* that it is his voice, *it does not give him the impression* of being his own... . Acts other than speaking are also involved... . Everytime the subject moves he cannot believe that [he] is doing it himself... The state in which the self feels that its acts are strange and beyond its control will be called here *alienation of personality* or *depersonalization.*"[7]

In the classic *Un Cas de Depersonnalisation*, Dugas refers to a quote from a case studied by several of his contemporaries:

"I exist, but outside real life...my individuality has completely disappeared; the way in which I see things makes me incapable of realizing them, or feeling that they exist. Even when I can see it and touch it, the world appears to me like a phantom, a gigantic hallucination...I am perfectly conscious of the absurdity of these ideas, but cannot overcome them."

Dugas pointed out that the comments make perfect sense to one of his patients, but are "likely to be unintelligible to those have not had the experience...

"...The subject feels himself a stranger amongst things, or if one prefers, things seem strange to him. It is not that such objects have visually changed or appear different. It is that the subject himself has changed in relation to the said objects..."

Dugas viewed depersonalization as a form of apathy, a 19th-century term that was earlier associated with stoicism, implying a kind of indifference to fleeting earthly temptations. In time, psychology latched onto the word to imply a loss of vitality and "life."

"Because the self is that part of the person that vibrates and feels, and not what merely thinks or acts, apathy can be truly considered as the *loss of the person*, " Dugas noted.

Many who experienced or researched depersonalization in the 19th century, including Kraepelin, Dugas, and Janet could not help but deduce that it was in some way a variation of *déjà vu*.

But later on, J.C. Nemiah, one of the most notable psychiatrists of the 20th century, made a clear distinction between the two phenomena. In *déjà vu*, what is, in fact, new, alien, and previously unexperienced is felt as being familiar and as having been perceived before. In contrast, in depersonalization what is actually familiar is sensed as strange, novel, and unreal. The one, in other words, is the obverse of the other, and the two phenomena are therefore better considered as distinct entities.[8]

Pierre Janet, well known for introducing the words "dissociation" and "subconscious" into psychology terminology, considered depersonalization to be a manifestation of "psychasthenia," an antiquated term for any nonspecific condition marked by phobias, obsessions, compulsions, or excessive anxiety.[9]

Certainly, phobias, obsessions, and excessive anxiety often accompany depersonalization or mark the beginnings of it. But Janet also stressed the presence of a *sentiment d'incompletude*, an experience of incompleteness that many observers found well-represented in Dugas' source for the term "depersonalization," Frédéric Amiel's diary, *The Journal Intime*.

"What characterizes the feeling of depersonalization ... is that the patient perceives himself as an incomplete, unachieved person," Janet wrote. People with long-term Depersonalization Disorder have sometimes reported these feelings. Their *not rightness* may present itself as a distinct sense of something missing, such as their soul, or their personality. Their lives on the whole, having been spent in the Neverland of depersonalization, seem wasted, fruitless, and devoid of the kinds of achievements others easily take for granted.

Janet's theories brought about a shift in the predominant thinking on depersonalization. He believed that all psychic activity was either primary or secondary. Primary psychic activity encompassed everything that was evoked by external stimuli—from knee jerks to memories. Secondary psychic activity was a background echo elicited by representations of primary acts. By conferring a feeling of vividness (*l'impression de vie*) upon primary experiences, this secondary echo creates the illusion of a continuous flow of psychic activity: "thousands of resonances, constituted by secondary actions, fill the spirit during the intervals between external stimuli, and give the impression that it is never empty."[10] Dysconnectivity between these primary and secondary brain processes could result in depersonalization-like symptoms. Janet's language was different, but his theory remains surprisingly accurate and contemporary. Disconnections in the processing of incoming information does play some role in the most current thinking about DPD.

Janet's reference to the illusion of a continuous flow of psychic activity also seems to bear relevance to the illusion of the self, or *skandas*, which we look at later in a discussion of Buddhism.

Further Inquiries

As the twentieth century emerged, depersonalization began to be viewed in terms of the loss of some brain mechanism that causes the *feeling* that "my experiences are indeed mine."

In the 1930s, Heidelberg psychiatrist Wilhelm Mayer-Gross left Germany as the Nazis came to power and began doing his research at Bethlem Royal Hospital in London. His now-famous paper, "On Depersonalization," reviewed case histories, theories, and subsequent speculations up to that time in an attempt to clarify the true nature of the disorder.

In looking at prior literature, Mayer-Gross noted that patients' symptoms were two-sided, involving changes in the selves, but also changes in the environment around them. Noting these two aspects of the disorder, he named the latter sensation *derealization*, a term which is used to this day.

Mayer-Gross believed that depersonalization was an expression of a "pre-formed functional response" of the brain, analogous to catatonia, or seizures. He took exception to theorists who focused on isolated symptoms of the disorder, such as increased self-observation, loss of emotional response, or impairment of memory:

"It is a characteristic form of reaction of the central organ, which can be set going by different causes... The difficulty of description by means of normal speech, the defiance of comparison, the persistence of the syndrome in the face of complete insight into its paradoxical nature—all these point to something more than purely psychic connections."[11]

Mayer-Gross recorded another important observation which holds particularly true for people like myself and others whose stories are told herein: "Depersonalization and derealization often appear suddenly, without any warning. A patient sitting quietly reading by the fireside is overwhelmed by it in a full blast together with an acute anxiety attack. In some cases it disappears for a short period, only to reappear and finally persist."

Convinced that depersonalization was founded in some cerebral dysfunction, Mayer-Gross did not see a lot of point in psychoanalytic attempts to treat the condition: "Writers make abundant use of hypotheses about narcissism, libido-cathesis, etc.," he wrote. "I have found it difficult to gain any fruitful idea from such suggestions or from the suggestions of psychoanalytic writers about depersonalization. The disagreement between them is rather discouraging."

Psychological Theories

Despite Mayer-Gross's feeling that there was not much to be gained by psychological theorizing about depersonalization, a lot of thought did go into the psychology of the condition in the 20th century, particularly concerning the idea that depersonalization serves a purpose as a "defense mechanism."

Depersonalization has been linked to a poorly integrated ego or sense of self, resulting from the presence and activation of conflictual and inadequately integrated parts of the self (known as partial identifications or self-representations). This likely explains the higher frequency of dissociative experiences among adolescents, for example, where the developmental task of identity formation has not been fully completed. Indeed, the onset of depersonalization often occurs in adolescence.

Sometimes, observations of psychologists, psychiatrists, or neurologists brought unique speculations to the ongoing discussion of depersonalization. The famous Austrian neurologist Paul Schilder, director of clinical psychiatry at New York's Bellevue Hospital in the 1930s, was particularly interested in consciousness in children. This knowledge of young people may well have laid the groundwork for his observations in a well-known paper, *The Treatment of Depersonalization* written in 1939:

"I am inclined to stress the fact that the patient with depersonalization has been admired very much by the parents for his intellectual and physical gifts. A great amount of admiration and erotic interest has been spent upon the child. He expects that this erotic inflow should be continuous. The final outcome of such an attitude by the parents will not be different from the outcome of an attitude of neglect."[12]

Schilder goes on to say that the parental attitude of considering the child a "showpiece" rather than a complete human being eventually results in deep dissatisfaction. Initial self-adulation, stemming from an identification with parental attitudes, will ultimately be followed by emotional emptiness even though intellect remains intact and the person may appear quite normal or even successful to others.

Schilder's observations come to mind when I recall several young people with whom I corresponded for a period of time through *depersonalization.info*. They have been the exception, but they are worth mentioning. These individuals came from upper middle class households in which they were the only child. They were usually attractive young women who had consistently invested much in their appearance, even as their parents had invested much in their well being throughout the course of their lives. They all shared a history of life at home going their way. They appeared to be, frankly, quite spoiled. What they attempted to describe as depersonalization was invariably vague, and more of an annoyance, a hindrance to their moving on in life rather than a disorder they could clearly describe. Their frustration bordered on tantrum-like behavior, at times, and they wanted to be cured immediately, certain that they had invested enough of their precious time in pondering inexplicable fogginess and lack of interest in anything other than their own unhappiness. I referred several of these people to noted psychiatrists whom I trust, but to no avail. They were, in the end, convinced that neither the professionals nor I had any idea what they were going through. Perhaps we didn't. And perhaps they were not suffering from depersonalization at all. They seemed to have far too much ego that so desperately needed protecting. Or, perhaps they were locked in a stage of self-scrutiny that outwardly manifested itself in hostile ways. They possessed a lifetime history of thinking about themselves. Now they were impatiently thinking nonstop about their changed selves. As Schilder wrote: "All depersonalized patients observe themselves continuously and with great zeal; they compare their present dividedness-within-themselves with their previous oneness-with-themselves. Self-observation is compulsive with these patients. The tendency to self-observation continuously rejects the tendency to live."

Schilder also made some astute observations about the "automaton" aspects of depersonalization, which he called "negation of experiencing." He commented: "In clear cut cases, the patients complain that they no longer have an ego, but are mechanisms, automatons, puppets—what they do seems not done by them, but happens automatically... . raw materials of their somatic [body] sensations are unchanged... . Their lack of memory images is not a *loss* of imagery, but rather an *inhibition* of existing memories. Such patients fight, defend themselves against their perceptions; they negate internally their entire experience, and prevent themselves from experiencing anything fully."

Nonetheless, many patients may remain capable of complex achievements, which, however, are experienced as fake and without deeper meaning—part of the false, showpiece self.

Other psychologists theorized about the fractured self as well. Jacob Arlow, one of the better known ego psychology theorists, agreed with other contemporaries who felt that depersonalization represents the outcome of intrapsychic conflict, "in which the ego utilizes, in a more or less unsuccessful way, various defenses against anxiety. The split in the ego which results in the dissociation between the *experiencing* self and the *observing* self takes place in the interest of defense." Depersonalization, he believed, boils down to a specific set of reactions of the ego in the face of danger. These reactions consist of a split into a participating self and an observing self—the danger is experienced pertinent to the participating self, and can thus be distanced from the observing self.[13]

Arlow was one of the few psychologists to bring up the similarities between dreaming and depersonalization. Indeed, feeling as if in a dream is one of the more common complaints among depersonalized patients. Two characteristics of depersonalization, feelings of unreality and the split of the sense of self into an observing self and a participating self, are prominent in dreaming.

Altered Sense of Time

Distortion of time perception is a frequent complaint of depersonalized individuals; it is often mentioned today on depersonalization-themed websites and in personal stories. In a 1946 paper, "The Depersonalization Syndrome," H. J. Shorvon reviewed aspects of his study of 66 patients. One-third of these complained of changes in time perception. Shorvon cited a statement by Aubrey Lewis that time consciousness "is an aspect of all conscious activity; it is essential to all reality. In *déjà vu* there is a brief inability to actualize the present, which in consequence is projected into the past."[14] Of time disturbance in depersonalization, again Shorvon quoted Lewis, who said:

"They [time disturbances] illustrate many of the outstanding features of the disorder; the inability to evoke the past readily or clearly, to distinguish the present from the past or future; there is paradoxically the increased quickness with which time passes though it seems to drag along, the seeming remoteness of the recent past, the unconfirmed feeling of the inability to judge the length of time."

Paul Schilder adds that "the present is a concept which has meaning only in relation to experiencing personalities. The inanimate has no past, present or future...Cases of depersonalization, whose total experience is splintered, all have an altered perception of time. In extreme cases, time seems to them to be at a standstill, or the present seems to be like the distant past."[15]

The Phobic Anxiety-Depersonalization Syndrome

Aside from the seminal work by Mayer-Gross, Martin Roth's paper on the Phobic Anxiety-Depersonalization Syndrome is particularly relevant for many people caught in a cycle of panic-anxiety-depersonalization. The relationship between panic and depersonalization is cited often, and we explore it more thoroughly in later chapters. Certainly, panic and anxiety do play major roles in the overall experience of many depersonalized people, even though in others it hardly or never enters the picture at all.

Many people with whom I have compared stories have lived through periods of acute anxiety, panic attacks, and ultimately complete, mind-numbing "pure" depersonalization. Over time, one recognizes that a cycle is underway. A series of panic attacks, or free-floating anxiety, is triggered by a period of excessive stress, or even extreme involvement in a project that need not be negative at all. The anxiety eventually subsides, and settles into either excessive rumination about the apparent hopelessness of the condition in general, or a complete loss of feeling.

Panic and DPD are duly noted by the most recent research at the

Institute of Psychiatry in London. "The association between depersonalization and panic spans along a continuum of severity," writes psychiatrist Mauricio Sierra. "At one end, we find patients who experience transient depersonalization only during panic attacks. In some patients, however, depersonalization outlasts the latter and is present between attacks. At the other end of the spectrum, patients experience continuous depersonalization even after complete remission of recurrent panic attacks."[16]

It seems that in the latter instance, the series of panic attacks becomes the trauma that then triggers depersonalization. In time, exhaustion with the depersonalization itself may lead to anxiety again, and then panic, which starts the cycle all over again. This was the cycle with which I lived for many years, and the many stories submitted to *depersonalization.info* have assured me that I have never been the only one trapped on this particular treadmill. But so has one other important fact: Oz Janiger, the doctor who first recognized and treated my depersonalization, had experienced the very same thing decades earlier. Martin Roth himself had treated him, not long after publishing his theories about the Phobic Anxiety-Depersonalization Syndrome.

Obsessions

The obsessional aspects of depersonalization have not been ignored through the years, though Sir Martin Roth in 1960 pointed out the major difference between obsessional states, such as contemporary obsessive-compulsive disorder (OCD) and the kind of obsessiveness present in depersonalization. Roth identified a particular subgroup among depersonalized individuals that included patients fraught with ongoing free-floating anxiety and excessive rumination. Depersonalization, in any context, does not involve classic obsessive rituals like hand washing or outwardly eccentric compulsive behavior. Roth remarked: "Obsessional features commonly present, though rarely in the forefront of the picture, are a compulsive self-scrutiny and preoccupations with fears of disease, insanity, or loss of self-control."[17]

Roth also pointed out the distinction between DPD and classic phobic states which involve fears of specific acts like flying, or objects or creatures such as snakes or spiders. "The free floating anxiety which is said to be characteristic of anxiety neurosis proper, is very common in the phobic-anxiety-depersonalization state," Roth observed. But these patients are unable to suppress their anxiety altogether by avoiding feared objects or situations in the way a person with a phobia might. If the center of the fear is the self, or existence itself, escape or avoidance is impossible.

Evan Torch, who observed that there is a particular type of patient whose obsession is observing himself or his "vegetative functions," further explored the obsessional components of depersonalization. Torch wrote, "Even in a typical case of hypochondria, conversion neurosis, or depression *in the background of an obsessional person-ality,* it is not hard to see how continual, repetitive preoccupation with one's self can lead to a feeling of unreality, based in no small way on the fact that even to a philosopher...the question of just where to locate centrality of 'self' or 'being' is an uncomfortable one to face.[18]

"Truly depersonalized people are often very competitive and somewhat anxiety laden," Torch says. "They are not only battling with depersonalization, but often the world, too, and the DPD emerges as if the brain is setting up a shield for them. There should be some secondary gains from this—the brain now has this to focus on, rather than the other things. But the brain doesn't seem to realize that that's more painful than the problem.

"It doesn't really matter what set it off," Torch adds. "All that matters is that the DPD has staying power. So the question is, why can't a person with chronic depersonalization give it up? Because true DPD is an obsession, not an affective disorder. This is much harder to get rid of. You can't wake up and forget that you constantly hyperscan yourself. You have to accept it, and try to understand the fuel behind it."

Among patients with DPD, Torch, like Roth, also noticed a particular subtype of the disorder which he called the "intellectual-obsessive depersonalization syndrome." This subcategory, Torch said, is composed of a complex combination of alternating states of depersonalization and obsessive self-scrutiny. The end result is the "burned out" depersonalization patient, who, although still fully in touch with reality, refuses to acknowledge its intrinsic meaning.[19]

Viewing One's Self

One of the many intriguing metaphors used by depersonalized people is that they feel as if they are viewing themselves from outside, as if watching themselves in a movie. Depersonalization can involve an unpleasant sense of self-observation, or an exaggerated hyperawareness of one's self. The split between the observing and the acting self can, at its most extreme, become an out-of body-experience, although for most people it is not. Near-death experience researchers Noyes and Kletti explored this split when discussing partial or complete depersonalization among accident victims. For the 66% of the normal subjects who suddenly depersonalized, the condition appeared to be "an adaptive mechanism that combines opposing reaction tendencies, the one serving to intensify alertness and the other to dampen potentially disorganizing emotion."[20]

Cleary, the consensus of most theories about depersonalization is that it is a natural response intended to distance the self from overwhelmingly painful or conflictual impulses or feelings. But the symptoms one might experience during the course of Depersonalization Disorder are broad, and some may be less noticeable, or less verbalized because of the presence of others that seem most pressing.

The concept of depersonalization as a defense mechanism against overwhelming traumatic stress makes good sense. The subsequent lack of feeling and emotionless automaton behavior seem completely reasonable, even valuable.

"The data presented suggests that depersonalization is, like fear, an almost universal response to life threatening danger," say Noyes and Kletti. "It develops instantly upon the recognition of danger and vanishes just as quickly when the threat to life is past."[21] This description certainly describes the purpose and usefulness of transient depersonalization, which Noyes and Kletti were discussing in the context of accident victims. In the face of life-threatening danger, normal depersonalization is an adaptive, even life-saving mechanism that is considerably more useful than this process gone awry, which locks a person in heightened awareness and dampened emotions long after any perceived danger has past.

Time and again, the variety of internal and external stressors to which depersonalization may be a response has been amply illustrated and discussed. But reliance on a single premise may result in a limited diagnosis that may do little to help the patient. Depersonalization ultimately involves a constellation of unpleasant symptoms that have been discussed in earlier chapters and theorized on by the writers we've mentioned here.

In the last decade new information about the biological underpinnings of DPD has emerged, and new research into effective treatments has been conducted at the Institute of Psychiatry in London and at Mount Sinai Medical Center in New York. The highlights of this research will be examined in later chapters.

Symptoms Clarified

In 2001 psychiatrists Mauricio Sierra and German E. Berrios reviewed the nature of complaints voiced by people diagnosed with DPD. By comparing the older literature with the newer research, they were able to identify two clusters of symptoms that emerged more often. The nonchanging core symptoms include visual derealization, altered body experience, emotional numbing, loss of agency feelings, and changes in the subjective experiencing of memory. The distress caused by these particular problems is probably why they are reported most frequently. The second cluster of symptoms, including unreality experiences not related to vision, mind-emptiness (subjective inability to entertain thoughts or evoke images), heightened self-observation, and altered time experience are less likely to be reported by a patient first and foremost."[22]

Ultimately, much of the early theorizing about DPD was rooted in existing biases of the times. And, the patients' emphasis on the most pressing symptoms influenced the initial and limited formulation of what Depersonalization Disorder involved.

All of this information, the theories formulated over a century, and the more recent inventory of the ongoing essential core symptoms has laid the groundwork for a new era of research which may now combine traditional wisdom with new brain imaging technologies.

REFERENCES

1. Hunter, E.C., Phillips, M.L., Chalder, T., Sierra, M., David, A.S. (2003) Depersonalization Disorder: a cognitive-behavioral conceptualisation. *Behaviour Research and Therapy*, **41**, p 1451-1467

2. Sierra, M. (2009) Cambridge: Cambridge University Press. *Depersonalization: A New Look at a Neglected Syndrome*, p 8

3. Pizarro, J., Silver, R.C., Prause, J. (2006) Physical and Mental Health Costs of Traumatic War Experiences Among Civil War Veterans. *Arch Gen Psychiatry*. 2006: 63: p 193-200

4. Sierra, M. (no. 2) p. 12

5. Krishaber, M. (1873) *De la Neuropathie Cerebro-Cardiaque*. Paris:Masson

6. Simeon, D., Abugel, J. (2006) Oxford: Oxford University Press. *Feeling Unreal: Depersonalization Disorder and the Loss of the Self.* p 51

7. Dugas, L., (1898) Un cas de depersonnalisation. *Revue philsophique*. 55, p 500-507.

8. Nemiah, J.C., (1989) Depersonalization Disorder (Depersonalization Neurosis), *Comprehensive Textbook of Psychiatry, Vol. 1, 5th Ed.*, Kaplan and Sadock, Williams & Wilkins, Baltimore. 20: p 1039

9. Janet, P., (1903) *Les Obsessions et la Psychasthenie*. Paris: Alcan.

10. Janet, P. (1928) *De l'Angoisse a l'Extase*. Paris: Alcan

11. Mayer-Gross, W. (1935). On depersonalization. *British Journal of*

Medicine and Psychology, 15, p 103–126.

12. Schilder, P. The treatment of depersonalization. *The Bulletin, Psychiatric Division of Bellevue Hospital,* 1939, p 260.

13. Arlow, J.A. (1966). Depersonalization and derealization. *Psychoanalysis: A general psychology* (pp. 456-477). New York: International Universities Press.

14. Shorvon, H.J. (1946). The depersonalization syndrome. *Proceedings of the Royal Society of Medicine, 39,* p 779–792

15. Schilder, P. (1953). *Medical psychology.* New York: International Universities Press, p 310.

16. Sierra, M. (no 2.) p 73.

17. Roth, M.R. (1960). The phobic anxiety-depersonalization syndrome and some general aetiological problems in psychiatry. Journal of Neuropsychiatry 1:293-306

18. Torch, E M. (1978). Review of the relation between obsession/depersonalization, *Acta Psychiatria Scandinavia, 58,* 191–198, p 194

19. Ibid.

20. Noyes, R., Jr., Kletti, R., & Kupperman, S, (1977). Depersonalization in response to life threatening danger. *Comprehensive Psychiatry, 18,* p 375–384

21. Ibid.

22. Sierra, M., & Berrios, G.E (2001). The phenomenological stability of depersonalization: comparing the old with the new. *Journal of Nervous and Mental Disease,* 189, p 629–636.

4   Voices From the Void

To live is to suffer, to survive is to find some meaning in the suffering.

— Friedrich Nietzsche

Nothing relays the reality of depersonalization more than personal accounts from people who experience it. Their voices sound familiar because to the outside world, they usually seem no different than anyone else. When given the opportunity, however, they often open up with an honesty rarely found in autobiography, eloquently revealing their private silent suffering.

The following stories all appeared on *depersonalization.info* between 2002 and 2010. Some have been edited for length, and in some cases grammatical or spelling errors have been corrected. The names also have been changed, to protect the identity of each contributor.

This sampling, out of the hundreds submitted, reveals consistent themes within the context of very diverse lives. In some cases, the individual suffers from chronic, full-blown Depersonalization Disorder. In others, comorbidity with other conditions is self-evident. Most important, the details so candidly revealed go well beyond the brief patient accounts usually quoted in medical literature. Often, the latter are created from composites of different patients, or fictionalized quotations employed to illustrate various points. These stories are real. One of them may have been written by a close friend, a neighbor, even a spouse, son, or daughter. Individually, they reveal people ready to admit to every aspect of their pain, as a whole, they represent a community based on shared experience, and an uncanny ability to listen each to the other, and understand completely. They are presented here as a permanent record not subject to the transitory nature of cyberspace.

Adam's Story

I'd smoked pot since I was about 16. I had resisted for a long time, being a total control freak even at that age, but once I tried it I just had too much fun. For a number of years I had no problems. I simply enjoyed myself and suffered the typical paranoia of being regularly stoned. At the age of 20 I broke down another resistance and decided to try LSD. I had no problem with pot, and I wanted a bigger buzz. Three times I took LSD. In the first two instances, I helped the experience along with alcohol. The experience was sometimes tame, but mostly just like being drunk and tense. I had some fun and again, no problems. The third time I made the mistake of smoking a bowl to bring on the LSD. It took about 30 minutes. It started as a restless feeling, which grew into nervousness.

I wasn't sure what was going to happen. What exactly was I doing? As the LSD started to have a serious effect it dawned on me what I was doing. I had the idea that I really wasn't prepared to lose my mind in a drug experience. I then suddenly knew that this was exactly what was happening. I was, in one way or another, going to 'lose it'.

Once the thought entered my mind, that was it. The fear grew worse, which predictably set off a chain of panic and fear. Reading a number of people's descriptions of DP I can piece together a lot more of what happened that night. I know that I immediately felt disconnected from my self, for the first time truly seeing that my thoughts and my sanity were in some way not under my control. With the LSD there was nowhere to go, no retreat or safety. Panic, and a sense of losing one's mind or self are very common to DPD. But since it was a drug experience, although it was horrible and lasted for hours, it eventually settled. As the LSD wore off I began to calm down. I distracted myself and eventually managed to get to sleep. When I woke up the next day, things were simply not right. People's voices were different. Colors were different shades. Of course much of it was typical of LSD after effects. It was the nervousness, the lack of anything familiar that was the problem. I made it through that day and continued to slowly calm down. But as I went to sleep that night, the experience returned. It wasn't that I felt unreal, but rather a recurring thought, the thought that I was going to "lose it." Fear came with the thought and very quickly the panic attacks re-surfaced. This time there was no drug to wear off. This time I really felt out of control.

DP itself wasn't really my main problem at this point. I was dealing with blind, raging panic. I could only stop myself from having attacks by being distracted. My concentration was capable enough that I could study or engage in various absorbing activities. But as soon as my mind had a second to itself, the memory triggered what was happening and the panic attacks returned. It wasn't really until some weeks later, when the panic started to subside and when I began to gather my wits again, that I noticed how strange things seemed.

The view, looking down at my arms and legs, seemed very strange, not unreal, just questionable, as if it didn't have to be that way, as if the true me didn't really belong in the world and I was only supposed to be an observer. Looking back, I realize that it was, in fact, a defense mechanism. Being absorbed in my own thoughts was unpleasant, unbearable. The constant panic was my worst nightmare, so my mind had chosen to displace itself. My new view of the world was not being in it, rather being just slightly outside. In this way the DP actually progressed over time. The intense feelings died down but the perspective of not being directly in the real world developed and became a lot more permanent. Over the years, my concentration has become worse. I've become a lot more prone to stress and emotional problems. The world itself developed a sort of haze or fog. Nothing seemed entirely clear anymore and I couldn't look at something and really "see" it the way I thought I used to.

In many ways it was as if I was still on LSD, when every time you look at something, it seems new, different or interesting. As if there is nothing you can really grab on to. The intense aspects of my DP have certainly faded over the past two years or so. Being more distracted, my panic attacks are basically gone and my life is relatively normal. I am left simply feeling slightly depressed, constantly nervous and not quite able to really relax and let myself go. In some ways it's opened up my mind to many different ways of looking at the world. This is actually not all bad, although a lot of spiritual exploration can be incredibly intimidating. I am at the point now where any resistance I had to medication is gone. I've been like this for too long. I am more than aware that the symptoms are mostly to do with anxiety and I know that there is something I can do about that. I may also have found a therapist who is willing to work through things with me. In this way I am hoping to get back in touch with a more authentic version of myself. For me, DP has come about because something scared me so much that I have turned away from reality itself. I do understand that for many of us it's easy to question that reality, but I don't think it's as flimsy as it sometimes appears. And while it's good to be open to any interpretation of what is happening here, I don't believe that feeling disconnected from your own thoughts and feelings is the right way to be. DP, for me, is a case of self-denial, not self-loss, or the loss of something created as an illusion to make life easier. I have become disconnected and put up some barriers. These barriers stop me from enjoying my life and feeling as if I am a part of what is going on around me at every second, even feeling as if "I" exist at all. And while I sometimes think that this disconnection is closer to the truth than what I had before, I still know that DP is a step in the wrong direction. It gives us some interesting things to think about and experience, but ultimately it is a partial creation in itself and not somewhere where I think anyone wants to end up.

Allan's Story

For years I have attempted to recount my experience with depersonalization as a full-time condition. And every time I've tried I've stopped, for the simple reason that I first knew this illness nearly 30 years ago, and to relay everything I've experienced, felt, or endured during that time would literally take hundreds of pages.

I have lived a successful corporate life wearing a mask. When intelligence or reasoning was involved, the parts of my brain responsible for those things have never failed me. But to most of my co-workers, I was an enigma. I was fair and generous, comical, and seemed to display perceptive insights into corporate bullshit and the falseness of life in general.

A number of years ago I read *The Stranger in the Mirror*, by Marlene Steinberg, MD, thinking that at long last something concrete and comprehensive had been written about depersonalization—the thing with which I had been loosely diagnosed. But I found myself challenging what appeared to be the major premise of the book, namely, that DPD, or dissociative illnesses in general, almost exclusively stem from trauma or childhood abuse. While I have complete empathy for people who have endured such abuse, I never did, unless one considers smoking hash in college some form of self-abuse.

It is hard to believe that a single bowl of hash, not laced with anything else, can throw a person into an entirely different state of being, an entirely different world. But today, more and more evidence is proving this to be true.

In college in the 1970s everyone smoked pot and hash every day. It was just part of life, along with drinking, occasional LSD, and sex, engaged with the casualness of shaking hands. I had smoked pot four or five times with little effect. Then, the last time, I experienced a profound sense of terror unlike anything I had ever known. I knew I had damaged my brain. Yet I was, somehow, able to sleep it off and I was fine for two or three days. Then, for no reason at all, this terror came back out of nowhere, and persisted nightly for another three nights. I had felt perfectly normal the day after smoking the hash, but now, as the panic returned, a different feeling began to take over. Everything seemed strange somehow and it was as if my personality had no purpose. I couldn't participate in conversation, I couldn't laugh, I couldn't be tender with my girlfriend. It was as if I had disappeared and all that was left was a cloudy, unpleasant, headachy feeling that no amount of aspirin would remove.

I will not attempt here to relay all that happened in the next decade or so. I will stick to the facts of what has been clearly spelled out as being symptomatic of Depersonalization Disorder.

The sense of strangeness and fear of what was wrong persisted every moment in the weeks and months that followed. Familiar objects, people, and places all seemed unpleasantly unfamiliar. I couldn't concentrate at all. My perception of myself as a funny and talented guy disappeared. A zombie-like demeanor replaced the "charm" that had once marked my presence. My "self" seemed like an illusion inside, and every word or action presented to others seemed false and not worth doing.

This state of mind exhibited subtle changes over time. For a long while every thought going through my head seemed "weighed" or overly loud, excessively present. I was completely unable to experience the quiet, unobtrusive stream of consciousness that I had once enjoyed. Every thought was like tall letters running along the side of the Goodyear blimp.

I withdrew from college and returned home to live with my parents. I tried to research my condition, but everything I read led me to "psychosis," "schizophrenia," and "severe mental illness."

In a strange coincidence, or perhaps a gift from some merciful God, I learned that my old girlfriend from high school was going through the exact same thing. It was still a living hell, but I had been spared having to go through it completely alone.

While our relationship remained plutonic, we began to explore what was wrong with us, and looked for a cure. Because of this shared experience, it became clear that it had all begun with the hash, despite the normal days that had followed the initial panic.

We visited a psychiatric clinic, filled out page after page of questions, none of which seemed relevant, and then met with a low-level psychiatrist who told us that he might be able to help us with a few years of psychotherapy.

At the time, phrases like "panic attack," and "obsessive-compulsive disorder" were virtually unheard of. You were either depressed, schizophrenic, or "manic-depressive." Valium and lithium seemed to be all you could get in a prescription (even though there were many effective drugs available at the time).

We passed on the psychotherapy, and concluded that the pot had caused it all. Perhaps it would get better in time. For my-ex-girlfriend, it did, after a year. For me, it lingered.

The acute depersonalization, as defined in all the manuals today, lasted about two years, then came and went for several more. I went on with my life, graduated college and began working. I also began to fall into periods that could only be described as deep depression. It was different than the depersonalization. In DPD, you fight, you struggle, and you somehow look forward to improvement or resolution. You can even distract yourself through work or romance. In depression, however, the battle is over. You are ready to sink into "the void" and die, with no trace of you left behind. It's beyond feeling as if things are meaningless. Your mind becomes fragmented, fearful, and then resigned to somehow end it all.

Seeking help from more qualified doctors, some anti-depressants pulled me out of these dark holes every time, usually within a few weeks. Perhaps these episodes were already built into my genetic make-up. I have accepted the fact that depression and acute anxiety, two sides of the same coin, may have erupted in me no matter what. But depersonalization was decidedly different, and for the first few years that I mentioned earlier, the symptoms of pure DPD, as they are now recognized, were clearly present. Depersonalization has, in many ways, defined my life, for better or worse. Thankfully, mental health research and attitudes of the general public are emerging from the Dark Ages. Hopefully, many will be spared from altering their lives to suit the problems in their heads.

Maya's story

I may have experienced it from the very beginning of life, I really don't know. I was born in Poland and adopted by Americans at 1½ years of age. I include this fact because I think there are some links with adoption and DP. I don't really know, but would like to know more about it. The first experience with depersonalization that I can remember is sitting in my parents' room on the floor looking into a mirror on the back of a door. I remember thinking/ feeling that I wasn't alive. I think it scared me a lot, but I don't really recall. I think the feeling was always there.

Then when I went away to college my first year two things happened. I did mescaline one night. Usually, when I drank alcohol there would be a point when I just suddenly snapped back into reality. I don't ever recall feeling that snap back into reality after I took the mescaline, but I am still not sure how much that experience really matters in terms of DP. Another thing that happened (the big thing) was one day about a month after I tried the mescaline—I went into a fog. It just happened one day, which has always seemed so strange to me. Every psychologist (that I have seen for depression) has not felt that depersonalization is related to the mescaline. Only one thought it might be. The DPD disturbed me for years. When I told close friends about it they seemed to appreciate it, but I always sensed that they didn't realize it was really something I lived with 24/7. Once I was talking to a best friend about it and I think he just got scared himself, thinking about whether we are truly alive or not. I learned that it is dangerous to tell some people about it, because it scares them.

I struggled with college and withdrew a few times. My adoptive mom died, and there were some other deaths and attempted suicides of close friends. As a result, I think, I became depersonalized all the time. Later on, after I graduated from college and was working, I thought back to the DP and it seemed so distant, not because I didn't still experience it every day, but because I had stopped focusing on it and went on with my life. I am not preaching—I was just lucky I was able to do that eventually. I have read several stories on the depersonalization websites by people who speak of "DP episodes." I don't have episodes. I feel like my life is always just one big episode. I don't even feel like this is a dream because if this was a dream there would have to be a dreamer. I don't just feel like I don't exist; I feel like nothing exists!

It was the worst in college, when it was like I couldn't feel or see anything past an inch of my skin. A therapist tried an exercise with me where you hold a rock and feel it. I didn't exist, so neither did the rock. In the last ten years I have only *really* seen the world or the room around me for about a total of twenty minutes. I just *saw* the outside of my house and part of the block I live on for the first time the other day. Usually these experiences of actually seeing my surroundings only last about a few minutes. Everything always looks so much smaller than how I thought it was when I was just floating though it with the DP.

The newest development for me is that I randomly started reading this book *The Drama of the Gifted Child*. I don't claim to be an abused child at all, but for some reason this book really reached me in a way that started really pushing my DP buttons. Sometimes when I was reading it I was really feeling completely not alive. Normally I would have just calmed myself down then somehow distracted myself as I have learned to do. But this time I decided I was just going to let my feelings go and feel not alive. Influenced by the book, I decided not to run from my feelings and let myself simply experience them. It was pretty scary, but I was able to do it.

One of the things that has also changed is that I have started thinking a little more about I guess what you call spirituality. (Maybe it's because I just recently moved out to California). I am not saying I believe in God. But for so long my depersonalization has been so tied to bad feelings, really bad feelings, and the sense that life is totally pointless, and the world is going to hell in a hand basket. Maybe that is depression—it's hard to sort it all out. But now I allow myself to think that it might not all be bad, and that there might be something out there, and it has made the depersonalization somehow different. I allow myself to feel what I do, without fighting it as much.

I haven't drawn any final conclusion about if there is something more or life after death, but it has definitely made it a different experience to open myself up to that possibility. Finally, I've noticed that the depersonalization is much worse after I've taken an early evening nap, and slept too long. Instead of waking up rested, I feel horrible, almost suicidal. Sometimes it will take nearly an hour to feel better.

Bernadette's Story

I'm scared of myself, I'm scared of people, I'm scared of the world I live in and the life I'm leading. These thoughts hide behind fake laughs, awkward movements, and sunken eyes, they consume me. I feel their intensity as I stare at this blank page. Every move-ment of my pen is the result of a forceful nudge from some trapped version of me, to a hand I don't recognize. I look up at my reflection in the mirror and I don't see myself anymore, my face is dead and old, there is nothing there, I look and feel like a comatose patient. There is a definite subjectivity to how I have come to view the world, I am removed from the experience of watching, as I observe a group of friends sitting and talking, almost as though I see them through a life size television. A few years ago I would have tried to view this experience as empowering, having convinced myself that I felt detached because I was somehow better than these superficial, shal-low people that surround me. But now I know it's because I'm dead, and I have nearly lost the energy needed to pretend to be alive.

I wrote the passage above on a napkin when I was 17 years old, before I knew anything about depersonalization and before I had even dreamed about getting help. I am now 21 and have recently left hospital where I was admitted for three weeks after suffering what my GP called a "nervous breakdown." It was a Monday morning I was getting prepared for university that afternoon and filling in some forms for my part-time job, I try very hard to keep myself distracted from the invasion of thoughts that eat away at me and that Monday was no exception. As I was finishing my jobs the thoughts began to creep in, suddenly my mind was a flurry with antagonistic debates and rhetorical questions, what was wrong with me, was I going insane? And if I was, why was it taking so long? Then the last thing I remember was putting down my pen and staring as hard as I could at my reflection in the glass cabinet a few meters in front of me. I didn't recognize myself. In fact its been so long since I did recognize myself that I don't know if I ever will again. I'm dead I thought, and with what was either my body finally giving up under the weight of my own thoughts or an act of rebellion on my part, trying to take back control of my body by "deciding" to lose my mind once and for all, I found myself in a psychiatric hospital.

I don't remember waking up on my first day in the hospital because I never remember waking up, most of my life has felt like a dream, my memory is dreamlike and I have trouble separating fact from dreamlike fiction. As I walked around the hospital at a speed that seemed much slower than everyone around me, I did something I have not done since I was a child and unfamiliar with the laws of the universe. I laid on the floor, curled up and clutching my knees, closed my eyes and begged whatever Mighty Power may exist to let me please wake up, or perhaps if I would never awaken, to let me die. With that thought and right on queue, my thoughts began to harass me, "maybe you are already dead, perhaps this is your punishment for being such a self-absorbed emotional robot...never knowing whether you are asleep or awake, living or dead." I quickly picked myself up hoping not to have drawn attention to myself, however it was too late and a few concerned nurses had gathered around me. They asked me what was wrong and I tried without much success to explain it to them. As I fumbled through the vague descriptions I began to feel that intense burning panic. I sounded sane enough, but what I was saying was far from sane. Were they buying my performance? Would I personally give it a good rating? Perhaps I should have thrown in some hysterical screams for dramatic effect.

Later that day my mum and a family friend came to visit, they hugged me and their eyes showed genuine concern for my well-being, but I didn't feel it. I looked at my mum's hand holding my own hand. She was squeezing it, but I felt nothing, no love, no squeezing, all I felt was a general disgust and a burning desire to tell her to stop touching me. It was not because I thought she didn't love me or because I didn't love her. I do and she does but I didn't want her to touch me because I didn't want to feel that nothingness, it made me think I was some sort of evil entity. It has been so long since I felt anything genuine, besides fear and my own forced pain that I inflict on myself by trying to get close to people who treat me poorly, because it is familiar. I think, perhaps, if this person hurts me enough I will feel something again, but I never did, I simply forced out those predictable tears that have become second nature to me, and waited for the real feelings to follow.

After a week in hospital I had settled into the routine well, since it allowed me to maximize my distractions, but the activities weren't enough, so I began to try and help the other patients through their problems. My desire and efficiency in helping them sort out welfare issues, or liaison with their fed-up family members caused some of them to question whether I was in fact a patient or perhaps an informer of some kind sent to spy on them. When I was confronted with these theories I simply laughed and thought to myself, I still am the best actress around, people still buy my performance. But was this caring and helpful person the performance or was it the old me trying to force its way through? I began my performing career at a young age you see and now almost 15 years later I have forgotten which parts of my so called identity are me, and which are merely part of my automatic performance. I spend so much time distracting myself by caring for others. Do I really care, or is it just easier than thinking about or trying to take care of myself?

I settled into the routine of antidepressants and counseling. The drugs robbed my mind of the cognitive ability to obsess over my own thoughts, but it didn't reattach me to my life, it didn't wake me up. The counseling began to help. Slowly I allowed myself to feel pain, but I'm still not sure what the pain is from. My memory is so confused I can't connect the traumatic events in my life (that I can remember with any sort of affect.) I am home now and still going to the hospital as an outpatient and hopefully if I put in the work I will one day wake up, but perhaps I won't but at least I know I'm not alone and there are many people going through something similar.

Alex's Story

About 18 months ago while at work something changed inside my brain. It was instantaneous. I looked around and everything seemed different, like nothing was real, like I was in a dream or a movie or under the influence of drugs. An unbelievably hot rush of fear swept through my body (my doctor tells me it was panic) and I headed straight for the toilet. I tried to shake it off but I couldn't, then it hit me, either one of my workmates had spiked my lunch or I was going nuts and would surely be committed. Even the thoughts in my head seemed somehow askew. I spent the rest of the afternoon at work completely paranoid and self-conscious. I didn't go to work for the next five weeks. I endured panic attacks and transient Agoraphobia. I did all the basic tests and everything was fine. The only way I could describe it to my GP, family, and friends was a feeling of "displacement." I compared it to the feeling of when you're suddenly awakened from sleep by a ringing phone. You fumble around, neither awake nor asleep. I didn't go to see a neurologist or a psychiatrist because the episodes that caused the Agoraphobia had subsided. So I went back to work, but there was this weird thing with my perception, like a haze in my brain. My vision was clear but something about it was blurry, as if I were looking through someone else's eyes. I have never been the same since. I worked for an entire year completely spaced out, depersonalized. Every day was hell, constantly evaluating how I felt and constantly asking myself what is it, what's wrong with me? Strange sensations, and strange thoughts.

During the year the DP didn't stop me from doing anything, I traveled, socialized, drove and skied. I had no Agoraphobia and I didn't feel overly anxious, but no matter what I did it wasn't the same as before, nothing looked the same and nothing felt the same. I was the walking dead, like I was no longer a part of the world; in it, but somehow not part of it. Everything seemed surreal, with a feeling of displacement as if I was in a dream or a trance, an altered state of consciousness. I would have momentary feelings of "phasing out" then "phasing in" again followed by fear from the knowledge that the feeling of "phasing in" is a result of having "phased out". I also had a constant concern about not being able to predict one of those "hot fear" episodes that initially brought Agoraphobia and paranoia.

I feel that my brain is slow to interpret visual images, and changes in light. For example, if I'm sitting in a room doing whatever, and then I get up and walk to another room, the new setting throws me, like I need a minute to get used to what I'm looking at. That applies to any changes in my environment. My brain needs a minute to register what I'm looking at. When I'm outside on a sunny day and drifting clouds block the sun, the sudden change in light makes me feel strange for a minute until I get used to it.

I was constantly drowsy, no matter how much sleep I'd had. I endured a constant awareness of self-awareness, and an inability to concentrate and focus. I felt physically weak. Even with all of this I was in a generally positive and optimistic frame of mind. There where fleeting instances through the year where I thought, "What if you stay like this forever?" But the thought was too much to bear and I would snap myself out of that sort of thinking before I got into it. I honestly thought that whatever it was, it would go away just as quick as it had come to me. I maintained my social life and did the things I always did for fun, but it wasn't the same, it wasn't fun. I couldn't feel *anything*. Sometimes I thought I may be dead and not know it, and sometimes when talking to people I would think to myself "did he just say that or did I imagine it?" On occasion I would get an abrupt feeling that I was falling into a void, but it would only last a split second. Sometimes things seemed so unreal, like I could see past them or was falling away from them, it was as though I could walk through solid objects. They didn't seem transparent, just not real. When I was really bad I would have tense limbs, like my legs didn't want to co-operate with my brain, as well as balance problems, as if I were going to fall over.

I noticed things through the year that made it worse—when I was tired, or after a long driving stint (4 or more hours). Also, exercise made me worse. I also felt weird in well-lit areas and under fluorescent lights. I did find one thing that actually made me feel kind of normal again—getting drunk.

As for my past, as a child I always thought and analyzed too much, but I was the "strong one in the family," and never had mental issues before this. I did some drugs, but none for three years before this happened, once or twice I had somewhat similar feelings to this with pot. I was never happy in my work but loved life outside of work. I was very social, loved traveling, and couldn't wait to go away camping, skiing or hiking. I've always loved nature and was drawn to its beauty. Unfortunately I now can't appreciate it like I used to. I know it's beautiful but I can't "feel" it's beautiful. I have always experienced excessive déjà vu (twice a day minimum) and it always made me feel uneasy.

Toward the end of last year I'd had enough, I wasn't getting any better and I thought I better go and get a referral to a neurologist. Christmas was approaching, however, and I had a trip planned with friends, so I didn't see him. I went on my trip and when I went back to work in January, I was hit with panic attacks late on a Thursday afternoon. All I could think was "no not again." I haven't worked since. Along with the panic, Agoraphobia has gotten really bad. It's this that incapacitates me. I honestly think I wouldn't get panic attacks, and the resulting Agoraphobia, if I wasn't depersonalized. When it all began, I'm positive I depersonalized first then suffered a panic attack, but it may have been the other way around. If I could just get rid of the panic and Agoraphobia, I'd be able to attack the DP, which is now worse than ever.

Since January, I have been to neurologists and clinical psychiatrists. I was diagnosed with severe Depersonalization Disorder, with panic and Agoraphobia as secondary symptoms. My doctor said that in my case it was genetic (my sister has Temporal Lobe Epilepsy.) Later my doctor told me that DP and anxiety were one and the same, but he didn't seem too sure about it, so I subsequently changed doctors. I've had an EEG—it was clear. But an MRI showed a localized thickening of the Cortex at the left temporal lobe. I have tried four different anti-depressants (Lovan, Cipramil, Avanza, Zoloft). Some made me worse; others had no effect (except side effects). The only thing that has sort of helped is Xanax, and I've even had small panic attacks on Xanax particularly in crowded public places.

I write this in the hope that people out there suffering from DP and anxiety may read it and know they're not alone. It has also made me feel a little better putting this in writing. I don't know what DP is except that it is a horrendous condition that robs you of your very soul. Most of the doctors down here in Australia either don't have a clue or don't recognize it is as anything but a symptom. None of the crap I've had to put into my body has helped, so my faith in doctors down here is non-existent. I'm seriously considering flying to New York to see a specialist. I can't take it anymore. I am an empty shell of what I used to be. I want my life back.

Jared's story

I walk feeling alone in the world. Everyone is here but at the same time they're not. I feel empty. Is anything what it appears? Am I the only one here? Am I the only one that sees? Where are everyone's eyes? Why don't they see what I see? Did they close their eyes to the place I see and feel?

I feel completely hollow. I feel as unreal as the perceived objects around me. This body I occupy seems foreign to me. It's as though I am borrowing it for some undefined reason. I know the feeling will pass, but then will my eyes be closed? The pressure at the base of my head is a chilling reminder of death, the few moments of awareness before I pass to the other side. Perhaps this pressure opens my eyes. Perhaps it isn't really there. Perhaps this feeling isn't real.

I touch things around me to verify they are really there. Even though I can physically feel them my mind perceives that they truly aren't there. If they aren't there, why can I touch them? I feel tired and weak. How my body moves to write is strange to me. Am I really moving my body, or am I just a spectator that is observing this body moving?

The page turns, and the sound of the paper moving is interesting. The sound of this reality is interesting. I know these sounds exist, but why do they now sound hollow? The walls around me are the same as ones from my everyday memory of this place, but they somehow look like cardboard. Like one gentle push would make them all collapse. It's not really that they look different, but somehow my mind tells me they are cardboard. I feel air blow across my feet. I seem larger than normal. My head is so quiet. Why can't I hear all my thoughts. Perhaps the thoughts of this feeling are louder than my regular thoughts. The world seems so quiet. Am I really the only one here? How can I be the only one? If I am the only one here then how can I truly learn from these figures that appear the same as me? If they can't see what I see, then how can they teach me about the things that surround me? If I can't learn about this place then I am puzzled as to why I am here. Am I here to play as a pawn in something's sick game? How can I become a true player of this game?

The page turns again. I don't feel like writing any more. Rather I feel as though I should contemplate my existence in the quiet ordered hollowness of my mind. Perhaps stimulating my senses will jolt me back to myself. But once back, how can I handle things knowing my eyes are again closed? Although I hate this feeling, in some way I am glad that I get to see the world with open eyes. I will miss this feeling as it starts to pass, and will again hate it. Perhaps writing this down will help me remember more clearly what I can see as this person. Perhaps in time I will understand what this feeling is. Perhaps this feeling is a way for me to learn the hidden truths of this reality. Perhaps I will never know.

Linda's Story

I am a 51-year-old woman, and have never spoken to a doctor about my episodes of unreality. They have, thank God, lessened greatly over the years, and have never become chronic.

I remember as a child of about five being in the garden and suddenly thinking I had just been born. I couldn't remember the person I had been before that time (although I am quite sure that I hadn't forgotten my parents or other important people or things.) Around that time I also remember being in a lane having strange thoughts about things not having a beginning or an end, but just going round and round. I couldn't explain how I felt to my mother, although I tried.

My feelings of depersonalization didn't start until I was about ten or eleven. They were episodes that lasted from a few seconds to several minutes, but were the most awful feelings I had ever had. I never felt that I was the only one to feel this way though, because my elder sister had what she called the "far-away" feeling, and shortly after my first episode, my younger sister had her first attacks.

There was usually a recognizable trigger for me, which was either an unexpected sensation—a bright light, a loud noise, or an unexpected, sudden event. I would have to shut my eyes and stand exactly where I was because I didn't really believe I was in control of myself. Everything around me seemed like a dream. Luckily my friends got used to it.

As a youngster I dwelt on thoughts of life, the universe, and everything. I had dreadful panic attacks, usually in the middle of the night, about "nothingness" and "eternity."

Unlike others, I had never experienced any truly traumatic experiences prior to my first episodes, nor had I smoked dope or taken ecstasy or acid. I am lucky. As I said, these attacks have lessened greatly, and now occur only periodically. I hope that soon there will be a proper cure for those people living with this condition on a daily basis.

Lenora's Story

For the longest time now I was convinced that I might have a brain tumor or something; perhaps not. I have been seeing a psychiatrist for some time. She prescribed Zoloft which I have been on for a little over a year. It has helped with my depression, but not with these rather startling episodes I have. I try to explain them to her. Her best conclusion is "panic attack." I have had panic attacks, but they seemed to be triggered by this depersonalization.

I suppose this has been with me my whole life. It wasn't until recently that it has started affecting my daily life. It was one episode that started it all. I was driving with my sister. We were on vacation and it was my turn to take over the wheel. I was fine for a while, but then I noticed myself drifting... I could see my hands on the steering wheel, but they weren't mine. I was somehow behind myself looking at these hands and wondering how it was my flesh. I couldn't get out of it. I couldn't understand or comprehend anything happening. I tried controlling my body but I was trapped, watching from a distance. I could see the cars in front of me on the expressway, but they were so odd to me. I couldn't understand or judge distances between them. They seemed like robotic monsters. It was frightening, as if I was asleep all this time, inside myself and now I had awakened to this new, odd world. I kept thinking focus, focus on the road, but I was lost in these thoughts, confused and scared. We had to pull over and my sister took the wheel. This has frightened me a lot and now while I drive I cannot think too much or I will leave myself again as I did that day.

These thoughts and feelings seem to also take over while I'm talking to people or explaining something to them. I am an artist. So in the middle of a critique I find myself drifting away and I am again lost inside myself. I can hear myself talk, but I have no control over what I'm saying, almost as if I am on autopilot. I then get confused and stumble over words.

The fear that I am turning schizophrenic crosses my mind many times. Sometimes I get scared of my body. I will be lost in thoughts and notice that I'm actually a human, as if I never saw one before. I am often disturbed by my own presence and turn shy, as if I were someone else. I don't feel human at times, like I'm an identity that was never fully connected to my physical being. I am a straight girl, but I have found myself startled by the fact that I have sexual organs at all. Then I start to think that what really makes me a certain sex is my body. My mind seems to be wandering as if I could float from body to body. It's odd at times, and I often feel alone. I have trouble explaining it to my boyfriend or family without sounding crazy, but at least I now know that there are others like me with similar experiences .... I wonder what it all means...what's happening to us all?

Matthew's Story

I have experienced depersonalization for my entire life. I am 33. I was adopted after being born with Temporal Lobe Epilepsy. For as long as I can remember I have always felt like a stranger unto myself. Even as a toddler I remember looking in the mirror and wondering who I was looking at. Sometimes I would get in trouble for telling stories about what things I thought I had done but actually hadn't—my subconscious was that strong even back then. Late in high school, and for a short time after, I smoked pot to excess, at least a half ounce a day for about two years straight, until I ended up completely paranoid. During this time I had also dropped acid twice, smoked and snorted cocaine and indulged in some mescaline once.

In 1989 I fell from a roof while at work and landed head first on a set of concrete stairs. I suffered a crushed left wrist and forearm, demolished left hip and a left orbital implosion which severed my left optic nerve and left me with left temporal lobe bruising due to the incredible amount of swelling. This tragic event killed me for three minutes and the odds were 60/40 against me, but I made it. The subsequent lawsuit left me with a net worth of over $500,000, which just helped to let the illness gain more power over me, because with the money, I could be anyone I wanted to be. even though I had no idea who "I" was. Needless to say, the money was gone within five years.

At one time I was taking a combination of 6mgs of Xanax, 30 mgs of Valium, 500 mgs of Depakote, 360 mgs of Endoral and 50 mgs of Prozac all in one day. My resting heart rate before the Endoral was 140 beats per minute. Now it is around 80 bpm, (blood pressure was always fine.) This was due to an over production of adrenaline, cause unknown. Cushing's Syndrome may also be a factor, though I need to see an endocrinologist for tests.

When I was young the only way I could deal with it was to push myself to the limit causing my body to use all it's adrenaline. The way that worked the best was to drive at insane speeds down roads that would have killed normal people but with my focus and desire to expend that adrenaline I could drive through downtown Boston at over 120mph, blowing red lights and dodging pedestrians. Though the best was 140+mph police chases either on the highway or through the suburbs of Boston (they could never catch me). My mind was thinking so fast and so caught up in its self that I literally couldn't drive slow. If I did, you would swear I was driving drunk. During recent neurological and psychiatric testing, doctors calculated that my brain was operating at more than six times the speed of a normal brain, as determined through the Rorschach test. My IQ is 145. Taking Endoral was my idea, not my doctor's. It has been a godsend for anxiety and panic but I am still taking the Xanax so I can stay somewhat in touch with reality. My combination of illnesses is overly frightening to me due to the nature of the thoughts that invade my mind from my subconscious—very morbid, delusional and fanciful thoughts of homicide or suicide, fantasy thoughts and "what if" thinking. Sometimes I'll hold my arm out, look at it and not believe that it is part of me, more like I am an alien inside someone else's body. Looking at the world through someone else's eyes. Speaking of eyes, I am blind in my left eye, so I have no depth perception, hence two-dimensional vision that just makes everything even more surreal. Sometimes I'll look around and it's as if I am walking through the little city they show at the beginning of "Mr. Rogers' Neighborhood." Often I'll be walking out of a store back to my car and I'll see my car yet I can't believe it's mine, even though I know it is. I'll just think, "Wow, I actually have a car."

Sometimes with the "what if" thoughts that float through my mind I just feel as if there is no hope and I want to die. Add in the depression and guilt from a divorce and even I am surprised I am still alive. Also I have many memory lapses, such as driving to work and not remembering certain parts of the drive. The same can occur during any activity, working, surfing the net, watching a movie, making love, etc. It is like I wake from a haze not knowing where I am or what I was doing. It takes but a few seconds to recover but is very odd. Now, to make matters worse, my wife has left me because she can't live with my illness any longer. We were together for 10 years then right out of the blue, just a week after our sixth wedding anniversary, she said she wanted a divorce and that it was too late to fix anything. All I want is for people to understand, is that too much to ask and why is society so afraid of psychological pain? I am afraid to wake up tomorrow.

Pam's Story

I'm really pleased that I have found a website where people can submit their stories re: depersonalization. I am 53 years old and have been depersonalized since I was 19 years old. I think it can be traced to when I was 12. I was transferred to a new school, and I was considered bright. I became very conscious of myself and started having panic attacks when asked to read at school. I am sure that it was because I felt I wouldn't measure up in the new school.

I became so terrified of English lessons that I would tremble, become breathless, and feel acute embarrassment. School became a nightmare. I began experiencing absences of time. I looked through medical dictionaries to find the cause and discovered epilepsy. I didn't want epilepsy and so I decided to hide the "absences" as best I could. Eventually, after a couple of big seizures, I was diagnosed with epilepsy although I was loathe to admit that I had suffered any lapses in time. The doctor who diagnosed me was so annoyed about my trying to hide my symptoms that he laid into me, listing all I could *not* do in life, such as get married, have children, drive etc. etc. All my fears exploded into reality.

I returned to college and began thinking about life—why I was me, and if I died I would still be me, therefore trapped forever. I thought about other people. I wondered who they were and how they could be them, if they weren't me. I wanted to be someone else, someone without epilepsy. My mind became overwhelmed with thoughts about existence and one day, when I was walking along a college corridor, I felt something click inside my head. I felt distanced and different and the familiar surroundings appeared strange. I remember going to the library and sitting down trying to wait for these awful, weird alien feelings to pass.

They never did, but I have survived.

Michael's Story

When I was born nearly 48 years ago I suffered from a birth defect known as Congenital Diaphragmatic Hernia (CDH). Due to a malformed diaphragm my stomach and intestines went up into my chest cavity and displaced my heart and lungs to the left side. I was a dark blue when I was delivered because I couldn't breathe and I had to be resuscitated.

Twenty-four hours later emergency surgery was performed and my internal organs were placed where they needed to go. I was apart from my mother from the instant I was born and for the next two weeks. My first experience with human existence and reality was pain, fear and isolation.

I don't remember much about my childhood except that one day when I came home from school (I was eight years old at the time) I saw my mother being taken out of the house on a stretcher and put into a van. Nobody told me what was going on. My parents were strict Christian Scientists and they didn't believe in doctors or sickness. I was told very early that everything was an illusion and that I couldn't trust my five senses. I was always afraid and I probably didn't ask anybody anything about what was going on.

A few days later I came home from school and my dad and my uncle from England were there in the house. My dad said, "Mom isn't coming home," and then got up and left. I remember him walking past me as I sat on the floor. I felt one of the first chills of unreality race down my back. Nobody ever talked about mom and I felt very alone and scared. My dad didn't talk to me or my older sisters and brother about anything, really. He was very cold and isolated and didn't care about us.

I've suffered panic attacks from eight years old until today and I have felt unreal on and off for all of my life. I remember asking my father and brother "Am I really here"? when I was 10 years old. They sneered and walked away. All my life I've been trying to explain to non-DPs the misery and unreality I've felt periodically throughout my life. My father went to prison a few years ago for sexually abusing two of his grandkids. After he got out of prison he told me that he had psychologically abused me when I was a child.

When I suffered panic attacks as a little child, and up to this day, the world instantly became unbearably terrifying. I would look at objects: my bedside lamp, the walls, the door and they had no meaning. I didn't know who I was or where I was or why or where anything could ever be. Life was an impossibility. All I knew was a rapidly mounting terror feedback in my head. I would be forced to run down the "unreal" stairs in a blind panic and rush outside into the night. My dad never knew what I was going through and wouldn't have cared anyway.

Many times I would be standing barefoot in the snow at night during winter in my underwear trying to connect with something that was "me". The expanse of the Universe, infinity, eternity, constantly tormented me. Where is anything? What possible meaning could anything have even if it were real? "I" am just an unknown thing experiencing fear and pain in a forgotten, and non-existent place and time. I tried to explain my torment to people and they'd reply, "If you're not real, then how come you have a body"? Circular and confusing misery and depression. I tried to explain that my "reality shield" was broken. They didn't get it. I'd get glimpses of all of eternity and it drove me close to insanity. It strikes randomly. Do I get to go to heaven for having suffered so much? I only tried marijuana a few times in high school because every time I tried it, it would trigger a panic attack. Life sometimes doesn't make any sense. Sometimes depersonalization goes away and I'm left angry and exhausted that I've been treated this way. I have had wonderful moments in my life, but this constant dwelling and pondering has reduced the quality of my life. I'm getting older and that fact is depressing to me. I wake up every morning with a knot in my stomach. I suffer from having the emotional maturity of an 8-year-old while inhabiting a 48-year old body that is starting to ache more and more as it ages. My wife left me and took the children. We've been separated for two years. She is a non-DP and never understood my torment. Who does?

Five years ago my reality shield broke for good and I spent the next several years in a permanent low-grade panic attack. I've tried psychiatrists, drugs, holistic medicine, exercise, and diet. What's the answer? I sometimes get awful DP sensations from falling asleep after getting home from work and then waking up half an hour later. Total existential nausea. I'm very grateful that *depersonalization.info* "exists." I've been looking all my life for someone who understood this misery. I want to become "real," even if it's only online.

Nan's Story

I was the sixth child. My brother was born 18 years earlier and two boys and two girls died in infancy before I was born. My mother did not want another child because she could not bear another loss. Nonetheless, I was conceived and in spite of her efforts to abort, I was born healthy. She hovered over me. In fact one psychiatrist said it was smother love that I received. Each sniffle, or pain became a death knell in her mind.

When I was seven, I needed my tonsils out. She would not agree to having it done in the hospital because her children had all died in the hospital. I had mine removed on the kitchen table with ether. I suspect it was poorly administered since there was no equipment to monitor. It was horrible for me and the awful smell lingered in the house for days. It was then I felt unreal. I never truly awakened. In November my dad had a fatal hemorrhage and two years later I witnessed my mother beaten by her mother and niece. The DP became more intense. School was a nightmare. My mother said it was nothing and I would be fine. I was an A student in spite of DP.

I graduated and since we could not afford college or university I began to work. At age 18 I saw the first of many psychiatrists. None understood depersonalization. I was hospitalized, assessed, endured shock treatment and medication. I was much worse, but continued to work. No one knew what was happening to me because I had learned to act. I never met anyone who said they felt unreal, so I assumed I was alone. I wanted to die but could not give my mother more pain with the loss of another child. I married, had children and completed my education in this haze called living.

I am now in my 50s and some meds help, but I still live in this shadow of life. Not until I punched in the letters DEPERSONAL-IZATION on my computer did I realize I was not alone. I have coped because I had to for my mother, husband, children and now grandchildren. Do I still think I am insane or going that way? Yes.

Would my friends and family think so. No. They see me as a normal, competent individual with a terrific sense of humor. I have been a social worker for many years and an author. I am currently working on a book. Does any of this give me pleasure? Only in terms of how much I can escape the pain of DP.

Charles' Story

I am 67 and live in England. I have had DP since I was 12, and so that's 55 years of living with this incapacitating problem of feelings of unreality, and all the other feelings that go with the condition.

I came from a hard family, with an alcoholic and violent father. Although my mother did not drink much, she also could be quite violent. I had one sister, two years younger. My father loved fighting and used to go into pubs and clubs to cause fights and beat the unwary victim quite badly. Then he would come home and beat my mum, Nanny, and me. My mother usually beat me afterwards to get rid of her frustration and temper at being beaten herself. My sister always got off free and my Nan was my only defendant. Later in life my Nan told me my father used to knock me around in the cot when I was very small because he could not stand my crying. My father had six brothers who were all like him, only he was the worst. His brothers used to bring their wives to our place on a Friday night. My father would smack them around because they were not doing what their husbands expected of them. I used to lie in bed listening to these poor woman scream for my father to stop hitting them. It was dreadful.

Reasons for the start of the DP? I am not sure. When I was born in 1943 and only a few months old, a V2 rocket from Germany landed on a house in the road and virtually destroyed the street. I was buried under rubble and was found two days later by fireman, apparently physically uninjured.

As a young boy everything I did was wrong. I was constantly smacked for the slightest infringement of any of their rules. You were not allowed to cry if you were hit and you were hit until you stopped crying.

My mother is still alive but my father was killed when I was eighteen. In all that time I can never remember, even on one occasion, when they cuddled me or told me they loved me.

The first time I had any idea something was wrong with me was when I was 12. I was playing football at school. For some reason I looked down at my hands and my mind said they are not yours. I just started screaming and running in every direction in absolute horrendous fear. The fear was based on the premise that if these were not my hands, whose were they? The teachers caught me; an ambulance came and took me to a hospital. My parents were called in. The doctors told my parents they thought I might have a brain tumor. Obviously I did not. I was put under a psychiatrist, and given Valium. I was in a dreadful mess. In between getting what I came to call the "bad heads," I was just like a zombie. Just a pair of eyes observing what was going on. I just felt that the me, my identity whatever it is that makes you feel like yourself, just disappeared. So I lived with the two problems. One was the feeling of detachment and being in a dreamlike state. And the other, which was far worse, was this extraordinary terror of realizing your mind is totally rejecting who you are. There were common triggers to this but sometimes no triggers at all. Mirrors did it. Looking in a mirror often brought on a bad head in as much as my mind said that reflection was not me. The dark, but only when I am on my own. I have driven down dark country lanes at night on my way home from work and had screaming fits as my eyes watched my hands on the steering wheel and my mind saying that's not you driving.

When this first started, I came home from school and sat on a wall near my house. I was far too frightened to knock on the door to be let in as my mind used to say "what if they do not know you." I use to wait outside until it got so late they started looking for me and then just dragged me in and hit me because I was late. This happened every day for two years.

When the bad heads occurred in the house they used to grab me and pour cold water over my face and tell me that would make me feel better. It never did.

I was also under strict instructions never to tell anyone about how I felt, because I would be taken to a mental institution and locked away. Shortly after my eighteenth birthday I felt a lot better. I had met a girl and we started dating. I still had the bad heads but I told her, and she was great with me.

We married and had two children. I trained as an electronics engineer on aircraft radar. We decided to immigrate to Canada in 1966 when I was 23. I was to go first and my wife and children were to follow when I was set up. I had been and was still taking Librium, Nardil, and Tofranil. The day I was due to leave by boat from Dover to Quebec, my bad heads started. I was so ill I could not speak. My fear was so bad, I was incapable of even the simplest of conversations.

I could not stop crying and I was begging them all to let me stay. My whole family had come to see me off. They told me I was stupid and to pull myself together. We had let our flat go and my wife was living with her mother until she could join me. I had no choice. I got on the boat not knowing anyone and in, as far as I was concerned an alien and unfriendly place. I had the worst six days of my life. Constantly in fear, missing my family, and so frightened of being on my own. I arrived at Quebec and got on the train for Edmonton in Alberta. I was so ill on the train someone gave me some Mogadon tablets, which left me virtually knocked out. I had a job as an Electronics Engineer with Westinghouse. As soon as I arrived at the hotel, someone called a doctor and I was put in a mental institution for three weeks. They told me I was nuts. I was given heavy medication and made to paint things and interpret cards etc. I was eventually sent back home, as I could not afford the treatment. My whole family was disgusted with me on arrival back home. They said I was weak; I was again put under a psychiatrist and was again put on a mixture of Nardil and Tofranil. I was prescribed that for 10 years. I was later on Stelazine for 10 years and then Parstelin for 11. The doctors always said it would fade when I got older. It never did.

I have always had pressure jobs. I decided to change jobs. I got a degree in business studies and ended up as a general manager of a hypermarket until 2009.

I have had times when I have felt better but even to this day I have never felt totally me. It always seems as though somewhere along the road I have created this personality, which has a very thin veneer and can crack at any time. I feel one of the hardest things about DP is trying to pretend you're normal when you're dealing with people, when all I want to do is run away.

I suffer in silence and I try to explain this all to people—nobody apart from fellow sufferers knows what I am talking about. I suffer also from insomnia and find that sleep deprivation can make the DP worse. I am still very nervous when looking in mirrors for shaving. I hate being in the dark alone, and when by myself I turn all the lights on, even when I sleep. I have a shelf full of self-help books. They all talk about the power of the mind that can solve your problems. I always felt that when I was in the phase of the "bad heads" my mind was never functioning well enough to apply the lessons the books were trying to impart to me. Having said that, I have just read the book *Feeling Unreal* and found it very helpful, although reading about DP made me, in some ways, more alienated.

This last year has been bad. I am back with a psychiatrist and a psychologist. My current psychologist feels that the DP is/was caused by childhood trauma. He felt that both my parents had mental problems of their own. I was put on Fluoxetine (Prozac) six months ago. Although it lifted me a little it did not help the DP. I had a bad side effect; it gave me Sleep Paralysis, which was awful. But I stopped Prozac, it went away. I was then put on Risperidone, but apart from feeling a little happy, no real change in the DP.

Although a nice guy, my psychiatrist seems to not really under-stand DP. He always looks so confused when I explain how I feel. I am now getting panic attacks several times a day, and he is asking me if I want to go back on Stelazine. That seems to show how little he knows, if he is asking me about a choice of medication.

I feel alone, in panic, and a prisoner inside my own head.

5 Transformers

If the patient can tolerate the experience of unrealness for a time, he can make for himself a new reality which is more solidly grounded for his own needs and perceptions, and in a sense more "real" than his old compromises were, however comfortable and familiar they might have felt.

—J. S. Levy and P. L. Wachtel

While eating away at your soul, depersonalization takes your life. Months, years, even decades go by as you search for a cure or a way to adapt to it. If your ability to hope remains, you build your plans around a future when you are normal again. You may, like Frederic Amiel, develop a career from the places your mind takes you, all the while living with the dull pain emanating from the dreams of what might have been. More likely, your interactions with the world center around the single goal of looking presentable and performing normally. People are not very accepting of mentally disturbed individuals and you do everything in your power to convince whomever you encounter, and yourself, that you are decidedly not one of them. You fear many things, but the thought of doing something crazy is the most terrible. Some out-of-the-ordinary act will surely reveal that things in your head are simply *not right*. Sadly, appearing normal may become your primary ambition.

But it doesn't have to be that way. There are people in the world today who have faced DPD head on and accomplished what they wanted to, become what they wanted to, despite its cruelty.

Now let's look at people who have faced the Filth, the Nine Circles head on and emerged to go beyond trying just to be normal, surpassing the childhood dreams that so often consume normal human beings. Each of them, and many like them, have chosen not to hide their issues with depersonalization, but transcend the stigma of mental illness to create in their individual venues of expression.

Laughter from the Void

In April 2007, an independent film entitled *Numb* debuted at the Tribeca Film Festival in New York City. The movie, starring Matthew Perry, Mary Steenburgen and other, lesser-known Canadian actors marked the directorial debut of Harris Goldberg, a screen writer already well-known in Hollywood for *Deuce Bigalow: Male Gigolo*, *Without a Paddle*, and other broad comedies. But no one knew just what to expect from *Numb*. A distinguished cast, and the Tribeca premiere suggested a dramatic departure from the teenage comedy genre.

Dr. Daphne Simeon and I were in the audience at the director's invitation, and we were, very likely, the only ones who knew what the film was going to be about. We wondered how the topic it addressed, Depersonalization Disorder, could possibly be dealt with in a romantic comedy. "Do no harm" we thought silently as the opening scenes unfolded.

I had gotten to know Harris during a period of several years. We had discussed our mutual experiences with this condition as he wrote the screenplay and I finished *Feeling Unreal: Depersonalization Disorder and the Loss of the Self* with Dr. Simeon.

Our book was published before Harris's movie was produced and it had received excellent reviews from the psychiatric community. Now it was time to see how the film *Numb* would portray this mysterious, highly internalized condition to a general audience, and whether or not it would hold up against critics who, like most doctors, had never even heard the term "depersonalization."

The plot of the film proved to be relatively simple. Matthew Perry smokes pot and his internal and external worlds are never the same. The endless attempts to find a cure for his strange affliction lead him through a very typical trail of doctors and clinicians—his frustration and pill popping lay at the heart of the biggest laughs. Perry tries every imaginable medicine, and working from the premise that what caused it all might cure it, he even resorts to smoking the biggest bong in screen history. Nothing works, even a visit to the Mount Sinai clinic run by a rather chilly Paula Simon, a tongue-in-cheek homage to Dr. Simeon.

In addition, a love interest appears, making the protagonist doubly frustrated and impatient with the knowledge of how good life would be without this thing called "depersonalization."

Perry finds no cure, only the resolve to try to look forward to the future with hope, and his new girlfriend. Sometimes, that is all one can expect, we knew.

The film was successful in bringing an unknown condition to light, albeit to a relatively small audience. The same can be said for *Tarnation* and *Feeling Unreal.*

Having gotten to know Harris before the film and in the years that have followed, I am in awe of how much he has been able to accomplish despite chronic DPD. I remember talking with him when he was working on the "Numb" script, held up in his apartment, working 12-hour days—obsessive, but in a constructive way.

In our conversations he would invariably revert back to his less constructive obsession, namely worrying about whether "it was the pot" that caused the DPD, and what life would have been like if he had never smoked. My reassurances never seemed to penetrate.

"It would have happened anyway," I told him. "The same thing happened to me. Maybe life would have been different if we both never smoked pot. But who doesn't at least try it…like a half a percent of the population?

"We simply have a predisposition to depersonalization, and the pot triggered it. Who knows what else might have done the same thing. But I suspect it would have exhibited it in some way," I concluded time and again, trying to convince myself as much as I was trying to convince Harris.

Numb was a good movie. It was something of value that never would have existed if he had not gone through the things he depicted on screen, I finally told him. Neither would *Feeling Unreal*, nor this book.

"The movie was terrifyingly autobiographical," Harris says. "It was almost journalistic. The story was actually fairly easy to write, and it was relatively cathartic.

"I don't think there's anything in there that didn't actually happen. And I think that's why it's resonating so much. I seem to get the same reaction every time, where people sort of tap into what's going on with this character. I think with all the stress of what's going on—Blackberrys and cell phones and things—more and more people are developing anxiety disorders and panicked reactions, and they don't know what to do, and it's hitting them hard. I get calls from all over the place, looking for advice. And I have to say, "well, I'm not a therapist—this is just something that happened to me.""

From an early age, Harris Goldberg was en route to a distinguished career as a screenwriter, actor, and comedian. Still in his twenties he had written and produced films like *Deuce Bigelow* and *The Master of Disguise.*

"I have always had an obsessive style," Harris says. "And I have always been ridiculously anxious. As a kid, I never went too far from home or I became too anxious. I worried about health issues, and about 'what if?' this or that would happen. But I had that kind of self-deprecating humor that saw me through the uncomfortable times to garner the perception of being the charming kid with the quick wit... But of course, it's bullshit and an extreme defense mechanism.

"I never did a drug or drank a beer until I was 29," Harris adds. After I had moved to L.A. and partnered with my brother, I tried pot. It made me laugh almost to the point of panic. I felt some feelings of depersonalization then, and wondered if they would go away. They did."

Harris says that he smoked pot approximately 30 times as a way to alleviate racing thoughts and nighttime anxiety.

"I would wake up in the morning feeling clear headed. But as the day and the stress progressed, I noticed, day by day, feelings of depersonalization without knowing what they were."

In the early 90s, Harris hooked up with a new writing partner, and the workload resulted in physical and mental exhaustion.

"I went out one night and shared a joint with my new partner and a friend. I was told it was strong marijuana. I inhaled twelve hits in half an hour. Then, severe panic set in. Racing heart. Adrenaline shooting through the body. I was so high I didn't think I'd ever get out of it. After they walked me around outside for hours, I finally started to come down."

Everything was normal the next day, Harris adds. But he made the decision to book a flight back to his home in Canada five weeks into the future. During those weeks he suffered three 30-second panic attacks, then returned to a manageable numbness.

Once back home, however, things changed drastically, Harris says. "I saw my old house, my parents, my grandmother, and severe depersonalization symptoms began to come to a head. I experienced horrible vice-like headaches, crying spells, depression, and chronic depersonalization."

Harris' family doctor prescribed Xanax. A neurologist's thorough examination revealed nothing out of the ordinary.

"Then one night I went to an emergency room because I couldn't breathe. I thought I was having a heart attack. I was hyperventilating."

Again, according to the doctors, nothing was wrong. When he returned to Los Angeles, Harris was chronically depersonalized, day and night.

"I wouldn't leave my apartment. But I forced myself to write nonstop," he recalls. Over the course of the next several years he was seen by some 30 therapists, psychologists, and psychiatrists. He tried more than 20 different medications, as well as cognitive behavioral therapies to break his cycle of stress, worry, excessive rumination, and the rest of his personal Nine Circles. Nothing helped. I suggested that he try one of the older antidepressants, one I hadn't noted on his laundry list of failures. He tried it for a month to no avail.

"Now, years later, as much as I rationalize or try to accept things as they are, I am still haunted by 'why did I smoke that pot?' he says. Even though I was feeling a little depersonalized months before that last pot experience, in my gut I consider that last time the straw that broke the Jewish writer's back."

Harris says that Dr. Simeon's assessment was that the milder feelings of depersonalization were a good indicator that the disorder was going to surface eventually, with or without the trigger of pot.

"I don't think anyone really knows," he says. I must have spent about $100,000 during the decade before *Numb*, mostly getting well-known doctors to reassure me that this would have happened anyway.

"The reality is, I find it difficult everyday to deal with the DP. I feel like I've lost a good portion of my life to it."

Reflecting on the experience now, Harris attributes chronic depersonalization to his biological make up, the stresses of life in general, as well as those to which he specifically subjected himself.

"I think I'd been building up a lot of stress over a period of years when I was working nonstop. And I had a sort of fear of stopping—like if I stopped, everything would end. I think that came from my predisposition for anxiety.

"When I smoked pot the last time, it triggered my first anxiety attack, and my body went into this chronic state of "flight", as in "fight or flight" reaction. Your adrenaline system gets all out of whack, and even though you're not in any real danger, your body is perceiving everything that way —a kind of overload. Then comes a constant state of detachment, like you're watching a movie. That happens to everybody at one time or another, but it usually only lasts for a minute or a few minutes. I had it chronically. And I didn't know what it was. It was a nightmare.

"A lot of people—thousands and thousands—still don't know what it is, and they start to panic about it. And just like a panic attack, once it starts, it feeds on itself in a sort of spiral."

In our conversations through the years, Harris and I learned from each other. Much of the childhood anxiety he described was similar to my own, though I had long discounted it as being indicative of some predisposition to anxiety or DPD. It was periodic and did not pervade my entire childhood. But for several years, I too was hesitant to leave the house. I always took a towel along just in case I had to throw up. This nervousness seemed to emerge from my stomach. I never thought I was going crazy. But I was always afraid that I would somehow embarrass myself in the outside world.

Secondly, both of our onset triggers were the same. We each had smoked pot a few times and then confronted panic when we respectively smoked stronger substances with greater "enthusiasm." Yet over time, Harris' symptoms seemed to be locked into the "pure" depersonalization that I knew constantly for only a few years. My DP seemed to follow a different path through the decades, following tributaries that led to acute anxiety, clinical depression, DP, improvement, and then a repetition of the cycle. His DPD, as far as I could tell, seemed to remain locked in that horrible Neverland that marked only the beginnings of my extended voyage. Much like many of the "non-drug" participants in Mount Sinai's 2008 study (see Chapter 8), his depersonalization to a large degree played out by making him what would ultimately become his expression of it all—numb.

A third similarity emerged. Harris's obsessiveness centered largely on his regrets about ever smoking pot. Mine focused on the self, existential mysteries, or any number of imaginary fears stemming from the essential "aloneness" of the self. It is the same obsessiveness—just different thoughts pursuing different paths.

Interestingly, "Numb" which emerged directly from his depersonalization, proved to be a cohesive, funny, and valuable film contribution to the cultural depictions of mental disorders. However differently DPD chose to present itself to each of us, we have come to agree that, somehow, the creative process taps into a totally separate part of the brain. And this is a positive revelation, because only through the "mediating intellect" can the true nature of a disorder that affects feelings and emotion so strangely be adequately represented, and ultimately understood, by an audience beyond those who suffer from it.

The Crazy Train

When I first encountered the hashish-induced "blow" that hurled me into the Nine Circles, some 10,000 miles away in Sydney, Australia, lived a young musician who for four long years had been traveling the road on which I had just taken my first steps. His name was Robert Daisley.

Daisley's words have been known to millions of people who never knew he wrote them. For more than 30 years as a bassist and studio musician he has been laying down the foundation upon which some of the classics of rock and roll have been built. In the 1970s and 80s Daisley played with Mungo Jerry, Ozzy Osbourne, Uriah Heep and Black Sabbath.

Unlike others in his field, Bob's DPD did not emerge after years of hard living or drug abuse. It started before his musical career ever took off and indeed influenced some of his most successful musical efforts. Bob tells his own story as follows:

"My first experience of Depersonalization came in 1966 at the age of sixteen when I was working at an office in the city of Sydney. I was also in a band at the time — something I took seriously and wanted to make a career of. I was working some nights as well, which led to tiredness, albeit moderate most of the time. I'd experienced some physical and emotional pain prior to when the Depersonalization kicked in so I suspect it could have been a contributory ingredient. My spine had been injured in a bad fall down some steps at work and I'd lost the band I was so fond of when the key figure left to join another group. There had been some other incidents, but those were the main and worst ones. One day at the office I walked into the men's room and came out a few minutes later a different person. It was just a normal trip to the loo to 'water the horse,' wash and leave, but something strange came over me as I looked into the mirror. I began to look into my own eyes and mentally talk to my mind behind the eyes in the mirror. It only lasted a few seconds and then something snapped and the weirdest feeling of separation came over me. I remember saying out loud, "Oh, what was that?" All of a sudden the reflection in the mirror seemed like a stranger and I couldn't relate to myself. It was like I'd lost contact with myself and didn't know who I was. I was a stranger to myself and couldn't snap out of it. I walked out of the men's room and began slapping my own face, hoping it would go away but it didn't. I felt out of sync with myself and couldn't grasp who I was. Trying to get in touch with myself again was like standing with your back to a mirror and turning around quickly enough to get a glimpse of the back of your head, which of course is impossible. I knew my name and what I looked like, but it was like 'the self' was a stranger and I was looking on from somewhere else, and when I spoke, it sounded like it was coming from somewhere else.

"I hadn't ever had any drugs and my alcohol intake had always been moderate and very limited, so I thought I was going mad. On my return home from work, nothing had changed and even the next morning after a night's sleep, the strange, unreal feelings were still with me. They stayed. I became very depressed because of it, and it didn't take long before I couldn't function at all. My mum phoned my boss to say I wouldn't be returning. Obviously, my parents were worried, and concerned about the state I was in. They arranged appointments with psychiatrists, analysts, and anyone they thought might help. Being in this strange mental state, and at such a young age, I couldn't explain my symptoms or feelings properly. I had no terminology with which to try to explain what I felt. So no one understood or was able to help in any way. Professionals insisted that these symptoms were part of depression, but I just told them in so many words that they were putting the cart before the horse. I wasn't depressed before I experienced my seeming 'loss of self' and my inability to relate to my own reality. This just added to my frustration, as not only was I not getting any answers, the doctors didn't understand the question. I was given Stelazine, a drug for anxiety and psychosis, but it did nothing.

"I'd watch television incessantly, as it took my mind, or what was left of it, off my conscious awareness of the problem, but as soon as it was switched off, I'd be hit with the separation from my 'self' relentlessly. Various friends came to visit me in support and hope that it would help, but nothing changed. (The weird thing about the condition is that on the outside, to everyone else, you can seem 'normal.')

The mental aggravation made me suicidal, which caused more

conflict because all I wanted was to be cured of whatever this strange phenomenon was and to live life—I didn't 'want to die.' I was living a lie and living in a nightmarish hell.

"Although the sensations came in varying strengths and degrees, the condition never ever really left completely, and seemed as though it was always waiting to be felt and acknowledged at any time I became conscious of it or focused on it. It wasn't until 2007 when I watched the movie *Numb* that I got to grips with the full story and the term for the condition, 'Depersonalization Disorder'. It's only in recent years that research and studies have been carried out on the condition again after many years of neglect, and it's said that it affects 'artistic and creative types', which was also mentioned in the movie.

"So when I was hit with all that, I didn't know what was going on and no one could comprehend what I was trying to explain and no one could help. In strange synchronicity the soundtrack to my life was on the airwaves with the release and success of a song in the charts entitled 'They're Coming to Take Me Away, Ha-Ha', written and performed by Jerry Samuels as 'Napoleon XIV.'

"Research into Depersonalization Disorder was apparently put on the back burner from around the early fifties until the late 90s. But back in 1966, no one I tried to converse with about my problem had a clue of what I was going on about. (Other than maybe Napoleon XIV.)

"Feeling suicidal a lot of the time, I started to question life and its meaning, and developed a seeking mind with a quest for answers to the mystery of existence and consciousness. I was still only sixteen and found the whole thing overwhelming, but I couldn't bring myself to the point of suicide, even though life was a nightmare, and being honest, I didn't have the courage to end it all, I just wanted answers.

"I began reading various books, visiting psychics and holding séances, and of course had my mum's, dad's and sister's support throughout. After weeks that turned into months, I'd come to terms with living in a twisted reality and knew that if I wasn't going to end my life, wasn't going to get relief or find help, I had to learn to live with it and get on with trying to go forward. To everyone else, I appeared 'normal', but they weren't in my head, and although a lot of the time I was 'numb', it was by no means 'comfortably'. I've had much success in my musical career and have made references in my lyrics to my experience with depersonalization, most notably in well-known songs such as 'Crazy Train,' 'Diary of a Madman' and 'Suicide Solution' among others. For me, having what seems to be a 'handicap' has sometimes been an uphill climb, but I'm proud of who and what I am and wouldn't change anything if it would mean losing any of that, even with 'Mister DP'."

Bob Daisley's story is one of hundreds of thousands, or millions. It illustrates a case of chronic, relentless depersonalization that emerged seemingly from nowhere, though the physical and emotional stresses he mentions would easily have been enough to set off the condition that lay beneath the surface all of his life. Drugs were not the trigger as might be expected from someone in the rock-and-roll scene, just the slings and arrows of life. Like others, he was still able to achieve great success in his chosen field, and as is often the case, the creative energies within him proved to be a way to channel his thinking away from the not right-ness of his individual self.

I have always been curious about creativity and DPD. Again and again, the idea of creating a new, better self that transcends the disorder tends to emerge. Success, ambition, competitive drive—they all stem from the ego, they say. Yet I have encountered many people who have been enormously creative and successful, when the one thing that was supposed to motivate them, the ego, was diminished or damaged beyond recognition.

In light of this, I asked Bob Daisley whether he thought DPD had hindered his creativity or whether it might have helped it in some way?

"It might have hindered it at times, but I began to realize that by being how I was, made me who and what I was, so if I'd been normal, whatever that is, I may not have been as creative or have been able to become the 'me' I became…whatever that is.

"I'd say that depersonalization made me become a person with a seeking mind, and definitely more spiritual. Maybe I experienced DPD because I was like that anyway, so it might be a bit of a 'chicken-and-egg' situation," he added.

Like Bob, many people, in time, adapt to depersonalization. Sometimes they feel they have no choice but to do so. This can lead to a channeling of the mind's energy into other directions, as Bob was able to do with success, or it can lead to an endless trail of doctors, medication, even hospitalizations. Part of the problem stems from the difficulty Daisley mentioned—the inability to verbalize the experience clearly.

To the degree that Bob Daisley's long experience with depersonalization did affect his creativity, his unique expression of it has joined the works of Frederic Amiel, Jean Paul Sartre, Poe, Camus, and others as part of the literature of DPD:

Diary of a Madman

Screaming at the window
Watch me die another day
Hopeless situation endless price I have to pay

Sanity now it's beyond me there's no choice

Diary of a madman
Walk the line again today
Entries of confusion
Dear diary I'm here to stay

Manic depression befriends me
Hear his voice
Sanity now it's beyond me
There's no choice

A sickened mind and spirit
The mirror tells me lies
Could I mistake myself for someone
Who lives behind my eyes
Will he escape my soul
Or will he live in me
Is he tryin' to get out or tryin' to enter me

Voices in the darkness
Scream away my mental health
Can I ask a question
To help me save me from myself

Enemies fill up the pages
Are they me
Monday 'til Sunday in stages
Set me free

What in Tarnation?

This rural colloquialism for damnation, or hell, was forever redefined by independent film maker Jonathan Caouette in 2004.

Tarnation, which now enjoys a large cult following, not only pushed the limits of Apple's I-Movie technology, but introduced the term "depersonalization" to an esoteric audience years before any other medium had breeched the subject. The film won eight major film awards while garnering five nominations for others, as well as critical acclaim at both the Sundance and Cannes Film Festivals.

At the heart of *Tarnation* lies the dysfunction that marked Jonathan's childhood and set the stage for dissociation early on. His mother, Renee LeBlanc, a child model, was subjected to repeated and unnecessary electroshock treatments after a paralyzing fall. This led to a plethora of psychiatric problems for Renee during Caouette's early childhood, culminating with his being subjected to physical abuse after he was placed in foster care.

"*Tarnation*'s importance is that it gave people from all walks of life an insight into a world that people usually brush under the carpet, or pass extreme judgement on," Jonathan has said. "People round off the mentally ill to the nearest drug addict, and just don't want to be involved. As a society, we have been hungry for this kind of insight into these hidden worlds, not the 'reality TV' we are subjected to now."

The film, which some critics have labeled narcissistic because of its intense focus on the subject (Jonathan), serves as a metaphor for Depersonalization Disorder itself. The lightning-fast, often-grotesque imagery, spliced from 8mm home movies and recent unscripted dialogues evokes *derealization*. The mental and visual search for the true self amidst pervasive dysfunction mirrors the fruitless rumination and self-observance found in DPD. Add in a variety of early traumas, including bad drugs, an archaic mental health system, damaged people, and a sentimental but on-target sound track, and the result is a film that, while not heralded as such, presents a specific disorder as no film has done before or since.

When I met Jonathan Caouette for the first time, it was, for lack of any more appropriate cliché, Fellini-esque. While driving his mother Renee from Texas to New York one last time, he and his crew emerged from a pair of SUVs with cameras aimed and rolling, like high-tech assault weapons monitoring their target's every move. The cameras paused long enough for introductions, then resumed.

We met on a winter night in an ancient building my wife and I had purchased purely because of its historic importance. Built in 1814, its main level once housed a coffee house that hosted many famous people of the early 19th century. For a few weeks in 1836, the rooms upstairs were home to Edgar Allan Poe and his 13-year-old cousin and bride, Virginia Clemm, as the two enjoyed their honeymoon. The rooms themselves, still illuminated only by candlelight and makeshift lanterns, are virtually unchanged from the time the newlyweds stayed there. It remains preserved in its original state, intentionally.

I was curious about Jonathan's depersonalization, as well as the possible relationship of creativity and DPD. I know from my own experience that there have been periods of creativity during periods of little self, but plenty of intellect. The mind, during this time goes to its own place that is creative, and the ability to create poetry, music, and art may in fact be enhanced by the complete focus on the creation rather than the missing self. It may be that with emotions and/or concerns about daily life obliterated, hopeless, or resolved, the mind is free to focus on what is verbal yet sometimes colored with the faint memory of emotion.

In the dimly lit ruin, Jonathan and I sat at a small table against a crumbly plaster wall and discussed depersonalization for the first time. The presence of his cameramen standing behind each of us, filming the entire conversation, completed the dreamlike montage. Renee and my wife sat at a table in the adjacent room, watching.

"I've often said that I use the camera as a weapon, or a shield, a way to make sense of things, " he said after I had commented about the rolling cameras.

As I knew from *Tarnation*, Caouette's depersonalization began with pot. He was born when I was enduring my second year of the condition. By the time he came around to "frying his brain," I had completed my 11-year search for the name of the condition we shared.

"When I was 12," Caouette recalls with slow, thoughtful deliberation, "I was in my mother's apartment... and I wanted to try pot. One of our neighbors was a drug dealer, so I went to his house and got a couple of joints. I smoked both of them very quickly, but I knew how to hold the smoke in and that it would get me stoned. (I was smoking cigarettes, too, at the time.)

"All I remember next was getting very, very tired and I think I passed out on my mother's bed. Then, I remember hearing myself laugh uncontrollably as if my arms were being held down and I was being tickled nonstop. I heard myself laughing and then the next thing I remember seeing was my feet outlining the parameter of my mother's apartment. And I remember my mother being there crying 'oh God, oh God.' I learned later that the marijuana was laced with PCP and dipped in formaldehyde.

"I confessed to my mother what I had done as I began to panic severely, and I kept asking her if this was the way it was supposed to feel? Was it like this in the 60s? I became completely dissociated, detached from my body and reality.

"My mother had her own issues going on at this time so the whole scene was horrible. Looking back I can put a name on it— total dissociation. And I can describe it differently now. It felt like somebody had scalped me and exposed my brain and put a bucket of Novocaine into my head, and all the Novocaine just slid down. After that it felt like a big liquid bubble of mercury around me.

"I had enough faculties during this unbelievable experience (we didn't have a working phone), and while I could see there was oncoming traffic, still in a complete dreamlike state, found a payphone and dialed 911. So I went to an emergency room where they shot me up with something. I woke up in a psychiatric hospital. I stayed there for about three weeks until I was reasonably stable on some unknown medications.

"When I returned home, it had pretty much worn off. Not long afterward, I remember watching Michael Nesmith, Whoopi Goldberg, and Bobcat Goldthwait on television, and all of a sudden it came back with a vengeance right there in my living room.

"I soon realized that it all came back when I veered away from the television. When I would look back at the television I was focused again. I think prior to becoming depersonalized you pre-program yourself to look at things that are not real. But when you're feeling unreal and you look at something that you remember as not real, it somehow makes sense. I wanted to fixate myself on something that is known to be not real for me.

"Then, about two months later I went to an amusement park with my grandfather and went on this water ride, and during the course of the ride, it all came back again.

"The panic returned with more intensity than ever," Jonathan says, and was decidedly not because of the ride. After convincing his grandfather to take him home, Jonathan adapted to a life of panic attacks, followed by a constant feeling of "everything looking a little twinkly, a little bright. I was very sensitive to fluorescent light," he adds.

Many of the symptoms of depersonalization emerged. What I had called the Nine Circles, Jonathan described as "synching out"— sights and sounds around him did not "synch" with his perceptions of them. One informed doctor even diagnosed him with Depersonalization Disorder, yet understanding it and treating it was another matter. Still, the film maker's venue is, after all, film. Pressing him for details about the precise sensations he experienced at the time is fruitless. The true expression of them can only be found in the work he now creates.

Despite the dysfunctional life with his aging grandparents and the mental roller coaster endured by his mother (not to mention his own battle with DPD) Jonathan was on his way to becoming not only a film maker but a skillful actor as well. Several scenes in *Tarnation* reveal fascinating home videos of an adolescent clearly searching for an identity and a self. Through role playing on camera, adopting clever yet disturbing effeminate personas and campy composites of past and present film sirens, Jonathan expressed a variety of selves, while also revealing his awakening sexuality. As time passed, the DPD lifted, Jonathan says. Still, at times things in his head were simply *not right*. But he was able to successfully pursue an acting career in New York. There he saw Daphne Simeon's ad in the *Village Voice* seeking candidates for Mount Sinai's first formal depersonalization study.

"When I saw that my jaw dropped because I thought I was completely alone in this thing that I had been suffering from since I was 12 years old," he recalls.

An acting commitment in Europe prevented Caouette from completing the Mount Sinai program.

"Then in 2000, I took a temp job where they gave me access to the Internet and told me I could use it. I came across the original DPD website, *UNREAL*. There were thousands of postings and stories and testimonies of people with their experiences. The first few days of this job I was on this website. Needless to say, I was let go. In retrospect, I think they were thinking 'lets see who he is by the kind of things he looks up', and they must have really wondered about me and all this business about feeling unreal. I was truly transfixed that I wasn't the only one, especially when I saw others whose DPD was triggered by pot."

Jonathan has lived with depersonalization off and on for more than 25 years, yet he was able to act on stage, create *Tarnation*, and envision new projects that are now underway. Has DPD diminished his abilities, or perhaps embellished them?

"I don't think I am quite as uninhibited or as spontaneous as I might have been, but on the other hand, I want to continue to explore film making on an existential level. I think there is a huge spiritual component to all of this.

"I find myself experiencing sort of a hypnagogic state—a place when you feel like you're walking along a fence and then you fall off the fence and jump up out of bed. It's a 'fever dream' place that I go to, where a plethora of information rushes into my mind. Everything makes perfect sense for a millisecond. Then it disappears. Where did it go?

"I want to explore the famous quotation—'we are not human beings going through a temporary spiritual experience, we are spiritual beings going through a temporary human experience.'" (Pierre Teilhard de Chardin 1881-1955).

"I'm interested in works that have to do with where we are, what we are, and the dreamlike nature of it all. Also parallel universes, the "multi-verse"—things like that."

What would have been different if we had not smoked the pot? It's impossible for either of us to say. His conclusion about DPD in general however, remains: "You do suffer, but good things can come out of it."

Jonathan, like others we have met in this chapter, seems to have channeled the mental confusion and identity crises of depersonalization into his particular artistic medium. Creative people who have suffered from depersonalization at some point, or chronically, are surfacing more than ever, but they have also been around for some time. (We will look at some of these "hidden" examples in Chapter 11.)

Ultimately, there are individuals who are able to somehow re-claim what has been lost of their personhood, "eat" their pain, and then re-invest the energy spent on worry into outward expressions of individuality. Often, the work that results is seen as narcissistic, or self-focused, which seems natural. The question "What's wrong with me?" wears thin and becomes an issue of "How Do I Express It?", particularly in people who have established some history of creative expression that may or may not have been born out of a strong ego or self-love. I've heard more than one writer state that serious writing comes from a separate place in the brain, as if the narrative plays out on its own, pre-written and in tact. The intellect, which has never been hindered by DPD, finds a new path and in the process, sometimes re-opens the doors to memory and past emotion as well. Perhaps this is part of why journal-keeping helps so much in DPD therapy.

Battling in the Trenches

Not everyone suffering with depersonalization is able to re-invest the psychic energy spent on it into successful creative outlets. Despite the intelligence and sensitivity common to many D-People, the majority are neither creative artists, nor talented musicians, nor child prodigies in any venue. Talent provides an inherent means of re-channeling that energy, but not everyone possesses talents that are immediately recognizable.

For most of her life, Sandy Gale has exhibited a knack for get-ting to the heart of the matter through her efforts as an advocate on behalf of the mentally ill. She is a talented writer, and armed with a master's degree in film, worked in production at 20th Century Fox in the early 1980s. But chronic and relentless depersonaliza-tion, coupled with clinical depression and severe anxiety, made her a "girl, interrupted."

Today Sandy is involved in numerous mental health advocacy programs, but her most impressive, ongoing contribution to awareness of DPD is her engaging website *dreamchild. net.*

Largely autobiographical and blatantly honest, the website has long established itself as an integral part of the DPD community. By skillfully analyzing her own past, Sandy has provided understanding for many who are curious about their own strange feelings.

Sandy states to her website visitors: "I want to say what I never thought I would say years ago; there is hope, there is reason to continue the fight. Depersonalization, depression, and anxiety are (in my opinion, in my case) neurological illnesses that can be treated or cured. "

Sandy traces many of her issues to genetics as well as upbringing. Her mother, a successful psychiatrist, was verbally abusive and withheld love and support. Her father, a thoracic surgeon, grappled with Obsessive Compulsive Disorder and anxiety in the days before effective treatments were available.

Sandy experiences depersonalization as part of an insufferable package deal that includes panic and depression. Her earliest feelings of strangeness occurred when she was only five years old, as her troubled mother took her on sight seeing trips around the world. Her mother, who was at times paranoid and may have had Borderline Personality Disorder (though never officially diagnosed) became sick with an unknown tropical illness. Nearby, in the strange hotel room, Sandy's young thought process led her into a mental shift:

"Afraid to disturb her I turned towards the blank wall by my bed and began to focus intensely on my body. I began to think, 'Who am I? What am I? What is this lump of flesh laying here? Why am I here? What is it to be alive, what is it to be dead?' These extreme existential thoughts took on a life of their own and manifested themselves as a physical sensation— a perceptual shift. I felt I was merely a thought. My body was merely a vessel containing the illusion of life, of the world, of the universe, all existence.

"At the time none of these thoughts or feelings were frightening to me and I could 'shake myself' out of the trance. But here was the beginning of the vicious cycle of over-introspection, over self-consciousness, and the physical manifestation of pure existential thought that would return to haunt me on and off throughout my youth and ultimately envelop me as an adult."

While as an adult Sandy has been diagnosed with Generalized Anxiety Disorder (GAD) and treatment-resistant depression, she feels that depersonalization and derealization are the most disturbing symptoms.

With eloquence befitting her high IQ and a lifetime of self-observation, Sandy explains her mental state in ways that become almost comprehensible to "normals," as well as doctors:

"Over the years I have used an endless number of metaphors and analogies to explain my DP and DR to doctors, family, and friends. For someone who has never experienced these feelings they are almost impossible to understand. I often pose the following questions to a healthy person who has not experienced chronic DP or DR: 'Have you ever experienced déjà vu?' The response is often 'Yes' and is described as an uncomfortable fleeting shift in perception —somewhat odd, but not troubling. I then tell them: 'Imagine if an experience like déjà vu never went away. Imagine that it came on with an intensity 100 times greater than what you have ever experienced. Imagine if that perceptual shift remained for the rest of your life?'"

She further describes the "loss of the self" in what she calls her Xerox metaphor: Take an original document and Xerox it. Take the Xerox of the document and Xerox that. Continue to Xerox each Xerox. The original document slowly fades away. This is how I feel my Self fading away. My arms often feel they are not attached to my body, as though they are not mine. It is as though I have phantom limbs that I can see. This is most disconcerting as one's arms and hands are so crucial to so many daily activities."

The details of Sandy's other symptoms throughout her life are offered in articulate detail on her website. They immediately hit home with people searching for solutions to their own mysterious disorder.

What is not mentioned is the tremendous degree of courage it took to expose herself completely to the world in this manner. She is neither venting, nor looking for sympathy, nor trying to work out her kinks by expressing them publicly. In the way that others have proffered poetry, film, and music to express depersonalization, she has offered her entire past, and what she can muster of a present self. Through her contribution people can compare experiences and follow their own paths of research and understanding. Through her personal insights, cited reference materials, and useful links to other sites, her web presence has become a guide for the lost, gently leading them from a place of fear towards the light of hope.

6 Diagnosing DPD

If you can't explain it simply, you don't understand it well enough.

—Albert Einstein

Depersonalization Disorder is not a mystery disease. Nor is it depression or psychosis. On the contrary, depersonalized people often describe themselves as being "too sane," living in a mental or physical world that seems "too clear." Still, it can be illusive and difficult to comprehend, even for the most experienced psychiatrist. Depersonalization is unique because it is experienced and *observed* at the same time. People who live with it seem to be able to understand each other relatively easily, while those who have not (including most doctors), respond to the words and the many "as if" metaphors with blank expressions.

"Depersonalization is not only a psychopathological phenomenon, but a kind of *ontological* mystery or *nosological* paradox," says California-based psychiatrist Elena Bezzubova. "Noticing it requires the observational capability of an experienced physician, or a natural scientist, and understanding it takes the reflective capacity of the refined philosopher. Patients who suffer from depersonalization may be described as people who proceed along the path that most of us stop dead at in the very beginning."

The degree of perceptivity Bezzubova alludes to is difficult to find anywhere, even in learned psychiatric circles. Psychiatry and psychology are not exactly *exact* sciences. A unique problem inherent to properly diagnosing depersonalization is the fact that the quickest, most accurate assessments come from a mere handful of professionals who have experienced the disorder, or the symptom, themselves. Psychiatrists and psychologists often pursue these fields of study because of their own mental issues or problems with their families or loved ones and, accordingly, a percentage of them are familiar with depression, anxiety, even abuse firsthand. While a doctor need not have experienced cancer, liver disease, or schizo-phrenia to properly diagnose it, DPD is somehow different. People who live with it are sensitive to the "as if" explanations used by others. But they may easily be mistaken for something they are not. You may find yourself talking to your doctor ad nauseum, only to earn back a condescending nod and a prescription for a new anti-depressant, even though you have emphasized the fact that you are not depressed at all.

Unless a generation of depersonalized young people opt to be-come psychiatrists, there's really very little way around this today.

A Closer Look at the Research

Publish or perish is one of the cardinal laws of survival, not only in academia, but in the psychiatric arena as well. As a result, study feeds upon study as each researcher makes a name for his or her self. This is how research slowly advances. Unfortunately, when it comes to something as subjective and often bizarre as depersonalization, the keen insights of some of the earlier psychological observers may be lost in the shuffle of statistics drawn from clinical drug trials or the applications of new technologies. Studies sometimes contradict each other and the methods resulting in publication may not seem particularly strong from traditional journalistic or evidential perspectives.

Findings published in the psychiatric journals do a lot of recycling. Read twenty papers written about depersonalization in the last thirty years and you will see the same names—Mayer-Gross, Cattell, Roth, Arlow, and in more recent years, Simeon, Sierra, Hunter, and others cited repeatedly in introductory paragraphs. Some of the material sourced can become gospel, at least for a while, simply because no other comparable study exists.

The issue of the prevalence of DPD in the general population serves as a case in point. In the late 1980s, Colin Ross, a well-known expert in dissociative disorders, conducted a community survey of about 1000 randomly selected residents of Winnipeg, Canada.[1] Us-ing the Dissociative Experiences Questionnaire, followed by an interview for those with elevated scores on the questionnaire, Ross estimated a 2.4% prevalence of depersonalization disorder. To date, this early survey supports the higher estimates of the handful of studies. More often, the numbers come in at between 1 and 1.4 percent, often extrapolated from some frequently cited research done by Y.A. Aberbigbe. (The questionnaire Ross used is one of the older diagnostic tools and it has largely been replaced by others that specifically address DPD, rather than dissociation.)

In 1995 Aberbigbe and colleagues tried to determine the prevalence of depersonalization and derealization over a one-year period in rural eastern North Carolina.[2] The method? A random telephone survey of 1008 adults. Each person was asked about depersonalization and derealization experiences they may have had during the prior year. Roughly 19% of those interviewed acknowledged depersonalization experiences, 14% said they had experienced derealization, and 23% said they had encountered both. Women and minorities reported higher rates. These are quite high rates for experiencing a psychiatric symptom for a one-year period.

Participants were asked the following question: "Sometimes people feel as though they are outside themselves, watching themselves do something, or feel as if their body doesn't quite belong to them, like a robot. Or they feel like they are in a daze or a dream. Have you had any of these feelings within the last year?" A simple "yes" put 19% of the respondents into the depersonalized category.

Similarly, to assess derealization, the interviewees were asked: "Sometimes people feel as though other people or objects around them appear strange or changed in some way—that their surroundings are not quite real. Have you had any of these feelings in the last year?" As stated earlier, about 14% of the people called said "yes," and on average these people experienced derealization about 26 times over the course of a year, ranging from just one time to once every day. About 19% of the total sample cited depersonalization and/or derealization experiences that were defined as more substantial, lasting at least one hour or occurring at least three times during the year. In other words, one in five people had depersonalization/

derealization experiences.

Aside from a whopping bill for the phone company, I don't think a lot was gained by this survey. Psychiatric disorders per se were not assessed, so it is not possible to know which of these people might also have suffered from clinical depression, anxiety disorders including posttraumatic stress disorder, or unspecified dissociative disorders. Some of them were likely chronic drug or alcohol users and I'll leave it to behaviorists to determine how many may have reacted to what could conceivably have been construed as "leading" questions.

However, when asked when their depersonalization and derealization tended to happen, their answers concurred with the trends found in later, more scientific research. Depersonalization appeared when under stress, when nervous or depressed, when thinking of disturbing past events, or for no perceivable reason at all.

Most recently, in 2009, a group of researchers conducted a "face to face" survey in Germany, based on a sample representative of the general population. Their findings showed the prevalence of DPD at 1.9 percent, based on responses to a revised version of the Cambridge Depersonalization Scale. Their observations confirmed what many in the psychiatric community are just beginning to realize: "depersonalization is common, it cannot be reduced to a negligible variant of depression or anxiety... more awareness about depersonalization with respect to detection and research is urgently required.[3]

The fact that Aberbigbe's numbers were backed up by earlier or later studies certainly lends considerable credibility to his conclusions, even though the methods at face value seem rather shaky. The actual number of people suffering from DPD remains elusive, however, until a massive in-depth study is done. I feel that the results of such a study would show that DPD is even more prevalent than assumed right now, and decidedly, the numbers may go up or down in direct relation to the use of, or the abstention from, drugs in the years ahead.

Growing Attention

In recent years, the large numbers of highly vocal people converging online, and the efforts of some key individuals in the arts, have done much to bring DPD out of the shadows; progress is steady, but slow. The debuts of movies *Tarnation*, and *Numb* promised to be huge strides forward, but distribution issues and the lack of understanding on the part of the mainstream media afforded these independent films cult status, but little else. Likewise, the publication of *Feeling Unreal: Depersonalization Disorder and the Loss of the Self*, and a few years later, *Depersonalization: A New Look at a Neglected Syndrome*, filled major gaps in medical literature, but suffered from lack of strong promotional efforts on the part of their publishers. (This is understandable to some degree since they were published by university presses rather than mainstream publishing houses.)

The only national consumer magazine article about Depersonalization Disorder as of 2010 was authored by freelance writer Ruth Konigsburg for *Elle* magazine. Unfortunately, the April 2007[4] article did little to affirm the prevalence of DPD in the world today. While not undermining the misery the condition can cause, the article essentially pitted "believers," against "non-believers" fueling the antiquated debate as to whether or not DPD really exists as a syndrome unto itself. The article quoted Harrison G. Pope, MD, of McLean Hospital, Belmont, Massachussetts:

"If I was betting, I'd say it's likely a nonspecific symptom, rather than a disorder unto itself. I'm saying that because in the course of my clinical practice I see it every day."

The "objective" reporting in the article also implied that Daphne Simeon was pushing an agenda to popularlize DPD as the disorder du jour:

"With her reputation now staked on depersonalization, it's not surprising that Simeon sees a hidden epidemic of it in our midst, but even some of her supporters don't share her belief that the disorder is widespread."

Some of Dr. Simeon's recruitment methods, such as running an ad for possible subjects in the *Village Voice*, were called to task as well:

"In Hystories: Hysterical Epidemics and Modern Media, *cultural critic and former Princeton professor Elaine Showalter argues... that advertising for patients, as Simeon did, attracts a suggestible population that is looking for an organic explanation for their personal problems. In Showalter's view, recent trendy disorders such as chronic fatigue syndrome and Gulf War syndrome gained traction because they tapped into deep-seated human narratives of victimization, which the media both reflects and propagates in an endless feedback loop."*

For a mainstream magazine, this pro-and-con approach is *de rigueur*. (Read a hundred or so 'women's magazine' articles and you will pick up on a very predictable rhythm, and a very formulaic style of writing.)

Investigative journalistic integrity aside, the credibility of most, if not all of the existing research is subject to a number of factors including, but not limited to: the questions that are asked, how they are phrased, the truthfulness of the respondents, their understanding of the questions, and what is being used as the criteria for DPD diagnosis by the individual researcher. This does not imply that clinicians are necessarily skewing things to meet their own agendas. What it does imply, however, is that given the mysterious and confusing nature of DPD itself, time spent with an insightful, experienced doctor or therapist who knows the territory is very likely a better investment than time spent with someone working exclusively from implications suggested by published statistics. Notes Konigsberg:

Simeon's estimate {1 to 2 percent of the population} is based on studies that she admits, in person, are inadequate. "We've been wanting to do a big epidemiological study, but it's a big deal to put one together."(The German study mentioned earlier now supports Dr. Simeon's conservative estimate, however.)

Still, even the most rigid, by-the-book psychiatrist has been given a point of departure since DPD has now been defined with some precision in every psychiatric diagnostic manual. Updates on research and treatment are published regularly and arrive in the doctor's mail every month. Trial-and-error treatments for the disorder remain ongoing, albeit on a scale limited by the syndrome's perceived obscurity as well as budgetary restraints. Your doctor doesn't have to be a shaman, philosopher, or top of his class. He or she just needs to recognize DPD for what it is and utilize the tools that are already available.

Much of the confusion about depersonalization arises from the fact that it can appear as a symptom with other disorders or emerge as a disorder unto itself in lieu of all others. If everyone who suffered feelings of unreality and detachment or loss of their "old selves," and fit the other criteria spelled out in the DSM or ICD, Depersonalization Disorder would be relatively simple to diagnose. When anxiety, panic attacks, and other symptoms are thrown into the mix, your family doctor, even a psychiatrist, is most likely to look at those symptoms first, rarely, if ever, determining that those other symptoms might, in fact, be part of what is decidedly DPD.

Depersonalization strikes at the individual personality. In doing so, its manifestations, under close scrutiny, may seem unique to the individual it affects. The specifics of what I had come to call the Nine Circles, the strangeness of certain things like the wind, the obsessiveness or compulsiveness that created the tormenting voice, may well have been my mind's *personalized* interpretation of the *depersonalization* process. Other people may or may not experience the exact same thoughts or sensations. But the changes going on in the brain that cause these specific thoughts are essentially universal. What emerges *because* of those changes is what makes the disorder a unique and very private hell.

Ultimately, Depersonalization Disorder is marked by a distinct sense of strangeness about your own being, and/or the world outside of yourself. Somehow, a major change has occurred, as if your old self has disappeared, yet you haven't become someone else. The mind struggles to make sense of this strange new world, and endless existential rumination likely follows. People with Depersonalization Disorder are neither clinically depressed nor anxious, except perhaps as a residual effect of the disorder itself. This distinction is absolutely necessary for a diagnosis of Depersonalization Disorder.

How Common is DPD?

Most people have experienced minor, fleeting depersonalization at some point in their lives, often following some traumatic or *unreal* event.[5] The prevalence of Depersonalization as a full-blown disorder has yet to be determined with certainty, however, as discussed earlier in this chapter. Ignorance of the syndrome, lack of media exposure, and misdiagnoses have all contributed to lack of adequate reporting of bona fide cases of DPD. One thing is certain, however—numerous factors, not the least of which is the growing use of drugs like marijuana and Ecstasy, have triggered an explosion of cases in the last thirty years.

Still, considering all the data, it's safe to place Depersonalization Disorder in 1 to 2 percent of the population.[6] While existing estimates are conservative, they still rank DPD higher in frequency than either of the better known disorders—bipolar disorder and schizophrenia.

In spite of the evidence, the ICD-10 and the National Institute of Health's Office of Rare Diseases continue to list depersonalization-derealization as a "rare" disorder.

The Institute of Psychiatry's Mauricio Sierra suggests reasons why DPD battles for recognition.

"Psychiatrists are still trained to believe that depersonalization disorder is extremely rare, and that, when present, it is usually a secondary, almost irrelevant symptom of another condition such as depression or anxiety," Sierra writes.[7]

Studies have shown that the average time from the onset of the condition until it is diagnosed ranges from 7 to 12 years.[8]

Other reasons include the fact that people who think they are going crazy often have no idea what they are looking for on the Internet or in a doctor's office. Many people opt to keep the condition quiet. They find this easier than trying to explain their bizarre symptoms to friends or family who will never understand what they're describing. If drugs are involved, young people are likely to keep their problems a secret from their parents for obvious reasons.

Patient Profile

Since the 1990s, the Department of Psychiatry, Mount Sinai School of Medicine, New York, and the Institute of Psychiatry, King's College, London, have investigated DPD through volunteer participants who meet the diagnostic criteria for the disorder. In 2003, both centers published articles in leading journals describing by far the largest series of patients suffering from DPD to be systematically studied to date. The Mount Sinai Research Unit's report, published in *the Journal of Clinical Psychiatry*, was based on a sample of 117 patients suffering from primary depersonalization disorder.[9] Each of these patients received an extensive psychiatric interview in person. The Institute of Psychiatry's report, published in the *British Journal of Psychiatry*, reported on 204 patients with chronic depersonalization; 124 were interviewed in person, while the rest were assessed by phone or internet by completing a set of questionnaires.[10] In other words, the British study included all responders who had depersonalization *symptoms*, of whom 71% actually suffered from primary DPD (as defined by the 4th edition of the *Diagnostic and Statistical Manual of Mental Disorders* [DSM-IV]), whereas the American study only included those with primary DPD.

Both the Mount Sinai and the Institute of Psychiatry research teams have studied adult DPD patients with an average age in their mid-30s. Many participants, of course, were younger or older. DPD affects men and women equally, the studies concluded.

The average age of onset of DPD was around 16 years in the 2003 Mount Sinai sample and 23 years in the Institute of Psychiatry sample.[11] Some people recalled their first experience in early childhood. In the Mount Sinai sample, 80% of the people described onset by age 20 and 95% by age 25, supporting the view that DPD is very much a disorder of adolescence; onset in middle or late age appears to be quite unusual. This means that it is not uncommon to find someone seeking treatment for DPD in their 30s after having suffered from depersonalization for about half their lifetime. The people who participated in these research programs had experienced DPD for as little as 3 months to as long as 6 decades.[12] Interestingly, these numbers are echoed by the 185 personal stories posted on *depersonalization.info* between 2002 and 2010. These stories revealed an average age of onset of 15 years. Approximately 40 percent of the stories revealed depersonalization as occurring with other issues such as panic, obsessive compulsive disorder (OCD), or anorexia, while several young women also engaged in cutting themselves.

Association with Other Psychiatric Disorders

A wide range of depressive and anxiety disorders may exist concurrently with depersonalization. On a lifetime basis, the following other disorders were present in the Mount Sinai sample (overlapping): two thirds also suffered from clinical "major" depression, one third from dysthymia (chronic low-grade depression), one third from social anxiety disorder, one third from panic disorder, one fifth from generalized anxiety disorder, and one eighth from obsessive-compulsive disorder.[13]

Importantly, when you compare DPD's age of onset to that of any of these disorders, none were found to begin earlier. This strongly supports the fact that depersonalization is a *primary* phenomenon, rather than one that sometimes accompanies these other disorders. It also suggests that struggling with DPD may lead to clinical depression or panic disorder if, in fact, an underlying predisposition to those disorders exists. I believe that this was the case in my own experience, resulting in what I call the "triple whammy" of terror—panic, depersonalization, and depression.

The U.K. research program found that people with stronger depression or anxiety symptoms also had more severe depersonalization symptoms. This suggests that both depression and anxiety can exacerbate depersonalization and make it more intense.

Onset and Course

The way that depersonalization disorder begins varies. In some people it happens very suddenly, and such individuals can typically recall the exact day and circumstances of how it started. This is certainly true for myself and for the people we met in Chapter 4. For other individuals, the onset of depersonalization can be very insidious, setting in over a period of weeks, months, or even years, or it may have started so far back that a person really cannot recall how it started (research shows about a 50/50 ratio of insidious versus acute onset). [14]

The course of the condition in the majority of people is ongoing. They may barely remember what it felt like not to be depersonalized, or they may refer to themselves as the "old" self and the "new" self, or as a "no self." In about a third of the people, the course of the disorder is episodic. It may come and go, and last for days, weeks, or months before relenting.

What Triggers Chronic Depersonalization?

Depersonalization Disorder, along with other psychiatric conditions, likely involves genetic predispositions followed by early life events that enhance vulnerability. Subsequently, later life occurrences may trigger the onset of chronic symptoms. (This likelihood is not a certainty, however.) Unlike some of the better-known psychiatric disorders, much less has been determined about this possible progression when it comes to DPD. There are many stories of people who cannot find a single reason why depersonalization began.

Some remember fleeting moments of depersonalization from an early age, before the disorder ever set in with permanence and severity. Some may not even recall passing instances of the symptom itself, but rather a willingness to distract or detach themselves from disturbing events around them. Often these moments are either forgotten or considered insignificant until later, when in the throes of DPD, a person begins to dig deeper into their past looking for evidence of some earlier indicators. With a predisposition to depersonalization, something eventually happens to trigger the actual onset of DPD. These triggers can be highly variable. The comment below, posted to *depersonalization.info*, is not uncommon for people who experience it at an early age for no particular reason:

How did it start? I remember as a child, about nine or so, thinking about the different parts of my body and how all of them put together made 'me.' I thought about it a lot. Then one day I was sitting in the car and I believe I had my first DP episode. I remember feeling as if I had just been born— everything and everybody was scary and strange to me, as if I was having a distorted dream about reality. The music on the radio sounded weird, my parents and sister looked weird. My mind went into an infinite loop, trying to comprehend how "I" could be "me." How can I be me? How can I be me? I asked myself over and over. I didn't panic, I was just scared. It lasted a few years, but in my adolescence it significantly weakened and I all but forgot about it.

Depersonalization Triggered by Drug Use

One trigger that has become readily and indisputably apparent is the use of drugs. Although not considered the most common trigger, in a sizable portion of the population, incidental or casual drug use, even one-time drug use can throw an individual into a chronic depersonalized state. This is frequently seen in people who post their personal stories on Internet websites or participate in some of the discussion forums on these sites.

Marijuana, Ecstasy (MDMA), and LSD seem to be the primary triggers, but DPD also can be precipitated by some less commonly used drugs like ketamine (special K), and salvia, as well as certain prescription drugs or hospital anesthetics.

How do drugs trigger DPD? While we will explore the possible reasons further in Chapters 7 and 8, one possible answer, according to Dr. Simeon, is that a very specific but unknown chemical trigger has tipped something off balance in the brain of a person who is already biologically vulnerable. This neurochemical change manifests itself in the form of depersonalization. (This is not brain damage, but rather a temporary or long-term dysfunction of existing neurochemical systems.) Other explanations for drug-triggered onsets are also plausible. The actual experience of the panic attack initiated by sensitivity to an overload of THC (pot's active ingredient), could be overwhelming and consequently throw certain people into an altered state of selfhood.

For most people, the issue of a "pre-existing diathesis", or preset likelihood of becoming depersonalized because of certain triggers, is difficult to accept. In high school, I considered myself absolutely "normal" mentally. I was even contemptuous of other students who seemed to regularly visit the school psychologist. I didn't understand "issues" and saw them as a problem of weak genes. There was no history of mental illness anywhere in my family. We were strong, determined, and vehemently individualistic. Our advice to the mentally troubled might have been typical: "Shape up and snap out of it."

Then, like millions of others, DPD raised its fearsome head. I was normal. I smoked pot and everything changed. Why? Would I have experienced this terrible thing had I not smoked at all?

Typically, psychiatrists will answer "yes" to the latter. Millions of people smoke pot everyday without triggering DPD. Clearly, there is something inherently different within the brains of people who do smoke pot and become depersonalized and in the brains of people for whom the other triggers set it off as well.

Depersonalization Disorder is not the only psychiatric condition that can be triggered by drug use, however. Some schizophrenic patients can trace the onset of their schizophrenia to the use of marijuana or cocaine. They may become psychotic, then stop using the offending drug, but the schizophrenia continues. The drug acts as a chemical trigger that in some way throws them over the edge, (presuming they were already biologically predisposed and vulnerable.) Panic disorder can emerge in the same way. An initial panic attack can be triggered by marijuana, for example, but people may then develop full-blown panic disorder that continues long after they've ceased using the drug. This is not to imply that these people are in some way psychologically weaker than others, or that they couldn't handle the drugs that their friends took frequently with apparent immunity. Their biological makeup is different, just as people have different blood types, different allergies, or different genetic vulnerabilities to certain diseases.

Onset of depersonalization brought about by drugs has been well documented and quantified by recent studies. Among the 117 subjects in the well-known 2003 Mount Sinai study,[15] 13 percent described a clear and immediate trigger with marijuana, whereby they smoked, went into a high, and then never came out of the depersonalized state. About 6 percent recounted clear triggering by hallucinogens. In two cases, the drug Ecstasy was the catalyst, and one case involved ketamine, which has long been known to induce dissociative states and is no longer used to induce medical anesthesia in humans. Similarly, the Institute of Psychiatry reported that a notable number of chronic depersonalization cases were triggered by drugs (40 out of 164). Of these 40 individuals, 20 attributed the onset of their depersonalization to marijuana, four to Ecstasy, two to LSD, and one to ketamine; the remaining 13 attributed the onset to drug combinations involving at least one of these drugs. Out of 185 personal stories gathered on *depersonalization.info* over an 8-year period, 68 people, more than a third, attributed their depersonalization to marijuana. Twelve people traced the onset to Ecstasy, and a substantial number (40 percent) mentioned panic attacks and anxiety, either as a result of smoking pot or concurrent with symptoms of depersonalization. The degree of drug use indicated in these stories is higher than indicated in the clinical research emanating from either of the DPD clinics. It is difficult to determine why, other than the fact that the accompanying anxiety that is often mentioned creates greater urgency to tell the story than exists in people who have gotten used to the disorder or feel more numb and indifferent. Or, it could simply reflect increased drug use among young Internet users and, therefore, increased depersonalization. Interestingly, about 20 percent of the stories are from people who first experienced severe depersonalization in early childhood (between five and 10 years of age), with no incidents of abuse, drugs, or inheritability.

Initially shunned by serious researchers because of its unscientific and sometimes unreliable nature, the Internet has now become a valuable tool for surveys and clinical studies, providing access to thousands of people who otherwise would never have been contacted. The Institute of Psychiatry in London realized this early on and now other centers of research consider the Internet a valuable research tool as long as the people interviewed pass the basic diagnostic criteria. Unknown to those who contribute their stories, the IOP website gathered both the personal stories (usually anonymously posted), and the website forums to gather fresh research data. Unfortunately, the site was discontinued once sufficient information for completing a study had been gathered. While this was no doubt disappointing to the many who visited the site, others, such as *depersonalization.info* and *dpselfhelp.com* were already underway, actively working on behalf of the patients, not the researchers.

The stories posted on *depersonalization.info*, all screened based on criteria spelled out in DSM-IV, clearly point to strong connections with pot and anxiety, even though a minority did allude to either some childhood trauma or no discernable source of onset at all.

Understanding the Symptoms

As explained earlier, some important symptoms of DPD often are overlooked because of the patient's emphasis on the predominant, or most unpleasant symptoms. In recent decades, diagnostic questionnaires have emerged in an attempt to fine tune the clinical definition of the disorder.

The first self-administered questionnaire to measure dissociative symptoms, which has now been in use for more than 20 years, is the Dissociative Experiences Scale (DES), developed in 1986 by Eve B. Carlson, Ph.D. and Frank Putnam, MD, two well-known experts in the field of trauma and dissociation. The DES has been helpful in diagnosing dissociative disorders, but not necessarily depersonalization. Out of its 28 questions, only a few relate to depersonalization and derealization experiences.

"It is very possible for a person to suffer from troubling depersonalization and still score quite low on the DES, which was designed with the more "severe" dissociative disorders in mind," Dr.

Simeon says.

However, a few items of the DES can be suggestive of the presence of DPD, especially when the remaining items are scored low. Such items have to do with classic symptoms like watching one's self from a distance, feeling outside of one's body, perceiving one's surroundings as unreal, or looking at the world through a fog. In particular, item 27 seemed particularly relevant personally in that it is the only place where I have seen the mention of "voices" such as the one that tormented me in the Nine Circles:

"Some people find that they sometimes hear voices inside their head that tell them to do things or comment on things that they are doing." (Mauricio Sierra has told me that of the hundreds of cases of depersonalization that he has encountered, only a handful presented this "voice" phenomenon.)

In 2000, the Department of Psychiatry at the University of Cambridge developed a self-administered questionnaire called the Cambridge Depersonalization Scale (CDS). The CDS specifically measures only depersonalization and derealization experiences and contains a wide range of questions covering such experiences. The scale has, according to its creators, proven to be a more reliable measure for quantifying the severity of pure depersonalization in the absence of other dissociative symptoms. Both the Dissociative Experiences Scale and the Cambridge Depersonalization Scale are now readily available online for anyone who cares to look at them. While many of the questions will be familiar to people experiencing depersonalization, they are not "checklists" for self-diagnosis. They have helped tremendously in the research involving groups of patients, and controls, but achieving a diagnosis of DPD, or anything else, involves many factors outside of these tools.

Further Fine Tuning

In a report published in *Psychological Medicine* in 2005, Mauricio Sierra and colleagues at the Institute of Psychiatry, London, pointed out that there was still no clear agreement among doctors, psychologists, and medical writers about Depersonalization's "constituent symptoms."[16]

In spite of its apparent symptom diversity, "there is the possibility that depersonalization could result from a unitary, pervasive experience of detachment which would equally affect all aspects of experience. However, the fact that not all symptoms are always present, or the fact that some seem more stable than others, or show different intensity, suggests that at least some of these symptoms belong to different "experiential" domains with potentially distinct underlying mechanisms." In other words, distill the patients' experiences further and it might be easier to discover the biological mechanisms behind them.

Through mathematical analysis of 138 DPD patients' responses to the Cambridge Depersonalization Scale (including degrees of severity), Sierra found that four well-determined factors could be extracted as distinct core symptoms of DPD. These are listed below, with abbreviated explanations of each factor:

1. Anomalous Body Experience.

Patients with depersonalization complain of a variety of changes in how they experience their physical selves. These may include:

a. A lack of body "ownership" feelings.

b. Feelings of loss of "agency," which result in the impression that actions occur automatically without the intervention of a willing self, in a robot-like manner.

c. Feelings of disembodiment, which can range from a non-specific feeling of the mind not being in the body, to heightened self-observation, to out-of-body experiences and autoscopic hallucinations (*seeing* oneself from outside the body). The latter two, however, are rare in depersonalization.

d. Somatosensory distortions, usually affecting the size of body parts, or feeling very light. These seem far less frequent in DPD, and were mentioned very little by patients in the study. Such gross somatosensory distortions are not characteristic of depersonalization but are frequent in schizophrenia, epilepsy, and migraine.

Examples of these sensations, and the other core symptoms are illustrated through stories posted on *depersonalization.info*:

"I go though moments when I feel unconnected to my body, although I remain in full control. I'll look at my arm and not even know it's my arm (mostly my right side). I'll look at myself in the mirror and completely not really recognize who is looking back at me. The worst part was the state of panic I would go into anytime something like this happened. I eventually went to a doctor who put me on Paxil for the panicking, which really had no effect. It didn't really make things worse for me, just had no effect."
   —From Katie's story

"About two weeks ago in school, I suddenly lost my sense of depth. Everything around me looked like one entire screen and it felt like I was watching the world go by, and my mind was on the outside, helplessly watching everything."
   —From Maya's story

"For a long time, my brain has felt separate from my body. It all used to be in tact and I never thought about it. Why should I? But when the change came, it suddenly became all I ever think about. I have no choice. My head feels full of air with my thinking, my consciousness somewhere nearby, but not in it. Once in a while, when I feel momentarily normal, I feel as if my mind has re-entered my head, with all connections back in place. Then, it's clear that thoughts start in the head and then make their way down through my mouth to communicate with others. That's how it should feel for me, and it should be as simple as breathing. But when I am not normal, my self is somewhere else, not connected to my body at all, even though my body still seems to work."
   —From Anton's story

"Many have been the moments standing in line somewhere and suddenly a brief dizziness passes over me, followed by a sensation

that I can only describe as being physically amorphous, devoid of substance—an empty thing. Everything seems distant, as if there was no possibility of me ever reaching it. So I stare at whatever it is, trying to figure it out. Put simply, I feel like an autonomous contraption, forced to exist, operating entirely on muscle memory and second nature."
—**From Nate's story**

2. Emotional Numbing.

Most patients with depersonalization report different degrees of diminished emotional experience. These include a loss of affection or pleasure on one hand or the loss of fear of situations that were previously avoided. Unlike the flat affect commonly seen in patients with schizophrenia or depression, the *expression* of emotions seems normal in depersonalization. Sierra et al attribute the lack of pleasure or displeasure associated with smell or taste to the subjects' inability to imbue objects or situations with emotional feeling, rather than a general inability to experience emotional states.

"Normally I go through every day, interact with people, go to school, go to work, hang out with friends or people who were my friends. They still talk, want to hang out—it's just different. But no one notices, I wear a fake smile, go through the appropriate actions and no one seems to care. No one seems to notice. The only person that has noticed something different is my mom. She mentioned she thought I might have changed. I'd like to be grateful for someone noticing but I just don't care. I don't even care about family anymore. They're just more people. I look at the world and see people like ants, just working to survive, evolve. Maybe this is just the next step in evolution, to eliminate the soul from the body. That's the feeling, almost like I'm soul-less."
—**From Tony's story**

3. Anomalous Subjective Recall.

Patients with depersonalization often complain of problems with remembering certain things. These include the feeling that autobiographical memories did not really happen to the person; the feeling that recent personal events happened long ago or had already happened (i.e. *de 'ja`vu*), and an inability to evoke visual memories of people or places.

"During this time it was very hard for me to concentrate and my memory would fade in and out like one that remembers their dreams. I started over-analyzing everything 'til I would make myself dizzy and sick; I still do this often. I would think back on things and my memory would often be distorted. The pictures in my head had me looking at myself from outside my body rather than through my eyes. Sometimes I think that's how I really saw things. When I did feel within myself I still didn't feel right, it didn't seem like my body that I was born into."
—From Sara's story

"I remember the first time I experienced depersonalization. It was like having an overwhelming sense of déjà vu, like everything that was happening had happened at some stage before, and if I could only concentrate, I'd be able to predict exactly what was about to happen. It always seemed just beyond my reach to pre-empt what someone was about to say or do. I also had the compelling feeling that I was actually just in a dream. My peripheral vision disappeared, and I couldn't hear or see very well. I had a pulsing in my head, and mixed feelings of euphoria, intoxication and terror. This felt disjointed and static, and very unsettling. It also became difficult to process what was happening around me and maintain a sense of where and who I was. This was my first DP attack, and I thought I was going insane."
—From A.D.'s story

4. Alienation from Surroundings.

Most patients with depersonalization describe feelings of being cut off from the world around, and of things around seeming "unreal." Such an experience is frequently described in terms of visual metaphors such as looking through a camera, veil, or fog, or living in a "bubble." Indeed, many patients claim that it is in the visual realm where "unreality" is most noticeable. In addition, clinical observations suggest that an inability to experience the pleasurable attributes of the things being perceived is a core feature of derealization. Articulate patients frequently attribute feelings of "unreality" to an inability to color their experiences with pleasurable feelings or feelings of familiarity. Depersonalization and derealization may simply reflect two different ways of describing the same experience.

"I suddenly feel alone inside my brain, alone in a distant and unreal world, as if a thick glass were located between the real touchable world and my pure consciousness. Like having a helmet put on, feeling like my brain is inside a bubble, with the sensation you have when you are diving into the water, mind alone, you only with your mind encapsulated in your head bones and living in a dream, an eternal non-ending dream. And every day you must tell yourself yes, you are alive, this life is yours, you are standing here in the world, that something pushed you off to the other side, and that man is your father, that other your brother. Why do they seem so distant? Why so strange?"
—From Arturo's story

Ultimately, the results of this Institute of Psychiatry study suggest that depersonalization represents the expression of several *distinct* underlying dimensions. "This finding is in keeping with long-held and currently neglected views that depersonalization constitutes a syndrome, rather than a symptom," Sierra states.

Complex analysis of the data also indicates that "the different components of depersonalization represent an integrated response, rather than the mere co-existence of unrelated phenomena.

"An understanding of depersonalization in terms of different interacting dimensions is likely to have implications for both clinical practice and research. For example, patients meeting the Diagnostic and Statistical Manual (DSM-IV) criteria for depersonalization disorder (i.e. chronic depersonalization not accounted for by co-morbid conditions) indicated more depersonalization symptoms on the Cambridge Scale than patients with anxiety disorders and Temporal Lobe Epilepsy, many of whom also suffered transient depersonalization experiences. From a research perspective, studies focusing on selective components of the condition such as emotional numbing and imagery impairments have proved promising lines of research."

A Further Update

A 2007 report by Daphne Simeon and colleagues[17] concluded that the DSM-IV, which uses a "single symptom criteria" for depersonalization does not do justice to the complexity of the disorder. The report published in *Psychiatry Research* suggested that depersonalization/derealization involves several dimensions that are not strongly related to each other. To reconfirm the point already established by the Sierra study, an internet survey posted by the National Organization for Drug-Induced Disorders (NODID) took responses from 394 affected individuals.

People visiting the NODID site, through *dpselfhelp.com*, were essentially asked for a self-diagnosis via questions drawn from the DSM-IV. The survey utilized the Cambridge Depersonalization Scale as its basis for diagnosis.

The final analysis of the responses indicated the prevalence of five factors that were, expectedly, very much in line with the Sierra study. The first factor, labeled "Numbing," described the blunting of emotions as well as pain and bodily drives such as hunger and thirst. This factor concurs with several neurobiological studies of Depersonalization Disorder that have demonstrated blunted emotional and autonomic indices, the report states. The second factor, labeled "Unreality of Self," captures the experience of detachment from the physical body, mind, thoughts, and actions. This factor is the most reminiscent of the DSM's current description of depersonalization. The third factor, called "Perceptual Alterations," includes distortions in visual, tactile, and body image perceptions.

"Heightened perceptual aberrations have been previously demonstrated in Depersonalization Disorder and may relate to altered brain activation in sensory association cortical areas," the authors of the study state. (We'll examine cortical disconnections in Chapter 7.)

The fourth factor called "Unreality of Surroundings" corresponds to the DSM-IV description of derealization.

The fifth factor, labeled "Temporal Disintegration," describes a disturbance in the subjective experience of time. The five factors in this substantially larger sample are quite similar to the four factors of the English study that preceded it. The main difference is that the factor labeled "Anomalous Body Experience" in the Sierra study appears to have been split up into two components, "Unreality of Self" and "Perceptual Alterations" in this study. This might in part explain why, in the Sierra analysis, "Anomalous Body Experience" made up the largest factor, followed by "Emotional Numbing," whereas in the Simeon analysis, "Numbing" was the largest factor, followed by "Unreality of the Self" and "Perceptual Alterations."

Of course this study clearly appears to have been influenced by the earlier one. One study involved in-house DPD patients and the other utilized an Internet survey. While it may begin to sound like the researchers are splitting hairs, if not simply repeating themselves, the DSM-IV is due to be revised in 2012. So clarifying the symptoms now may better define them for all the doctors who use the DSM as their primary reference. Hopefully the similar findings of these studies will, in the interim, contribute further towards clarification that will assist in diagnosing DPD more accurately. The issue of exactly where and how DPD should be placed in the diagnostic manuals remains an open question.

Temporal Disintegration

This term, mentioned in the study above, sounds frightening, but doesn't mean your temporal lobes are turning into dust. Rather, it refers to the alterations of time perception that are a large part of the depersonalized experience. A recent article in the *Journal of Trauma & Dissociation* by Daphne Simeon and colleagues,[18] took a closer look at the experience of time, which is an essential component to a cohesive sense of self. This study, which involved 52 people suffering from Depersonalization Disorder and 30 non-clinical control subjects (normals), concluded that temporal disintegration in DPD patients is not directly related to the core symptoms of DPD itself, but exists when the depersonalization experience involves more prominent "absorption."

Absorption, in psycho-lingo simply means a devotion to one act or activity only. When it's impossible to get the attention of a child mesmerized by the television screen, or a teenager lost in a video game, they are absorbed in it, literally. The specific scientific definition goes like this: "the use of one's full commitment of available perceptual, motor, imaginative, and ideational resources to a unified representation of the attentional object." In psychiatric absorption, the individual's consciousness is altered in a way that everything, including time, can be reconstructed into a "fantasy world." Thus, self-experiences are no longer anchored into perceiving time the way other people do. The individual may relive the past as reality, confuse dreams or television shows with reality, or simply stare off into space. Studies have generally shown that absorption bears some association with hypnotizability, imagination activity, and fantasy proneness, all of which are related to dissociative propensities. However, a small study comparing absorption between depersonalized people and "normal" participants reported no significant difference in absorptive experiences using a testing tool called the Tellegen Absorption Scale. This suggests that absorption may play a lesser role in chronic depersonalization than in other chronic dissociative conditions such as Dissociative Identity Disorder (DID). Given that absorption, but not depersonalization scores were highly predictive of time perception issues, Simeon and colleagues suggest that absorption is the main link to temporal disintegration in DPD. Depersonalization disorder does not always involve elevated absorption, Simeon writes. People experiencing depersonalization typically feel detached and unreal, but their consciousness continues to exist within a normal time construct. Although they feel *not right*, they may still be able to anchor themselves in the present. In contrast to chronic Depersonalization Disorder, acute *transient* depersonalization such as that occurring in THC-induction studies or during a trauma (peritraumatic dissociation) clearly involves a strong component of temporal disintegration. It may be that disturbances in the processes of attention, such as those seen in absorption, in some way act as the link between transient depersonalization and temporal distortions.

What about Mind Emptiness and the other Symptoms?

All of the symptoms I experienced while in the Nine Circles, feelings of "no self", "hollowness", "mind emptiness" excessive "self-observation," or even "split consciousness" (i.e., the mocking interior voice) do not seem to be adequately addressed by the research that focuses on the four or five core symptoms. Or are they?

People do not show up at their psychiatrist's office saying "I am suffering from anomalous body experiences." They describe certain sensations as best they can through metaphors, alluding to the states of mind described throughout this book. But these symptoms, which often defy interpretation, apparently emerge as manifestations of the very core symptoms that have been pulled out by researchers who have investigated depersonalization intensely. Heightened self-observation, for instance, seems intimately associated with "anomalous body experience," according to Mauricio Sierra.

"Patients often describe it as a kind of split of their subjective awareness into two minds: one which observes whilst the other goes through the motions," Sierra writes.[19]

Mind-emptiness, the frightening sensation of a hollow head containing no thoughts at all, is a frequent complaint that is suggestive of an absorptive state. "Heightened absorption in depersonalization is likely to have a negative, self-centered aspect to it, which may have the effect of 'freezing' the mind, rendering attentional and cognitive resources unavailable for creative and open involvement with the world," according to Sierra.

So the distillation of core symptoms that has emerged from the most recent research doesn't invalidate the many subjective observations and conclusions made by contributors to the DPD literature through the decades. Nor does it diminish the importance of individual symptoms that may not seem directly related to the clarified definitions of the disorder. What it does do is send researchers and clinicians down certain, specific paths of exploration in the hope of finding treatments that, while conquering the core factors, also traverse their many tributaries as well.

Classification Discussion

One of the more perplexing aspects of Depersonalization is its possible relationship to anxiety or panic disorders. What is supposed to be a defense mechanism, distancing the mind from horror, betrays its purpose and presents horrific sensations of its own.

As indicated earlier, the *International Classification of Mental and Behavioural Disorders*, 10th revision (ICD-10) places DPD within the category of "Other Neurotic Disorders," (F48.1). This listing contrasts the most recent edition of the *Diagnostic and Statistical Manual* (DSM-IV-TR) used in the United States, which places DPD among the dissociative disorders as classification (300.6).

Dr. Evelyn Hunter and colleagues at the Institute of Psychiatry, London, believe that there is compelling evidence to link DPD with anxiety disorders, particularly panic. This evidence builds a case for using cognitive-behavioral therapy as an effective treatment modeled primarily after that used with the anxiety disorders. We look at these treatments in detail in Chapter 10.

Hunter suggests that "if DP/DR symptoms are misinterpreted as indicative of severe mental illness or brain dysfunction, a vicious cycle of increasing anxiety, and consequently, increased DP/DR symptoms will result."

For many people, including several who have relayed their personal stories herein, panic has served as the unwelcome and unexpected introduction to chronic depersonalization wherein anxiety is no longer prevalent. For others, panic and or/anxiety do not figure into the experience at all.

But clearly, someone who feels detached from their former sense of self, or their surroundings, is experiencing dissociation. And the arguments establishing DPD as a dissociative disorder are valid and strongly supported. If hearing an internal, mocking voice, such as mentioned in the Dissociative Experiences Scale (DES) means that my depersonalization was dissociative, then I personally would lean toward that designation. Because I experienced panic and anxiety initially, and recurrently, I would lean toward the anxiety categorization as well.

While Hunter and colleagues acknowledge that subjective detachment from the external world and from private mental processes is dissociative in nature, they also stress that several of the primary characteristics of the other dissociative disorders, such as dissociative amnesia, fugue, and dissociative identity disorder (DID), are not typical of depersonalization. For instance, "D-People" do not typically experience significant periods of memory loss or identity shifts. Although there may be a sense of detachment from the external world, there is no loss of conscious awareness of the self or of the external environment in DPD. Also, unlike other dissociative disorders where there is typically a pattern of alternating between nondissociative and dissociative states, depersonalization, as a full-blown disorder rather than a transient symptom, is most often unremitting, with little fluctuation in severity. Finally, while recent research has found childhood emotional abuse to be a predictor of DPD, it is usually not of the extreme degree and type of abuse evidenced in cases of dissociative identity disorder. [20]

To Sleep, Perchance to Dream

In any discussion of depersonalization, few metaphors emerge as frequently as those relating to sleep. DPD is frequently described as a dreamlike state from which patients long to awaken. Life itself may seem like little more than a dream. And the nonstop mental anguish patients experience can be nightmarish at best.

Many of the things most people take in stride can seem quite strange to depersonalized people. But viewed objectively, the notion of sleep can seem rather bizarre to anyone who really thinks about it. Make believe you just arrived from Mars and are observing the human beings' ways for the first time:

"These beings, humans, somehow fall into a trance every day, close their eyes and disappear mentally from the world in which they live. Inside their heads they often enter other realms, which while purely imaginary, have become much of the subject of their prophesies, their interpretation of themselves, and poetry debating which state is actually true—the one they live in by day, or the one in their heads at night. Curious."

Humans have little trouble adapting to these essential nightly trance states. Often, we just fall into them. So philosophers have spent more time pondering the issue of dreams versus reality.

In his "Meditations," Rene Descartes asked if he could be really certain he was awake. "How often, asleep at night, am I convinced that I am here in my dressing gown, sitting by the fire when in fact I am lying undressed in bed ... I see plainly that there are never any sure signs by which means being awake can be distinguished from being asleep."

Yet sleep itself has rarely been explored in research relating to Depersonalization Disorder. Some people report that depersonalization feels dramatically worse after napping. Others feel more depersonalized when they are sleep deprived.

To date, sleep research and DPD investigations have yet to cross paths. Research involving sleep deprivation as a possible treatment for depression has shown that roughly 60 percent of the tested subjects show immediate recovery. The problem is that most of them relapse the next night. While this does not relate to depersonalization directly, it may imply some support to the theoretic idea that depersonalized patients need in some way to be "awakened" out of their dreamlike state, rather than numbed further by certain medications.

In 2007, one study published in the *Journal of Abnormal Psychiatry*[21] took what could prove to be the first steps toward further exploration of the sleep/DPD relationship. Working with 25 healthy Dutch undergraduate students (15 women and 10 men), psychologist Timo Giesbrecht, of Maastricht University in Holland and Mount Sinai School of Medicine, N.Y., attempted to determine if lack of sleep would result in dissociation in his subjects. The result, a paper entitled "Acute Dissociation After One Night of Sleep Loss" provided the first clinical evidence, through a series of dissociation scales and alertness tests, that dissociative symptoms do indeed intensify after a night of sleep deprivation.

"Our findings nicely fit with the notion that disruptions in circadian rhythms (the normal 24-hour biological cycle} affect wakefulness and arousal and have detrimental effects on memory and attentional control" Giesbrecht concludes. These disruptions in circadian rhythms might have something to do with the attentional deficits typically found in patients with dissociative disorders. Also, studies have shown that dissociation and depersonalization symptoms are related to lowered levels of urinal norepinephrine, a neurotransmitter regulating arousal and alertness.

An additional consequence of disruptions in the sleep–wake cycle of individuals scoring high on dissociation scales might be "the intrusion of sleep phenomena (e.g., dreamlike experiences) into waking consciousness resulting in feelings of depersonalization and derealization." Giesbrecht adds.

Clearly, the mysteries of depersonalization have captured the imaginations and the efforts of many researchers. Time will tell where it ultimately comes to rest in the diagnostic manuals. New studies will emerge along with new interpretations. Some of these may, in a philosophical sense, not question the existence of depersonalization, but view it in the context of how exactly it fits into a rapidly changing world. Is it truly a disorder, or an ever-expanding shift in human consciousness, destined in time to consume us all?

REFERENCES

1. Ross, CA: Epidemiology of multiple personality disorder and dissociation. Psych Clin N Amer 1991; 14:503-517

2. Aderibigbe, Y.A., Bloch, R.M., & Walker, W.R. (2001). Prevalence of depersonalization and derealization experiences in a rural population.
   Social Psychiatry and Psychiatric Epidemiology, 36, p 63–69

3. Michal, M.,Wiltink, J.,Subic-Wrana, C., et al (2009) Prevalence, correlates and predictors of depersonalization experiences in the German general population. *Journal of Mental Disease*, in press.

4. Konigsberg, R, Elle magazine (2007) April, p 246

5. Simeon, D., Abugel, J (2006) *Feeling Unreal: Depersonalization Disorder and the Loss of the Self.* NewYork: Oxford University Press. p 87

6. Ibid.

7. Sierra, M. (2009) Cambridge: Cambridge University Press. *Depersonalization: A New Look at a Neglected Syndrome*, p 54

8. Ibid.

9. Simeon D, Knutelska M, Nelson D, Guralnik O: Feeling unreal: a depersonalization disorder update of 117 cases. J Clin Psychiatry 2003;64:990

10. Baker, D, Hunter, E., Lawrence, E., et al (2003). Depersonalization disorder: clinical features of 204 cases. *British Journal of Psychiatry*, 182, 428-433.

11. no 5. p 88

12. Ibid.

13. Ibid.

14. Ibid. p 89

15. no.9

16. Sierra, M., Baker, D., Medford, N, David., A.S. (2005) Unpacking the depersonalization syndrome: and exploratory factor analysis on the Cambridge Depersonalization Scale. *Psychological Medicine*, **35**, 1523-1532

17. Simeon, D., Kozin, D.S., Segal, K., Lerch, Brenna, Dujour, R., Giesbrecht., T (2008). De-constructing depersonalization: further evidence for symptom clusters. *Psychiatry Research*, **157**, 303-306.
18. Simeon, D., Hwu, B.S., Knutelska, M., (2007). Temporal Disintegratiion
   in Depersonalization Disorder, *Journal of Trauma and Dissociation*, **8 (1)**, 11-24
19. Sierra, M. (2009). *Depersonalization: A New Look at a Neglected Syndrome.* Cambridge: Cambridge University Press, p. 143.
20. Hunter, E.C. , Phillips, M.L., Chalder, T., Sierra, M., David, A.S. (2003) Depersonalization disorder: a cognitive behavioral conceptualization. *Behaviour Research and Therapy*, **41**, 1451-1467.
21. Giesbrecht, Timo, et al. (2007) Journal of Abnormal Psychology, 116:**3,**
   p 599-606

7   The Biology of Depersonalization

Unless someone's chasing you down the street with a knife, there's nothing worth worrying about.

—Ed K

The words *above*, spoken by my college roommate still seem essentially true, many years after he mumbled them. I have never really *felt* them as true, but he was so different. Why was he able to ingest every illicit drug with impunity (at least up until that point), while I cringed beneath the covers in my bunk, eaten alive by fears that held no name or explanation?

The answers were near impossible to find back then, and they're anything but simple today. But in the last few decades, knowledge of the human body has increased exponentially, and continues to do so.

I don't know what happened to Ed. Nor do I think he could have carried on his excesses indefinitely. His carefree attitude and seeming immunity to fear and worry may well have continued for a lifetime. The reason is the same as why his eyes were brown and mine are blue—genetics. As we examine the possible workings of depersonalization and other states of mind, the simple fact that people are genetically programmed differently cannot be escaped. Things rooted in our genes can be overcome, but not denied. Ed's carefree attitudes and my perpetual angst each began developing in their own unique ways within the comfort of the womb.

To understand the many systems likely involved in DPD, and because depersonalization is so often a form of disembodiment (as if my brain were separate from my body), it is important to look at the brain-body as one integrated unit. It is, after all, exactly that. Despite the ancient concept of the body as the temple of the spirit, somewhat like a genie living in a lamp, the brain lives in a symbiotic relationship with the rest of the body. Dissociation is a severe disruption in

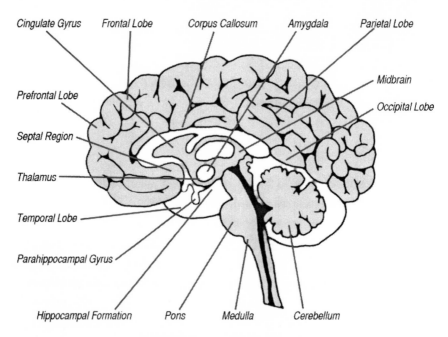

Cingulate Gyrus   Frontal Lobe   Corpus Callosum   Amygdala   Parietal Lobe

Midbrain

Prefrontal Lobe

Occipital Lobe

Septal Region

Thalamus

Temporal Lobe

Parahippocampal Gyrus

Hippocampal Formation   Pons   Medulla   Cerebellum

FIGURE 1: YOUR BRAIN

All drawings by Steven Doss

the normal sense of integration that most people rarely give a second thought. Reinforcing the idea of the mind and body as one cohesive entity can be a helpful first step toward mental re-integration.

Your Body Your Mind

"The mind is its own place," stands as one of poet John Milton's most memorable observations. And, as he noted, it can certainly make a hell of heaven or a heaven of hell. Mind is one thing. Something that only the individual truly knows. But brain and body are no longer perceived by educated people as two separate entities. The mind may be its own place, but it is housed in a condo that requires resident fees and interaction with the neighbors, like it or not.

Human beings cannot function normally unless all mental and physical components are in sync. Depersonalization does not separate your mind and body — it creates the *illusion* that they have somehow separated, and there are biological reasons why this occurs.

When was the last time your heart was broken, or you had butterflies in your stomach, or you were so frightened that a chill went up your spine? These expressions of emotion are more than bodily metaphors invented by ancient peoples with little knowledge of the brain. When the brain feels, or doesn't, the remainder of the mind/body system functions accordingly.

The gastrointestinal system, for instance, possesses its own self-contained nervous system, a mind of its own so to speak, called the Enteric Nervous System (ENS). The ENS can operate in the complete absence of input from the brain or even the spinal cord. This huge system containing hundreds of millions of nerve cells does more than regulate enzymes and food processing. It is also an efficient chemical factory that creates most of the neurotransmitters found in the brain. (Ninety-five percent of the best-known neurotransmitter serotonin is manufactured in the bowel before showing up in the brain).

A "gut" feeling is more than a figure of speech. Irritable bowel syndrome, endured by millions of Americans, correlates with low levels of serotonin, just like depression. Medicine now recognizes that many disorders of the gut involve changes in the Autonomic Nervous System, which regulates basic bodily functions such as respiration, digestion, and blood circulation.

For thousands of years, accounts of specific problems with the heart, bowels, head, and other parts of the body, as well as treatments for these ailments have been documented in a variety of texts. Depersonalization experiences also have been described, but often interpreted differently because of their cultural or spiritual contexts. It is fortunate, however, that the many descriptions of what we now know as Depersonalization Disorder have remained consistent in the literature of the past century or so. In 2001, Mauricio Sierra and German E. Berrios took a close look at 200 cases of depersonalization in the medical literature since 1898, dividing them into pre- and post-World War II groups. What they found was that "the phenomenology of depersonalization has remained stable over the last hundred years."[1] This tells us that we aren't dealing with a pop disorder, nor is DPD the "health report's" acronym of the week. It helps confirm the viability of Depersonalization Disorder as a singular, consistent syndrome within the body, despite vast changes in culture and society.

The Paths of Emotion

Depersonalization is often described as thinking without feeling. Lack of emotion becomes tantamount to loss of the actual self.

"Feeling itself is the basis of consciousness and underlies higher thought," notes emotion researcher Michael Jawer. "This statement is contrary to what many human beings (especially those of an intellectual bent) prefer to believe about themselves, but it is becoming generally accepted.

"When the nerve impulses, set off by body movements, reach [the lower brain] centers, a person becomes aware of feelings. The impulse doesn't stop at these lower centers, however, but passes on to the cerebral hemispheres, where image formation and symbolic thought take place."[2]

As pointed out by Maurico Sierra, some people readily attribute "unreality feelings" to a lack of emotional feelings that normally color perception, including that of our own bodies. "The idea that 'feelings of reality' might be determined by emotional feelings has been suggested previously in the literature," Sierra says, quoting research going back to the 1920s that stated, in part: "The feeling of the reality attaching to any idea is proportionate to our emotional interest in it."[3] For example, patients with depersonalization often complain that memories feel as if they really didn't happen to them. For many of them, autobiographic memories retain their factual aspects but seem devoid of the distinct feeling that accompanies the act of remembering.[4]

The idea that "emotional feeling" is a core experience, rather than just a reaction to an experience, has been neglected in neuropsychology, Sierra feels. It is likely, however, that in addition to a pathway of information processing leading to intellectual recognition, there is a parallel pathway in charge of assigning emotional significance to what is being perceived. There is evidence suggesting that these two parallel functions take place pre-consciously[5], which may explain why, when perception becomes conscious, it is already "emotionally colored."[6]

Recent research into the nature of emotional response has often employed a method similar to that of a lie detector. Technicians can measure a gut-level emotional reaction to a visual or other stimulus by observing the extent to which subjects sweat. This is accomplished with simple electrodes that measure an individual's Galvanic Skin Response (GSR), also known as skin resistance. In such tests, inanimate objects usually elicit nothing. But things that elicit fear, a threat, or an emotion, like seeing the familiar image of one's mother, show definite changes in the skin.

People with a disorder called *prosopagnosia* are unable to consciously recognize pictures of relatives, but still show evidence of *implicit* emotional recognition when their autonomic responses are measured.[7]

As a result, "Neuropsychological evidence is compatible with the view that the cognitive and emotional components of perception are independent of each other,"[8] Sierra says.

On the other hand, a failure to display normal autonomic responses while being able to recognize these pictures of relatives has been shown in patients with *Capgras Syndrome*.[9]

The possible relationship between the problems observed in these disorders and depersonalization have been brought up by V.S. Ramachandran, M.D., Ph.D., author of some of the Capgras research.

In discussing what he called *Capgras Delusion,* Ramachandran alludes to a case wherein a patient with a head injury resulting from a car crash emerged neurologically intact, but suddenly began to perceive his mother as an impostor.

In this patient, according to Ramachandran, the "wire" that goes from the visual areas to the emotional core of the brain—the limbic system and the amygdala—was cut by the injury. The visual areas in the brain concerned with recognizing faces were not damaged, but there was no emotion because the wire taking that information to the emotional centers was severed.

"If this is my mother, how come I don't experience any emotions?" the patient asked. It was difficult to acknowledge the woman visually without experiencing any of the feelings that had accompanied seeing her over the course of a lifetime.

To test the patient's claims, Ramachandran measured changes in the subject's skin resistance and the result was completely flat, "supporting the idea that there had been some disconnection between vision and emotion."

Ramachandran cites another syndrome he considers even stranger than Capgras—*Cotard's Syndrome*, in which the patient claims that he is dead:

"I suggest that this is a bit like Capgras except that instead of vision alone being disconnected from the emotional centers in the brain, all the senses, everything, gets disconnected from the emotional centers. Nothing he looks at in the world makes any sense, has any emotional significance, whether he sees it or touches it or looks at it. Nothing has any emotional impact. And the only way this patient can interpret this complete emotional desolation is to say, 'I'm dead, doctor.' However bizarre it seems, it's the only interpretation that makes sense to him."

Capgras and Cotard's are both rare syndromes. But Ramachandran believes that depersonalization, which he calls a sort of "mini-Cotard's" involves the same circuitry. Depersonalization is "more commonly seen in clinical practice ... in acute anxiety, panic attacks, depression, and other dissociative states. Suddenly the world seems completely unreal—like a dream. Or you may feel that you are not real. Doctor, I feel like a zombie. Why does this happen?"

Ramachandran suggests derealization, depersonalization, and other dissociative states are an example of playing possum in the emotional realm. The possum, when chased by a predator, suddenly loses all muscle tone and plays dead. Any movement encourages the predatory behavior of the carnivore who won't touch dead food. So playing dead is very adaptive for the possum.

Soldiers in battle or women being raped sometimes become detached from the circumstances as if they are watching it all happen. This is pure, classic dissociation. During such dire emergencies, the anterior cingulate in the brain, part of the frontal lobes, becomes extremely active. This inhibits or shuts down your amygdala and other limbic emotional centers, so you suppress potentially disabling emotions like anxiety and fear—temporarily. But at the same time, the anterior cingulate makes you extremely alert and vigilant so you can take an appropriate action.

In traumatic situations, this combination of shutting down emotions and being hyper-vigilant at the same time is useful, keeping you out of harm's way. It's better to be more possum-like and to do nothing than engage in some sort of erratic behavior. "But what if the same mechanism is accidentally triggered by chemical imbalances or brain disease, when there is no emergency?" Ramachandran asks. "You look at the world, and you're intensely alert and hyper-vigilant, but it's completely devoid of emotional meaning because you've shut down your limbic system. And there are only two ways for you to interpret this dilemma. Either you say the world isn't real—Derealization. Or you say, *I'm* not real, I feel empty—Depersonalization."[10]

Patients with depersonalization seem to experience a similar, non-delusional version of Capgras, Mauricio Sierra has said. In fact, a noted high prevalence of depersonalization in patients with Capgras syndrome or reduplicative paramnesia (wherein people believe a place has been physically duplicated) has given rise to the suggestion that the latter delusional states are in fact an elaboration of depersonalization experiences.[11]

Feeling and Hard Wiring

Depersonalization involves a lack of emotion, stress, fear, feelings of being hollow, mind emptiness, and the internal physiological changes that accompany these and other sensations. DPD is a master of disguises. Its symptoms are so varied, its co-morbidity so extensive, its actions so contradictory, its persistence so relentless that it's no wonder that it is so often misdiagnosed.

Some of the earliest 20th-century observers, such as Mayer-Gross, proposed what is largely believed today, that depersonalization is part of a "hard-wired" biological mechanism—a body mechanism that came into being somewhere along the evolutionary path as part of a response to life-threatening situations.[12] The existence of dissociating responses in different animals such as those who freeze in the face of imminent destruction (possums playing possum) provide evidence of this kind of system in the wild every day. But the mechanism in humans is likely what Mauricio Sierra sees as a "vestigial" brain response—like an appendix, it still exists but has long out-served its purpose.

Sir Martin Roth interpreted depersonalization's frequent occurrence in anxiety states as a protective brain response shaped by evolution, whereby "a state of heightened arousal together with dissociation of emotion served as an adaptive mechanism which enhanced the chances of survival in acute danger."[13] The other evidence for a hard-wired biological mechanism is the fact that depersonalization-like experiences often go hand in hand with Temporal Lobe Epilepsy (TLE).

Now let's look at the inner workings of the very things that make us human. Descarte's "I think therefore I am," has proven not only to be antiquated, but a verbalization of *thinking without feeling*, the very thing that can make depersonalization so disturbing. For the human animal, life must be colored by emotion, memory, and mood, underscored by familiarity. Thinking alone hardly does justice to the human experience.

The Brain and Its Tasks

Like other organs, the brain functions differently under different conditions. Basic bodily processes including respiration, blood circulation, heartbeat, digestion, glandular activities, and more are controlled by the Autonomic Nervous System. The ANS includes two branches—the parasympathetic nervous system that works when the body is at rest, and the sympathetic nervous system which speeds up the body's processes when needed. If some threat comes along, the sympathetic branch mobilizes to confront the situation through the influence of its nerves directly on the adrenal glands. The pupils in your eyes dilate, blood pressure rises, and more oxygen is delivered. At the same time, tasks handled by the parasympathetic branch— less essential things such as digestion, sexual arousal, and pupil constriction are hindered. When the threat is over, the parasympathetic branch resumes its duties. These two branches do not perform at the same time—one or the other does the job. It is interesting that in its way, the sympathetic system acts as if it *sympathizes* with your plight. However, it also has shown to be less than sympathetic, through its overactivity in people with anxiety disorders.

For decades, the media has made reference to left brain or right brain sensibilities. Incoming sensory information always goes to the opposite side, so the right hand sends information to the left hemisphere; the left hand sends it to the right hemisphere. Analysis, logic, and language reside in the left hemisphere. Face recognition, music appreciation, and holistic attitudes are housed in the right. The two hemispheres are separated by, and communicate through, a thick bank of nerve cells called the corpus callosum. One hemisphere may be dominant in an individual, but everyone utilizes both.

The human brain did not always look, or function, as it does today. The deepest structures within it are the oldest. The neocortex, which lies on the surface, enveloping and connecting the interior structures developed much more recently. One part of the cortex is the sensory cortex which is responsible for receiving sensory information from the sensory organs and deciphering it in terms of what we are familiar with—things that we already know inherently from past experience—a taste, a face, a touch, etc. This information is transmitted and processed via a network of interacting brain cells called neurons. Neurons communicate with each other via the various substances that together are known as neurotransmitters.

Sensory input, such as visual (sight), auditory (hearing), olfactory (smell), or somatosensory (touch), is first processed in the simplest sensory areas of the cortex called the primary sensory cortex.

Specific cortex areas throughout the brain receive the sensory information and then relay it to more complex sensory cortical areas known as the secondary unimodal association areas. So newly perceived objects are matched against pre-existing templates in various cortex areas. Appropriate templates exist for vision, smell, sound, taste, and touch.

The polymodal sensory association areas of the brain integrate all of the sensory input from these various sensory modalities. One such association area is known as the inferior parietal lobule, a portion of the parietal lobe consisting of the supramarginal and angular gyrus, strategically seated at the junction of the parietal lobe and the temporal and occipital lobes. (Figure 1.) Importantly, this area of the brain is also critical for something else—our ability to have a well-integrated body schema, that is, an intact and unified physical sense of self. [14]

The sensory association areas of the cortex are connected to the prefrontal cortex, which allow us to have thoughts about what we are perceiving, remember similar past perceptions, put them in context, and react accordingly.

Our reactions to what we perceive hinge on a system briefly mentioned earlier, and one of the most ancient systems in the brain—the limbic system. (Figure 2.) It includes the insula (not shown), the hippocampus, and a pair of small, bilateral structures with a name right out of a Vincent Price movie—the amygdala.

Recent neuroscience research tells us that the initial formation of emotional memories involves the activation of the two tiny, almond-size amygdala embedded deep in the temporal lobes. The amygdala (collectively known as amygdalae) plays a central role in a variety of instinctually driven emotional processes such as the conditioned fear response. (An example of this is when a lab rat immediately responds to a sound only because it has been paired to a mild electric shock in the past.) The amygdala is also involved in the automatic reading of emotional facial expressions, and the formation of explicit emotional memories.

The amygdala is an important part of the circuitry for fear. A

FIGURE 2: THE LIMBIC SYSTEM

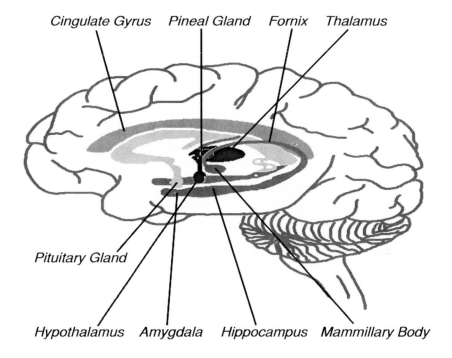

Cingulate Gyrus   Pineal Gland   Fornix   Thalamus

Pituitary Gland

Hypothalamus   Amygdala   Hippocampus   Mammillary Body

number of anxiety disorders in humans, such as social anxiety disorder, panic disorder, specific phobias, and Posttraumatic Stress Disorder (PTSD), all characterized by a heightened sense of threat, seem to correlate with overactivation of the amygdala when a person is presented with disorder-specific frightening stimuli.

In examining the fear processing circuitry, neuroscientist Joseph Ledoux discovered that two of the amygdala's dozen or more distinct divisions are particularly important. Stimulation of the central nucleus produces many of the expressions of conditioned fear: heart rate increases, "freezing" in place, and so on. A second area, the lateral nucleus, functions as a receiving station for information flowing from the cortex and thalamus, the two principal conduits within the brain for information coming from the outside world. "Thus the amygdala is able to monitor the outside world for danger," LeDoux wrote. "If the lateral nucleus detects danger, it activates the central nucleus which initiates the expression of behavioral responses and changes in body physiology that characterize states of fear."[15]

Fear activates the amygdala to stimulate the hypothalamus, leading to the release of hormones and other chemicals. Since it also activates the hippocampus and other cortical areas involved in memory, the result is a stronger, more enduring memory of a dangerous situation.

Interestingly, LeDoux discovered that the amygdala utilizes a fast track or "low road" for the conditioned fear response—a short, direct path from the thalamus to the amygdala. A lab animal hears a loud sound and freezes because of this pathway. A second path, a high road from the thalamus to the cortex and then to the amygdala allows additional time for the cortex to come up with an explanation for the sound.

The low road provides what LeDoux calls a "quick and dirty" response that can save your life when threatened. You jump out of the way of an oncoming bus because of this path. Then, seconds later, the high road provides the explanation and analysis of what has happened.

The Insula

Another important structure in the limbic system is the insula, which is responsible for registering internal bodily sensations, temperature, and pain.

The insula is a portion of the cerebral cortex folded deep within a fissure between the temporal lobe and the frontal lobe. It is divided into two parts: the larger anterior insula and the smaller posterior insula. These play a role in diverse functions that include perception, motor control, self-awareness, cognitive functioning, and interpersonal experience.

Research as early as 2001 identified the anterior insula as a crucial cortical region necessary for the experience of emotional feelings. Such findings are in keeping with the reduced insula activation found in patients with Depersonalization Disorder.[16]

According to Mauricio Sierra, the insula seems to be well placed to integrate signals from a variety of sources. It receives visceral, somatosensory, visual, auditory, and gustatory inputs, and has extensive reciprocal connections with the amygdala, hypothalamus, cingulate gyrus, and orbitofrontal cortex. Patients suffering what is known as "pure autotomic failure," unable to generate autonomic responses, also have trouble experiencing conscious feelings, including empathy.[17]

Functional Magnetic Resonance Imaging (fMRI) tests also have shown that the ability to experience feelings in response to emotionally laden imagery is related directly to activity in the anterior insula.

In fact, anterior insula activation appears to relate to a whole range of emotional feelings such as disgust, sadness, fear, reward experiences, categorization of facial emotional expressions, craving, and hunger or satiety states. So much activity suggests that the anterior insula is involved in the generation of emotions overall, rather than specific feelings, Sierra suggests.

The anterior insula is also thought to be the area associated with the pleasantness or unpleasantness of odors. Smell is certainly one of the oldest and most important of the senses. The "smelling brain," called the olfactory lobe, grew in tandem with the brain stem in early evolution and served the vital purpose of determining what was safe to eat or avoid, as well as detecting the scents of possible enemies approaching.

Michael Jawer notes that the anterior insula is also involved with our "highest and most cherished thought process—belief." Specifically, Jawer says, "research suggests that false assertions, such as 'torture is good,' trigger activation of the anterior insula... So when one reacts to a statement by saying, 'That sure smells fishy to me,' something more than metaphor may be at work."[18]

Many people with Depersonalization Disorder report a diminished sense of smell as one of their symptoms. It is interesting that some of the earliest researchers, such as Krishaber, the Victorian eye, nose, and throat expert mentioned in Chapter 3 interpreted depersonalization as a likely dysfunction of the senses themselves.

Smell triggers memories. Part of the human experience is sudden recollection, spawned by new information coming in through the senses. The aroma of frying chicken take me back to summers in Alabama at my grandmother's house. Certain blossoms in Spring evoke memories of people and places from the past. Motor oil on a heated engine reminds me of the old MG I drove as a teen. Take these smells away and the memories seem to disappear with them. The anterior insula and its actions regarding smell would seem to have plenty to do with our personal feelings of nostalgia.

The Posterior Insula and Feelings of "Embodiment"

Neuroimaging studies also have identified a network of parietal regions which seem to play an important role in the generation of embodiment and agency feelings: the inferior parietal cortex, the temporo-parietal junction, and the posterior insula. An early Positron Emission Tomography (PET scan) study of DPD patients showed abnormally increased activation of the angular gyrus of the right parietal lobe. This finding was particularly important because it also showed a "high positive correlation between parietal activation and subjective feelings of depersonalization."[19] (Interestingly, this little area is sometimes referred to as the Einstein area—dedicated to metaphoric and abstract thinking.)

Patients experiencing a lack of agency (sensations regarding movement), or the sensation that movements are being controlled by something outside themselves have exhibited increased activation in the angular gyrus. Similar subjective experiences are often reported by patients with depersonalization. Researchers currently believe that the right angular gyrus computes discrepancies between intended action and subsequently experienced movement, allowing any detection of a mismatch to be consciously experienced.[20 21] Mauricio Sierra suggests the likelihood that the observing of movements that do not seem to emanate from one's self elicits an "attentional orientation response" similar to that elicited by unexpected events.

In addition to the angular gyrus, the posterior insula seems to play a big part in integrating input signals related to self-awareness. Decreased activity in this region corresponds with a decreasing feeling of movement control. People with minimal insula activation report such a striking absence of feelings of agency that, when they move, it feels to them that they are watching the movements of another person. Also, studies of stroke patients have shown that lesions to the posterior right insula correlate with lack of ownership feelings regarding the existence or activity of their left side limbs.[22]

These studies have focused on the neurobiological underpinning of one aspect of DPD—agency feelings (being in control of one's actions). They indicate that while posterior insula activation correlates with the degree of self-attribution to movement, the angular gyrus in the inferior parietal cortex shows the opposite pattern, so that the lower the sense of agency, the greater the activity in the right inferior parietal lobe.[23] Another related and partially overlapping parietal region, the temporo-parietal junction, has been shown to play an important role in the experience of embodiment. Problems in this area, as well as electrical stimulation of it, can actually generate out-of-body experiences.[24]

The Hippocampus

Another important part of the limbic system is the hippocampus. The hippocampus is the seat of autobiographical memories—all the memories that make up the story of our lives—stored in the context of time, place, and details of what occurred. The encoding, storage, and retrieval of personal memories is a highly complex process involving the hippocampus as well as other extended cortical networks. Daphne Simeon has noted the belief among some neuroscientists that an autobiographical memory cannot be retrieved if an early "kernel" of the memory is not activated in the hippocampus, which serves as the epicenter of the distributed memory network in the brain. "Of course no autobiographical memory could be retrieved if it was not encoded in the first place," says Dr. Simeon. "But it appears that the memory difficulties experienced in depersonalization are more related to failures of this initial memory encoding. This makes it different than other dissociative conditions like amnesia, where the problem lies more with a state-dependent compartmentalization of memory and therefore difficulty in its conscious retrieval."[25]

Also, smaller hippocampi have been found in individuals suffering from a variety of psychiatric conditions associated with chronic stress, such as depression and posttraumatic stress disorder (PTSD). Stress appears to have a toxic effect on the hippocampus.

Sensation without Memory

As stated earlier, the amygdala and hippocampus are two very important subcortical structures in the brain. The amygdala is crucial to the initial processing of fear and other emotions before they're processed at a higher level by the cortex. The amygdala is the seat of emotional memory as well as the source of our immediate fight-or-flight response. The purpose of the hippocampus is the consolidation of information and the retaining of autobiographical memories. These two brain structures can operate quite independently of each other, resulting in two different types of memories being formed.

Joseph LeDoux suggests that the knowledge that a particular incident was terrifying is a declarative memory about an emotional experience, mediated by the hippocampus and its connections. In contrast, the intense emotional response evoked during the event (and at times during its later recollection) activates the implicit memory system and involves the amygdala and *its* connections. Under sufficiently intense or prolonged stress, the hippocampus can shut down through the mediation of the stress hormone cortisol. This can lead to impaired *explicit* conscious memory functions. At the same time, stress does not interfere with, and may even enhance, amygdala functioning. According to LeDoux, "It is thus completely possible that one might have poor conscious memory of a traumatic experience, but at the same time form very powerful implicit, unconscious emotional memories." [26] This distinction is crucial to understanding dissociative phenomena. Stimuli may activate the amygdala without activating conscious memories, eliciting an intense emotional state that the individual simply doesn't understand intellectually. The fact that the implicit system forgets and revises less than the explicit system over time, and also matures earlier in life, further fuels the dissociation just described, especially for early life events.

Another relevant part of the cortex is the medial prefrontal cortex, which is located inside the frontal lobes. The medial prefrontal cortex has important connections to the limbic, or "emotional," part of the brain, playing a crucial role in modulating and dampening our emotional responses. In some psychiatric disorders characterized by high states of anxiety and arousal, it appears that this area of the prefrontal cortex is *hypoactive* and is not adequately inhibiting the very active amygdala and other limbic structures. According to Daphne Simeon, one could predict that the hypoemotionality, or emotional deadness of chronic DPD might involve an inverse pattern: heightened prefrontal activity with greater inhibition of the limbic system.

More About Autonomic Response

Studying autonomic nervous system responses in depersonalization actually began in the mid 1960s. A patient suffering a panic attack showed skin resistance readings that were typical for anxiety when, abruptly, the skin resistance became flat and unresponsive. Her pulse rate also dropped. When questioned later, the patient described feeling more and more panicky, on the verge of crying out for help, when the anxiety suddenly subsided and was replaced by a strange feeling of detachment. Sounds appeared distant, vision was blurred and "swimmy," and the patient's limbs felt as if they did not belong to her.[27]

Other early studies of patients suffering with continuous, chronic depersonalization suggested that "the discrepancy between subjective and objective signs of anxiety is the fundamental characteristic of patients with depersonalization. In physiological terms, anxiety is experienced but is not translated into defense reaction arousal."[28]

A 2002 study conducted by the Institute of Psychiatry in England attempted to determine whether the Autonomic Nervous System's sympathetic responses weakened in depersonalized people when they were presented with emotional stimuli.[29] The skin conductance responses of 15 patients with depersonalization disorder, 15 "normals," and 11 people with anxiety disorders were recorded. They were all presented with things that normally produce a galvanic skin response, such as an unexpected clap of the hands or a sigh, as well as pictures with both inoffensive and unpleasant contents. (The latter included images of such things as dismembered bodies, snakes poised to attack, accidents, cockroaches, etc.) The results indicated that the depersonalization patients showed selectively reduced autonomic responses to unpleasant pictures, but not to neutral or pleasant ones. Also, the response to these stimuli took significantly longer in the group with depersonalization disorder. In contrast, responses to non-specific stimuli, (the clap and sigh) were significantly shorter in the depersonalization and anxiety groups than in the healthy controls. "These findings suggested the presence of both inhibitory and facilitatory {enabling} mechanisms on autonomic arousal, which pointed to a specific disruption in emotional information processing rather than a non-specific dampening effect on autonomic reactivity," Mauricio Sierra concluded. Somewhat expectedly, in spite of their slower autonomic responses to the unpleasant pictures, patients with depersonalization were perfectly capable of intellectually ranking their varied degrees of unpleasantness.

A more recent study compared the skin conductance responses of depersonalization disorder patients with those of anxiety disorder patients and normal controls, as they watched pictures and video clips of facial expressions of disgust and happiness.[30] The findings showed that while patients in the anxiety group exhibited increased autonomic reactivity to disgust expressions, depersonalization patients showed very similar responses to those of the "normal" controls. This was surprising, Sierra has noted, given that both the depersonalization and the anxiety patients had reported similarly high levels of subjective anxiety, as measured by administered anxiety scales. In other words, in spite of acknowledging that they *felt* highly anxious, the autonomic responses of depersonalization patients resembled those of healthy people rather than those of similarly anxious patients specifically diagnosed with anxiety disorders. Such findings confirm the conclusions of other studies that depersonalization in anxious patients has a blunting and selective effect on *autonomic* reactivity. This blunting also seems to be relative to anxiety levels.

This idea is supported by an earlier Mount Sinai study that compared the levels of urinary norepinephrine in patients with depersonalization disorder with those in healthy "normal" patients. In keeping with their higher anxiety levels, patients with depersonalization were found to have higher levels of norepinephrine than the normal group. However, within the depersonalization group itself, there was a striking norepinephrine reduction with increasing levels of depersonalization.[31] To conclude, it seems plausible to suggest that autonomic responses in patients with depersonalization are likely to reflect a balance between two opposing tendencies: an excitatory one determined by anxiety levels, and an inhibitory one determined by depersonalization intensity.

Functional Neuroimaging Studies

Over the last decade a number of studies using functional magnetic resonance imaging (fMRI) to examine Depersonalization Disorder patients have been published. Such studies are not only beginning to show evidence of dysfunctional brain activity, but also show how those abnormal findings relate to the autonomic changes already discussed.

One of the first neuroimaging studies, conducted at Mount Sinai, used positron emission tomography (a PET scan), to compare patterns of brain activation of eight patients with Depersonalization Disorder with normal controls as they performed a verbal memory task.[32] Although patients showed reduced metabolic activity in some association areas such as the right superior and middle temporal gyri, other association areas in the parietal and occipital lobes were more active than those in the controls. The finding of anomalous activation patterns in cross-modal association areas seems consistent with long-held views that depersonalization may result from a high-order failure of cortical integration.[33] The researchers reported a striking correlation between the subjective intensity of depersonalization and the degree of increased parietal activation.

Other studies using functional neuroimaging have been designed to explore the neurology of emotional numbing. The first of those studies used functional magnetic resonance imaging (fMRI) to compare the neural response of patients with depersonalization disorder with that of healthy volunteers and patients with obsessive compulsive disorder (OCD). Participants were scanned as they watched a series of aversive and neutral pictures. Expectedly, the depersonalized patients stated that they could clearly understand the content of the pictures, but failed to experience any subjective emotional response to them.[34]

While healthy control participants, as well as OCD patients, showed activation in the anterior insula in response to unpleasant and disgusting pictures, such activation was not seen in the patients with depersonalization. Other brain areas, such as the occipito-temporal cortex, known to be relevant in the response to expressions of fear and disgust, were also underactive in patients with depersonalization, compared with the two control groups.

A more technical, but important finding of this study was that depersonalization patients, but not the normal subjects, showed an area of activation in the right ventrolateral prefrontal cortex—a region that seems to couple its functions with the insula. During the presentation of unpleasant pictures, prefrontal activation only occurred in the *absence* of insula activation, which appears to be evidence of an inverse correlation. According to Dr. Sierra, the prefrontal area in question has been implicated in the evaluation of negative or aversive information, and on exerting control over both emotional experience and its impact on decision-making. For example, activation of this and other related frontal regions has been observed when normal subjects try to control their emotional responses to negative pictures by viewing the picture with a sense of detachment or by making believe that the images are in fact pleasant.[35]

Of course, to the layperson this research may seem confusing or intimidating. But it's important to understand that these findings do not represent brain "damage", but instead, subtle dysfunctions of existing brain systems. What's gone awry for the time being does not necessarily have to remain that way.

Little by little researchers have been able to sort out a variety of areas of the brain involved in depersonalization; the picture becomes more complete, and comprehensible, with every new research study. Each is a guidepost, pointing the way not only to the things that are *not right*, but possible new ways in which to treat them.

My personal reaction to some of the studies indicating minimal reactions to "aversive" images was befuddlement. Numbness is certainly a long-term symptom of DPD for many people, but so are many sensations that are frightening and intolerable. Emotional flatness is preferable to the constant feeling that you're going to go insane. It seemed to me that people going through the Nine Circles, as I knew them, would hardly be affected by pictures of cockroaches or car wrecks. And it seemed that there might be sociological factors involved as well. I grew up in a rough neighborhood in New York City were cockroaches were so common they were almost elevated to the status of pets. Aversive realities were ever present. So if I registered minimal responses to aversive imagery, would it be because I have DPD or because I have a greater tolerance to anything aversive or even offensive?

Ultimately, the message being relayed lies in the lack of autonomic response shown time and again by the research, as well as how parts of the brain "remember" while the individual does not, or vice versa. This is part and parcel of depersonalization overall, despite whether an individual feels detached, crazy, frightened, or numb. The way these internal systems act during DPD often illustrate the many contradictions that define its nature.

DPD and Epilepsy

Depersonalization is often linked with Temporal Lobe Epilepsy (TLE), a condition that has been systematically studied for many

years. Epilepsy has historically been an intriguing disorder, in part
because of the well-known figures who suffered with it. Vincent
Van Gogh likely suffered from Complex Partial seizures. Alexan-
der the Great suffered seizures, which in his time were considered
"the sacred disease," and Charles Dickens' descriptions of his own
epilepsy serve as case histories for neurologists to this day. One of
the most interesting, however, was the great Russian writer Fyodor
Dostoyevsky, who suffered a rare form of Epilepsy termed "Ecstatic
Epilepsy." Four of the major characters in his novels were epileptic,
most notably Prince Mishkin, protagonist of *The Idiot*.

Dostoyevksy suffered hundreds of seizures throughout his life,
and often it took him up to a week to recover as he experienced
"heaviness and even pain in the head, disorders of the nerves, nervous laugh, and 'mystical' depression."

Most curious are the writer's descriptions of ecstatic epilepsy as
he experienced it:

*"For several instants I experience a happiness that is impossible
in an ordinary state, and of which other people have no conception.
I feel full harmony in myself and in the whole world, and the feeling
is so strong and sweet that for a few seconds of such bliss one
could give up ten years of life, perhaps all of life. I felt that heaven
descended to earth and swallowed me. I really attained God and
was imbued with Him. All of you healthy people don't even suspect
what happiness is, that happiness that we epileptics experience for
a second before an attack."*[36]

Clearly, the ecstatic feelings Dostoyevsky described are unusual.
Yet depersonalization, in a way that is neither chronic nor particularly unpleasant, can accompany seizure activity. About a century
after the Russian writer's milieu, neurologist Wilder G. Penfield was
able to induce dissociation in people by stimulating specific areas
of the temporal cortex, the superior temporal gyrus and the middle
temporal gyrus.[37] As a result, he proposed the "temporal lobe hypothesis" of depersonalization in 1950, because he believed that he
had been able to interrupt the mechanism that assimilates memories
of sensory experiences. For example, stimulating parts of the tem-

poral lobe might interfere with the association of one's hand and body—the hand would no longer feel as if it belonged to the body. His hypothesis was later supported by other research which found depersonalization to be a common symptom among people with Temporal Lobe Epilepsy.[38]

In trying to understand his patients' vivid descriptions of being detached, or "far off and out of this world," Penfield interpreted what was occurring as an alteration in the usual mechanisms that compare immediate sensory perceptions with existing memory records. These brain mechanisms imbue our perceptions with emotional coloring and relevance. Perceptions both of the self and of the things around us should feel familiar, but in depersonalization they often do not. Our subjective sense of familiarity is diminished because these perceptions are not being emotionally tagged as "known" against pre-existing memory records.

The research on the relationship between depersonalization and epilepsy is ongoing, currently addressing whether or not depersonalization occurs in other seizure activity beside Temporal Lobe Epilepsy. Interestingly, some medicines traditionally used to treat seizures have been used successfully in treating depersonalization. We'll look at these more thoroughly in Chapter 9.

Depersonalization and Migraine

The precise nature of the association between migraine and depersonalization is currently unknown. The neurotransmitter serotonin, which appears often in the discussion of DPD, seems to play some part in migraines as well.

Depersonalization-like symptoms may occur as a component of migraine auras,[39] or may happen in the interval between termination of aura and the onset of headache (see below). Auras are a sensory phenomena that may occur before a migraine. Visual auras may include flashing lights, geometric patterns, or distorted vision. Some people may have aural auras involving sounds (usually buzzing), olfactory auras involving smelling odors not actually present, or tactile auras that present as a physical sensation. Some auras, known as *somesthesic* migraine auras, are characterized by dramatic distortions in body experience, such as magnification of body parts. These can be accompanied by depersonalization. A dramatic example of this is the so-called *Alice in Wonderland syndrome*, most commonly reported in children. This syndrome is characterized by the occurrence of a somesthesic aura often accompanied by depersonalization, visual illusions, and distortions in the perception of time.[40] Certain types of migraine such as basilar migraine seem particularly prone to altered states of consciousness, which may at times eclipse other, more common clinical features: "One must consider the possible diagnosis of atypical migraine when paroxysmal and periodic shifts of mental states are seen in a child or adolescent with a positive familial history of migraine, say some experts."[41]

In addition to its occurrence as a migraine aura, depersonalization also can occur during the interval between the termination of aura and the onset of headache. Such a period of time can last from a few minutes to a few hours and is known as the "free interval". A study providing detailed clinical descriptions on the "free interval" of 25 migraine patients experiencing visual auras found that 88% of them experienced symptoms suggestive of depersonalization. Though most had difficulty describing their sensations, they used terms like "unreal," "removed from surroundings," etc.

Back in 1946, the well-known psychiatrist Hyam Shorvon observed that frequently, the onset of depersonalization in a migraine sufferer seemed to coincide with decreased frequency, or even cessation of headache episodes.[42] It has also been suggested that some cases of depersonalization disorder could represent undiagnosed cases of migraine with prolonged aura, but considering how long depersonalization can last, today's experts consider this highly unlikely.

The HPA Axis

Two mind-body systems are involved in an individual's response to stress. One, which we mentioned earlier, the sympathetic nervous system, links the brain to the other internal organs and regulates things like breathing, heart rate, and digestion. In very stressful situations, this system diverts blood from the skin to the muscles, provides additional oxygen for breathing, and causes you to sweat, in order to stay cool inside.

The brain trigger for these reactions during stress is the hypothalamus, which stimulates the adrenal glands (located on top of each kidney) causing them to release the hormones noradrenaline and adrenaline. People who suffer from chronic stress register elevated levels of both hormones, often with side effects like high blood pressure, gastrointestinal problems, high cholesterol, and headaches.

A second system involved in stress management, and likely depersonalization, is known as the hypothalamic-pituitary-adrenal (HPA) axis (Figure 3). This system involves the hypothalamus, the pituitary gland, and the adrenal gland. In a time of stress, or a perceived threat, the HPA axis kicks in. First, the hypothalamus sends a corticotropin-releasing hormone (CRH) to the pituitary gland located just below it. The pituitary gland then releases a second substance, adrenocorticotropic hormone (ACTH) which travels in the bloodstream to the adrenal glands. They, in turn release a slew of other hormones, including cortisol. Cortisol prompts the liver to release glucose, which helps to recruit the energy required throughout the body to respond to a perceived threat. It's all pre-programmed to deal with something bad coming at you (like someone with a knife).

Stress is not all that releases CRH from the hypothalamus. The sleep/wake cycle does it as well. In healthy people, cortisol rises rapidly after awakening, reaching a peak within 30–45 minutes. It then gradually falls over the day, rising again in late afternoon. Cortisol levels fall in late evening, reaching a trough during the middle of the night. Anatomical connections between brain areas such as the amygdala, hippocampus, and hypothalamus facilitate activation of the HPA axis. Cortisol acts throughout many parts of the body and the brain via the glucocorticoid receptors, mounting an immediate stress response that effectively mobilizes necessary body and brain responses while shutting down energy-wasting responses that are a luxury in the face of acute stress.

Glucocorticoids have many important functions, including modulation of stress reactions. But in excess, they can be damaging. Atrophy of the hippocampus in humans and animals exposed to severe stress is likely caused by prolonged exposure to high concentrations of glucocorticoids. Deficiencies of the hippocampus may reduce the memory resources available to help a body formulate appropriate reactions to stress.

Finally, the same stress hormone cortisol works to shut down the acute stress response by inhibiting the actions of the pituitary and the hypothalamus through "negative feedback." In a normal individual, this is how the HPA axis does its job as a self-contained, self-regulating stress-response system. Like an electric fan in the engine compartment of a car, it should start when things get too hot, then shut off when things cool down. But sometimes it doesn't.

In some psychiatric conditions linked to early life stresses, or to extreme or prolonged stress, the HPA axis can go haywire, hindering an individual's ability to mount an efficient stress response with a built-in time limit. Tests conducted on laboratory animals have shown that stress in early life can result in a permanently disrupted stress response. Sound familiar? Clearly it smacks of the "defense mechanism gone wrong" explanation so often attributed to depersonalization.

Problems within the HPA axis have been extensively documented in individuals with Posttraumatic Stress Disorder. Do people with DPD exhibit this same dysfunction? Researchers at Mount Sinai speculated that dissociative disorders may in fact show a different kind of HPA axis dysregulation than what is seen in PTSD. A study comparing baseline cortisol levels showed that 24-hour urine cortisol was higher in people with DPD than in normal individuals—the exact opposite of what is found in PTSD.[43] This shows that these two disorders are in fact quite different from each other, despite the temptation to lump them together due to superficial similarities.

This study also used a challenge test known as the "low-dose dexamethasone suppression test" which is frequently used in psychiatric studies of the HPA axis. In this test, people are given a tiny dose

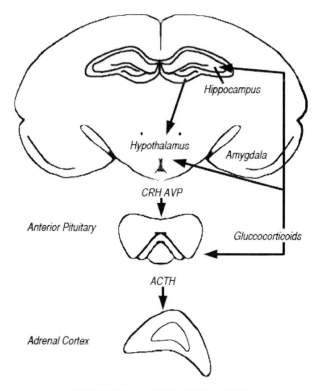

FIGURE 3: THE HPA AXIS

of a medication much like cortisol. This temporarily suppresses the body's production of cortisol in normal individuals. People who suffer from depression and PTSD exhibit different degrees of dexamethasone suppression than normal individuals. The study showed this to be true of DPD patients as well. Those with DPD suppressed their own cortisol production less in response to taking the dexamethasone. This pattern was similar to what is seen in severe depression, but people suffering from depression were excluded from the study. Follow-up studies further confirmed this same pattern of elevated resting cortisol and greater dexamethasone resistance in DPD.

In 2006, results from another study conducted by Dr. Simeon's Mount Sinai group showed cortisol levels in healthy comparison subjects and Posttraumatic stress disorder patients to be the same, while a group of dissociative subjects showed significantly elevated urinary cortisol levels. This demonstrates a distinct pattern of HPA-axis dysregulation in dissociation-depersonalization patients that needs to be further explored.[44]

Neurotransmitters, Obsession, and the Manufactured Self

When possible new treatments for DPD were examined in earnest in the 1990s, the new class of drugs, Selective Serotonin Reuptake Inhibitors (SSRIs) were the natural candidates to consider. These so-called "designer drugs" were specifically geared to inhibit the reuptake of serotonin into the presynaptic cell, increasing the levels of serotonin available to bind the postsynaptic receptor. (We'll look at how all this works in Chapter 9). Since substances such as LSD and pot, both of which affect serotonin transmission, trigger DPD, and because the disorder often presents symptoms that include anxiety and obsessive thinking, the SSRIs positive effects on serotonin seemed promising. Because they were designed to act on one system, SSRIs were more predictable and safer than some of the older meds, such as monoamine oxidase inhibitors (MAOIs), which acted on several neurotransmitter systems at once in more or less a shotgun approach. Serotonin seems to play a key role in depression, as well as anxiety; norepinephrine seems to relate more to pleasure—repeating an activity because of the reward it brought in the past. The efficacy in fighting depression through boosting serotonin levels was loudly touted in Peter Kramer's bestseller 1993 *Listening to Prozac*.

"Most antidepressants influence multiple sites on the same neuron," Kramer writes. "They may increase serotonin production at one end of the neuron, but also diminish norepinephrine or serotonin production through ordinarily less marked effects at receptors elsewhere on the same cell. Perhaps Prozac's extreme specificity is overwhelming to the neuron; the cell responds at one site, in one direction, and cannot, through mechanisms that otherwise allow neurons to 'compensate' for changes in state, return to a prior level of functioning."[45]

You cannot take serotonin directly in the hopes of increasing serotonin levels in the brain because it will not successfully cross the blood-brain barrier and will have no effect on brain function. Also, straight serotonin would activate *every* synapse it reaches, whereas SSRIs only *enhance a signal* that is already present, but too weak to come through.

SSRIs have shown themselves to be effective not only against depression, but also obsessive-compulsive disorders. Eric Hollander, MD, began treating OCD patients successfully at Mount Sinai in the early 1990s. Since obsessive rumination plays a large role in depersonalization for many people, it seemed logical that these drugs would be effective against DPD, at least in those patients that exhibited obsessive symptoms. When Daphne Simeon came on board, part of her job was to research the viability of these drugs in treating depersonalization. While some initial trials and experiences with individual patients showed promise using fluoxetine and buspirone, it didn't take long to see that SSRIs were not effective against intractable Depersonalization Disorder, even though they could help with the obsessive symptoms of many patients. They can also provide some benefits when combined with other medications.

Still, the overall failure of SSRIs in treating depersonalization is curious since, as mentioned earlier, so many indicators pointed to some serotonergic aspect to the disorder. For instance, DPD can be triggered or worsened by LSD, which is a serotonergic-acting drug (called a 5-HT2–serotonin type 2 receptor agonist*). Likewise, ketamine inhibits serotonin synthesis and metabolism.

One study by Simeon and Hollander looked at a varied group of patients not suffering from DPD. The group was a mixture of "normals," social-phobic patients, OCD patients, and borderline personality disorder patients. The study compared responses to the inducement of depersonalization and all kinds of other transient symptoms when people were given a one-time dose of either *meta*-chlorophe-

---

* An agonist is a drug that binds to a receptor of a cell and triggers a response of the cell. An agonist often mimics the action of a naturally occurring substance. In contrast, an *antagonist* blocks such action.

nylpiperazine (mCPP; a serotonin agonist used for studies such as this) or a placebo. It was found that mCPP produced a much higher rate of depersonalization in this diverse group than did the placebo, although importantly, it also induced more anxiety, more panic, and more dysphoria as well. The finding of anxiety, panic, and dysphoria is consistent with the literature by Drs. Roth, Torch, and others that describes DPD patients for whom these particular symptoms are a major part of their DPD experience.[46] But the specific role of serotonin in relation to depersonalization remains something of a mystery.

Depersonalization, through self-observation, existential ruminating, and analyzing what's wrong can often look like some *variant* of obsessive-compulsive disorder (OCD). While depersonalized patients don't engage in the typical OCD behaviors such as repeated hand washing or other rituals, they are often caught up in obsessive thinking, unable to get *out* of themselves. Whether it ultimately stems from an overall "anomalous body experience," feelings of unreality, or unacknowledged comorbidity, more than 125 stories out of 174 posted to *depersonalization.info* reflect this aspect of the depersonalization experience.

Sometimes, as we've seen, this type of thinking can occur at the earliest stages of the condition and could even be a defensive attempt to understand and make sense of the experience of unreality, which later flattens out into emotional deadness and an accepted feeling of "no self."

Obsessiveness has always been part of my personal depersonalization experience, as it has for Harris Goldberg and hundreds of others with whom I have communicated through the years. The object of this obsessive thinking can change from time to time, but at the heart of it is usually thinking whether or not one is going insane, thinking about what is wrong, and ultimately, thinking about thinking. The very act of thinking becomes tiresome, even painful—the sore tooth that the mind, looking into itself, cannot stop tapping. Some have likened it to an annoying song that you can never ever get out of your head, or endless static of a radio stuck between stations. The thoughts go round and round and end up nowhere.

The obsessive aspects of depersonalization exhibited by so many may well emanate from the initial overall sensations of strangeness, and the resulting concerns about maintaining one's sanity. But many people do fall into the kind of states observed by Evan Torch, MD, who coined what is known as the "intellectual-obsessive depersonalization syndrome." The difference I have observed in myself is that when depersonalization lightens up, or disappears completely, the tendency to obsess about something else continues. The mind can be like a helicopter piercing the dark alleys of a city with a searchlight. Eventually something on which to focus is uncovered.

Sometimes, when the strangeness of existence itself had momentarily diminished, I obsessed about a project at work, or someone who had hurt my feelings, or a literary masterpiece to be completed in the future. The latter revealed a fussy, perfectionist personality much like that of Frederic Amiel, the Swiss diarist who spent his life "practicing scales," but never composing the symphony of his dreams.

At times, this obsessiveness may have centered on a relationship, particularly when things were not going as I wanted them to. But when, for the moment, these obsessions resolved themselves, and there was nothing in particular to obsess about, I realized how much time had been wasted on my mental problems. In an effort to regain some of what other people enjoyed, I did everything in excess, as if to make the most of the normal periods while they lasted. Then, inevitably, perhaps in part because of these very excesses, my mind turned inward again. Depersonalization raised its head again, only this time I would question many of the things I had done during my more "normal" periods. Every expression of a personality, every argument, every joke, every challenge to my peers or my boss, every expression of beliefs or thoughts that were in any way a deviation from the mundane seemed extreme, ending with the question: "What was I thinking?" Reduced once again to a diminished sense of self, I questioned every action of the self I had exhibited during a time of full participation in life. It was very much like waking up after a night of drinking during which you made a pass at a friend's wife. You feel ashamed, humiliated, and want to apologize. People around me, however, thought I was amusing, or intelligent and perceptive because of my blatant honesty or my lack of concern for political correctness. People told me I should be a stand-up comedian. And yet, when this, a real personality emerged from within me, I feared that I was on dangerous ground, and inevitably retreated inside.

I have heard others relay very similar scenarios. Ultimately, I suspect that these episodes were an elaboration on the sense of unrealness of the self, coupled with obsessive tendencies. In my case, the path of excess took most of a lifetime to arrive at the palace of wisdom, as William Blake predicted. More often, and more frequently, it simply led back to one of the cycles some people find in depersonalization. The wisdom, if it could be defined as such, could be found in an attribute common to many depersonalized people—the ability not only to see through our own facades, but the illusions maintained by those who consider themselves "normal."

The Role of Glutamate and Opioids

One final neurotransmitter that seems to be involved in depersonalization is the amino acid glutamate. The brain contains a molecular device called the "NMDA (N-methyl-D-aspartic acid) receptor" which is widely distributed in the cortex, as well as in the hippocampus and the amygdala. Its purpose is to act as a receptor for glutamate, which binds to the cell to trigger a response. In this case it is involved in the process of memory.

When someone takes Ketamine, its effects are likely an excessive release of glutamate, which apparently provokes feelings of detachment and emotional numbing. This release goes beyond Ketamine's serotonergic actions and directly relates to one possible way in which DPD may be treated. We'll take a closer look at this in Chapter 9.

An additional system that may be related to depersonalization is the endogenous opioid system. As the name implies, opioids are natural substances that are opium-like, in that they are released in the body in response to pain. Endorphins, the best-known of these, bring on the "runner's high" that motivates many people to push themselves to their physical limits. Studies show that the endogenous opioid system is involved in the regulation of emotional and behavioural responses to stress.[47] When this system is triggered, people can endure a greater degree of pain, and their emotions can be suppressed. This system gone awry is suspect as a possible source of the emotional numbing that can be found in chronic depersonalization.

In addition to stress-driven activation of the opioid system, there is also evidence that chronic conditions such as depression and anxiety disorders may involve a dysregulation in the opioid system. Patients with panic disorder have abnormally high levels of endogenous opioids in cerebrospinal fluid, which increases after the induction of a panic attack with lactate, a chemical involved in the natural harnessing of energy during physical exertion. This panic-induced release of endogenous opioids is potentially relevant to depersonalization, since panic and depersonalization are so often linked.[48] Chapter 9 will look at how re-regulation of the Opioid system may play a role in treatment.

Clearly, Depersonalization Disorder has not been ignored by leading psychiatrists, psychologists, and clinicians, even though it remains highly unacknowledged by the general medical community as well as the media. The clinical research is clearly limited, and reading about galvanic skin responses and an under-activated insula does little for the person suffering with DPD right now, every minute of every day. What does this all mean, they wonder? So little is known about how to fix all these dysfunctions.

But just because there is no magic bullet to combat all the manifestations of this singular disorder does not mean it can't be dealt with or cured. The irregularities discussed in this chapter can and do change with treatment.

In treating some of these specific anomalies, the multitude of manifestations of the disorder are being often treated as well. In Chapter 9 we take a detailed look at what works and what doesn't.

REFERENCES

1. Sierra, M., & Berrios, G.E (2001). The phenomenological stability of depersonalization: comparing the old with the new. *Journal of Nervous and Mental Disease,* 189, 629–636.

2. Jawer, M. A., Micozzi, M.S. (2009) The Spiritual Anatomy of Emotion, Park Street Press, Rochester, N.Y., p.40.

3. MacCurdy, J.T. (1925) *Psychology of Emotions: Morbid and Normal.* London: Kegan Paul. P. 126.

4. Sharot, T., Delgado, M.R., Phelps, E.A. (2004). How emotion enhances the feeling of remembering. *Nature Neuroscience,* **7**, 1376-1380.

5. Halgren, E., Marinkovic, K. (1994). Neurophysiological networks integrating human emotions. In Gazzaniga, M. (ed.) *The Cognitive Neurosciences.* pp. 1137-1151. Cambridge, MA: MIT Press.

6. Sierra, M. (2009). Depersonalization: A New Look at a Neglected Syndrome. Cambridge: Cambridge University Press, p. 143.

7. Trandl, D., Damasio, A.R. (1985) Knowledge without awareness: an autonomic index of facial recognition by prosopagnosics. *Science,* **8**. 1453-1454.

8. Sierra, M. (no 6) p. 143.

9. Hirstein, W., Ramachandran, V.S. (1997). Capgras syndrome: a novel probe for understanding the neural representation of the identity and familiarity of persons. *Proceedings Biological Sciences,* **264**, 437-444.

10. Ramachandran, V.S., A Brief Tour of Human Consciousness; BBC Reich Lectures (2004) Pi Press, pp. 90-93.

11. Christodoulou, G. N. (1986). Role of depersonalization-derealization phenomenon in the delusional misidentification syndromes. *Bibliotheca Psychiatrica.* **164**, 99-104.

12. Mayer-Gross, W. (1935). On depersonalization. *British Journal of Medicine and Psychology,* *15*, 103–126.

13. Roth, M., Argyle, N. (1988) Anxiety panic and phobic disorder: An overview. *Journal of Psychiatric Research,* **22** (suppl 1), 33-54.

14. Simeon, D., Abugel, J. (2006) Feeling Unreal: Depersonalization Disorder and the Loss of the Self. Oxford: Oxford University Press, p. 106-107.

15. Restak, R., (2004) Poe's Heart and the Mountain Climber: Exploring the Effect of Anxiety on Our Brains and Our Culture. Three Rivers Press. N.Y., pp. 78-82.
16. Phillips, M.L., et al. (2001). Depersonalization disorder: thinking without feeling. *Psychiatry Research Neuroimaging*, **108,** 145–160.
17. Sierra, M. (no 6.) p.145.
18. Jawer, M. A., Micozzi, M.S (no. 2) p. 47.
19. Simeon, D. et al. (2000). Feeling unreal: a PET study of depersonalization disorder. *American Journal of Psychiatry*, **157,** 1782–1788.
20. Farrer, C., Franck, N., Frith, C. D. et al. (2004). Neural correlates of action attribution in schizophrenia. *Psychiatry Research*, **131,** 31-44.
21. Farrer, C., Frey, S. H., Van Hom, J. D. et al. (2008). The angular gyrus computes action awareness representations. *Cerebral Cortex*, **18,** 254-261.
22. Sierra, M. (no. 6) pp. 145-146.
23. Farrer, C. (no. 20).
24. Sierra, M. (no.6) p.146.
25. Simeon, D., Abugel, J. (no 14). P.109.
26. Ibid.
27. Sierra, M., (no.6) p. 132.
28. Kelly, D.H.W., Walter, C.J.S. (1968). The relationship between clinical diagnosis and anxiety, assessed by forearm blood flow and other measurements. *British Journal Of Psychiatry,* **114,** p. 611-626. Archives of General Psychiatry, **59,** p.833-838.
29. Sierra, M., Senior, C., Dalton, J. (2002). Autonomic response in depersonalization disorder. *Archives of General Psychiatry*, **59,** p. 833-838.
30. Sierra, M., Senior, C., Phillips, M. L., David, A. S. (2006). Autonomic response in the perception of disgust and happiness in depersonalization disorder. *Psychiatry Research*, **145,** p. 225-231.
31. Simeon, D., Guralnik, 0., Knutelska, M., Yehuda, R., Schmeidler, J. (2003). Basal norepinephrine in depersonalization disorder. *Psychiatry Research,* 121, 93-97.

32. Simeon, D. et al. (2000). Feeling unreal: a PET study of depersonalization disorder. *American Journal of Psychiatry*, **157**, 1782–1788.

33. Ackner B., 1954. Depersonalization: I. Etiology and phenomenology. II. Clinical Syndromes. *J Ment Sci*, **100**, p.838-872.

34. Phillips, M.L., et al. (2001). Depersonalization disorder: thinking without feeling. *Psychiatry Research Neuroimaging*, **108**, p. 145–160.

35. Beer, J. S., Knight R. T., D'Espolito, M. (2006). Controlling the integration of emotion and ccognition. The role of frontal cortex in distinguishing helpful from hurtful emotional information. *Psychological Science*, **17**, p. 448-453.

36. Frank, Joseph. (1990) Dostoyevsky: The Years of Ordeal, 1850-1859. Princeton: Princeton University Press. p. 195-196.

37. Penfield, W., & Rasmussen, T. (1950). *The cerebral cortex of man: a clinical study of localization of function*. New York. MacMillan, p. 157-181.

38. Roth, M., Harper, M. (1962) Temporal lobe epilepsy and the phobic anxiety depersonalisation syndome. *Comprehensive psychiatry*, **3**, 215-226.

39. Sacks, O. (1992) Migraine, 2nd edn. Reading, Berkshire: Picador, Cox & Wyman Ltd.

40. Todd, J. (1963) The syndrome of Alice in Wonderland. *Canadian Medical Association Journal*, **73**, 701-704.

41. Pelletier, G., Legendre-Roberge, J., Boileau, B., Geoffroy, G., Leveille, J. (1995). Case study: dreamy state and temporal lobe dysfunction in a migrainous adolescent. *Journal of the American Academy of Child and Adolescent Psychiatry*, **34**, 297-301.

42. Shorvon, H.J. (1946) The depersonalization syndrome. *Proceedings of the Royal Society of Medicine*, **39**, 779-792.

43. Simeon, D., Guralnik, O., Knutelska, M., et al. (2001). Hypothalamic-pituitary-adrenal axis dysregulation in depersonalization disorder. *Neuropsychopharmacology*, **25**(5), p 793–795.

44. Simeon, D., Knutelska, M., et al. (2007) Hypothalamic-Pituitary-Adrenal Axis function in dissociative disorders, post-traumatic stress disorder, and healthy volunteers. *Biol Psychiatry,* **61**, p 966-973.
45. Kramer, P.D. (1993) Listening to Prozac. New York, N.Y. Penguin Books. p 181
46. Simeon, D., Abugel, J., (no.14) p. 119
47. Cohen, M. R., Pickar, D., Dubois, M. (1983). The role of the endogenous opioid system in the human stress response. *The Psychiatric Clinics of North America,* **6**, p 457-471.
48. Sierra, M. (no 6) p.117-119.

8 Pot, Panic and DPD

I don't do drugs. I am drugs.

—Salvador Dali

Panic attacks, anxiety, drugs, and depersonalization appear regularly in stories posted on the DPD websites and in the medical literature. This clear connection is part of what fuels the debate as to where DPD should fall in the diagnostic manuals. According to the experts at London's Institute of Psychiatry: "There is compelling evidence to link DPD with the anxiety disorders, particularly panic."[1]

What drugs trigger depersonalization? What triggers panic? Is DPD brought on by drugs different than that caused by heredity, stress, or abuse? These questions have been given serious attention in recent years and the findings are not only compelling, but far outside the realm of pop culture's current assessments of recreational drugs in general.

Despite negative personal experiences, I do not consider myself an anti-drug activist. Since the beginning of civilization, no society has ever been free of mind-altering substances—none. Psychedelics, as something to research or utilize in cultural rituals, are part of a diverse human experience—arguably as essential as technology, religion, or politics. The problems arise when these substances become recreational and are viewed with the casualness afforded an after-dinner cocktail.

Marijuana, hashish, ecstasy, LSD, ketamine, and other illicit substances are not benign ways to get high for the moment. They carry inherent risks that science now affirms with a growing pile of data every year— data that is largely ignored by the media. These dangers can affect anyone, but they are particularly harmful to people with hidden predispositions to many disorders, not the least of which is depersonalization.

The Nature of Panic Attacks

The word "panic" originates with the Greek demi-god Pan, who was thought to inhabit the stretches of wilderness that separated the ancient Greek city-states. One of Pan's favorite diversions was to torment travelers walking the paths that meandered through the forests. Frightening them by rustling the bushes, he instilled growing apprehensiveness along their journey until they were consumed with fear, a state of near "panic" by the time they emerged from the forest. Many things can cause people to panic, but an intense fear of the unknown, as instilled in these travelers, stands out as one of the most primal.

Wilhelm Mayer-Gross noted: "Depersonalization and derealization often appear suddenly... a patient sitting quietly reading by the fireside is overwhelmed by it in full blast together with an acute anxiety attack. In some cases it disappears for a short period, only to reappear again and finally persist. This acute onset is most terrifying to the patient."[2]

"Most terrifying," is perhaps an understatement. It describes precisely my own experience, as well as that of countless others, shortly after smoking marijuana. The terror was beyond description.

Years before Mayer-Gross's 1935 observations, psychologist William James offered a vivid account of a similar type of panic onset in his classic work, *The Varieties of Religious Experiences*, published in 1902. In the chapter entitled "The Sick Soul," James relays the words of a French writer who has captured the flavor of the kind of panic many people have known as the event that triggered their own chronic depersonalization:

I went one evening into a dressing-room in the twilight to procure some article that was there, when suddenly there fell upon me without any warning, just as if it came out of the darkness, a horrible fear of my own existence. Simultaneously there arose in my mind the image of an epileptic patient whom I had seen in the asylum, a black-haired youth with greenish skin, entirely idiotic, who used to sit all day on one of the benches, or rather shelves against the wall, with his knees drawn up against his chin, and the coarse gray un-

dershirt, which was his only garment, drawn over them enclosing his entire figure.... This image and my fear entered into a species of combination with each other. That shape am I, I felt, potentially. Nothing that I possess can defend me against that fate, if the hour for it should strike for me as it struck for him. There was such a horror of him, and such a perception of my own merely momentary discrepancy from him, that it was as if something hitherto solid within my breast gave way entirely, and I became a mass of quivering fear. After this the universe was changed for me altogether.[3]

For some people, this narrator describes with uncanny precision the moment that marked the onset of their own depersonalization. It has also been suggested that it is an account of James' own experience with panic. The inexplicable sensations that the author explains so graphically go well beyond the clichéd images of sweaty palms or rapid heartbeat associated with spontaneous panic or anxiety attacks today. The certainty of imminent insanity, which unknown to the victim passes with the attack, lies at its heart. The mental image of men in white coats was among the first during my own experience.

Interestingly James includes this vignette in a chapter entitled "The Sick Soul." Depersonalized people, who sometimes say they have "lost their soul," may well recall a single episode like this as the very moment when their soul departed. Of course, others can experience this kind of incident once, or repeatedly, without the end result of chronic depersonalization. Panic attacks, or the stress of ongoing attacks, can ultimately lead to the numbing effect of Depersonalization Disorder. It seems that panic, whether spontaneous as the result of smoking marijuana, or even from excessive, intense focus on the self, can serve as the stress trigger that brings about DPD.

In his other well-known work *Psychology*, William James, writing about the Self, describes an excellent first-hand account of depersonalization specifically:

"I was alone, and already a prey to permanent visual trouble, when I was suddenly seized with a visual trouble infinitely more pronounced. Objects grew small and receded to infinite distances—men and things together. I was myself immeasurably far away. I looked about me with terror and astonishment: *the world was escaping from me*... I remarked at the same time that my voice was extremely far away from me, that it sounded no longer as if mine... In addition to being so distant, objects appeared to me *flat*. When I spoke with anyone, I saw him like an image cut out of paper with no relief...Constantly it seemed as if my legs did not belong to me. It was almost as bad with my arms. As for my head, it seemed no longer to exist...I appeared to myself to act automatically, by an impulsion foreign to myself...I had an ardent desire to see my old world again, to get back to my old self. This desire kept me from killing myself.[4]

On the other hand, depersonalization can, at times, provoke panic as well. In a moment of strangeness or mind-emptiness the mind suddenly catches itself, becomes overly aware of itself, and out of the blue panic emerges, often in situations over which an individual has little or no control. The *need t*o panic awakens, and the loss of connection to the things around you or within you (such as a normal, strong sense of self) does little to prevent it.

Some people exhibit an urge to compulsively "think" themselves into an anxiety state, even a panic attack. This is much like playing with a sore tooth with your tongue, or relentlessly picking at a scab. You do so, much like a child, to see what might happen. And you do it because you can. The frail ego, the lack of a self that would prevent you from doing self-destructive things, permits you to mentally proceed down paths normal, rational people would never begin to venture towards. This can make you your own worst enemy, obsessively grappling with internal oddities that seem considerably more frightful than any threat presented by the outside world.

Defining Panic Attacks

Panic means different things to different people. Like depression and anxiety, the words themselves have been diluted by their assimilation into popular culture. Some people experience palpitations and sweaty palms for a few minutes, fear that they are having a heart attack, and then later call the experience a panic attack. Others, such has those who endure absolute terror after ingesting any number of substances, relay an experience that is primarily *mental* in its presentation, followed by more comprehensible physical sensations. For these people, an overwhelming sense of fear and the intense need to flee defines a panic attack.

"The panic attack is a highly distressing subjective event that causes unprovoked, intense episodes of fear," states Robert G. Sacco, author of *Mystical Experience: A Psychological Perspective*. "Approaching the study of panic from a natural science paradigm, researchers have focused almost exclusively on objective characteristics," Sacco says. Panic is studied in terms of its prevalence, central nervous system underpinning, the environmental stimuli which precipitate its occurrence, and the ramifications which follow its onset.

"While the results yielded from these studies have broadened our understanding of the phenomenon, research continues to overlook the *internal* dimension of panic as experienced by the subject, limiting our understanding of what panic attacks mean," Sacco says.

The DSM-IV contains a separate category for panic attacks based on the recognition that these episodes can occur in several psychiatric diagnoses, not just panic disorder. A long-standing differentiation of panic attacks based on psychological versus physiological symptoms has appeared in psychiatric literature.

Citing recent literature, Sacco points out that panic exhibits two main symptom clusters: *respiratory* and *cognitive*.[5] The first cluster relates either to the hyperventilation theory of panic or to the suffocation alarm theory of panic. In contrast, the cognitive symptom cluster is defined by intense feelings of distress or fear, with cognitive symptoms.

My personal observation is that three kinds of panic attacks seem to persist in people who ultimately experience depersonalization. One is the spontaneous, out-of-nowhere variety, as described by James and Mayer-Gross. The second is of the ruminative, self-scrutiny variety wherein over concentration on the self, on the process of thinking, or thinking about the possibility of panic actually leads to panic, albeit of a slighter intensity. And the third is situational, which only appears under dreaded circumstances such as flying, being out of control of a situation, or in situations often cited by agoraphobics. (Chapters 9 and 10 will look at effective ways of dealing with these latter types of panic.) The latter two are related, I suggest, and stem from the lack of a clearly defined sense of self that faces the world with a confident, intact inner identity.

Psychologist Alicia Meuret and colleagues have identified three subtypes of panic attack, the last of which corresponds with my own experience: a *cardio-respiratory type* (palpitations, shortness of breath, choking, chest pain, numbness, fear of dying), a *mixed somatic subtype* (sweating, trembling, nausea, chills/hot flashes, and dizziness), and a *cognitive subtype* (feeling of unreality, fear of going crazy, and fear of losing control).[6]

Sacco points out that the "cognitive" subtype includes both depersonalization and derealization, as well as both the "fear of losing control" and "fear of going crazy"—the symptoms are most often associated with depersonalization experiences in panic attacks.[7] An interesting finding was that the fear of dying formed the most prominent dimension in the cardio-respiratory subtype, but not necessarily the cognitive type. (Based on the kind of attack I personally have known, dying is perceived as a fast way out of the panic, preferable to the panic sensation itself.)

When panic or depersonalization are not the primary culprits, free-floating anxiety often is. "Anxiety is being afraid when there is nothing to fear," says philosopher James Park. "We struggle with something in the dark but we don't know what it is."[8] This kind of vague, fruitless form of worry is often known as *angst*, which Danish philosopher Kierkegaard used to describe anxiety that has no specific object.

"In angst, we confront the fundamental precariousness of existence, our being is disclosed as unspeakably fragile and tenuous," Park adds. "And when we burst through the protective shell in which we try to encapsulate it, our anxious dread renders us helpless." The late Oscar Janiger referred to this existential angst as "The Blow of the Void"— a fundamental change in awareness that forces us to focus on those things most people permanently and safely lock away in the back of their consciousness.

Of course panic and anxiety involve physiological changes in the brain. Neuroscientists now know that at least three neurotransmitters are involved in panic—noradrenaline, serotonin, and gamma-aminobutyric (GABA).

More About Pot

In 2008, 25.8 million Americans age 12 and older had abused marijuana at least once in the year prior to being surveyed.[9] The 2008 "Monitoring the Future Study" funded by the National Institute on Drug Abuse (NIDA) showed that 10.9% of 8th graders, 23.9% of 10th graders, and 32.4% of 12th graders had abused marijuana at least once in the year prior to being surveyed. Pot is not a thing of the hippie's past, but of the adolescent's present. With it comes an ever-increasing incidence of Depersonalization Disorder.

Relatively few people today have ever heard of Depersonalization Disorder compared to the number who by now are familiar with THC, the active ingredient in pot. Although Cannabis sativa, or marijuana, has been in use for at least 4,000 years, it was not until 1964 that Israeli biochemists R. Mechoulam and Y. Gaoni isolated the principal psychoactive ingredient of the marijuana plant: delta-9-tetrahydrocannabinol (THC).

Delta-9-THC is the substance in the plant that produces the "high," that users crave. The marijuana plant contains more than 400 chemical compounds, of which 60 are cannabinoids—psychoactive compounds that can be extracted from the cannabis plant, or produced within the body after ingestion and metabolism of cannabis.

The most powerful derivative of the marijuana is from the pure resin removed from the leaves and stems; this is known as hashish. Its concentration of delta-9-THC is about 8 to 14 percent. Next in potency is ganja, which is commonly smoked in the United States. Ganja is made up of dried plant material taken only from the tops of unpollinated female plants. Known as sinsemilla, this version of marijuana has a THC content of from 4 to 12 percent. (In Holland there are varieties of cannabis for sale with delta- 9-THC levels averaging 20 percent, which has led to concern about the high potencies and the resulting psychoactivity.)

Targeting the Brain

Cannabis, like nicotine, is normally inhaled, and therefore has rapid access to the blood system. THC and its metabolites are fat soluble and easily penetrate the blood-brain barrier which controls the passage of many substances into the brain. After metabolism in the lungs and liver, THC moves rapidly to lipid-rich tissues in the body, including the brain.

Because THC and its metabolites are fat soluble, they may remain in the fatty tissues of the body for a long time. Later they are released into the bloodstream. There is substantial human variability in the metabolism of cannabis, but it is now proven that individuals who use cannabis daily are more at risk of triggering schizophrenia, depression, or depersonalization than infrequent users because of the slow release of THC. The time necessary to clear half the administered dose of THC differs for experienced and inexperienced users, with experienced users accumulating more THC in their systems. The plant constituent delta-9-THC has been found to produce many characteristic cognitive deficits in both human and animal subjects. It impairs the brain's functioning, particularly with chronic use. Numerous investigations have found that the most pronounced impairments are reduced short-term memory, locomotion disorders, altered time sense, paranoia, fragmentation of thought, and lethargy.[10]

The lingering THC in the brain also lends support to the theory that in time, a severe panic reaction may appear after smoking, even though one may have smoked pot with immunity several times earlier. If the THC does in fact build up, it will reach a point of overload in some individuals, prompting a severe reaction that never occurred before and was never anticipated. I have met many people who experience severe panic upon smoking pot one time, and others who only suffer panic after several occasions, usually within a time span of just a few days or weeks. In most cases, however, it does not result in chronic Depersonalization Disorder.

Marijuana research is in a new, exploratory phase, and scientists are tracking how cannabis consumption specifically alters the physical functioning of the hippocampus, cortex, pituitary gland, and basal ganglia.

It is known, however, that marijuana impinges on the central nervous system by attaching to the brain's neurons and interfering with normal communication between the neurons. As stated earlier, of the marijuana plant's 400 chemicals, 60 of them are cannabinoids—psychoactive compounds that are produced inside the body after cannabis is metabolized or is extorted from the cannabis plant. Tetrahydrocannibol (THC), the most psychoactive cannabinoid with the biggest impact on the brain, binds to and activates specific receptors, known as cannabinoid receptors. These receptors control memory, thought, concentration, time and depth, and coordinated movement. THC also affects the production, release or re-uptake (a regulating mechanism) of various neurotransmitters, the chemical messenger molecules that carry signals between neurons. Some of these effects are personality disturbances, depression, and chronic anxiety.

Marijuana also affects emotion. When smoking marijuana, the user may laugh uncontrollably one minute and become paranoid or panicky the next. This instant change in emotions has to do with the way that THC affects the brain's limbic system and the amygdalae, which, as shown in Chapter 7, serve as part of the circuitry for the most basic of human emotions—fear.

The fact that certain specific drugs may trigger chronic depersonalization while others do not, unavoidably leads to speculation about the underlying neurochemical systems that are involved. Experiments have shown that cannabis can induce depersonalization, with a large degree of temporal disintegration (time perception disturbances) in healthy volunteers.[11] Depersonalization-like sensations occurred during the time of intoxication, and related directly to the potency of the cannabis used. Sensations peaked 30 minutes after smoking and typically wore off after two hours.

In addition to acting as a partial agonist at certain cannabinoid receptors, inhibiting the transmission of the neurotransmitter gamma-Aminobutyric acid (GABA), as well as negatively affecting dopamine transmission,[12] cannabinoids block glutamate receptors such as NMDA at sites distinct from other NMDA antagonists.[13] Therefore their dissociative effect may be partly via NMDA (glutamate) antagonism.

Hallucinogens also act as agonists at specific serotonin receptors, and experimental challenge studies with the serotonin agonist meta-Chlorophenylpiperazine (m-CPP) have demonstrated the induction of depersonalization in a mixed group of social phobia, borderline, and obsessive-compulsive disorder participants.[14] The m-CPP also induced flashbacks and dissociative symptoms in a subgroup of posttraumatic stress disorder patients,[15] as well as dissociation in healthy volunteers.[16]

To date, the research clinics insist that no permanent brain damage occurs when one suffers a severe panic attack or when it leads to chronic depersonalization. This is something that has always concerned the sufferers I have interviewed through the years. But I think there is a misunderstanding about the very term "brain damage." What the experts are stating in fact is that there is usually no evidence of organic brain damage, as one would witness in a patient with a brain tumor or other organic irregularity. What does happen, however, is a mysterious dysregulation of certain brain systems. Therein lies both the problem and the mystery. Brain systems *do* go out of whack and patients battle through a morass of meds and therapies in their attempts to set things right again. We'll examine some of these systems and the deviations that occur in depersonalized people in Chapter 9.

Panic Redux

There is little doubt that the number of cases of Depersonalization Disorder has grown in recent decades because of the triggering effect of drugs, particularly pot, ecstasy, ketamine or hallucinogens. Research conducted by Dr. Simeon and colleagues[17] shows that depersonalization often follows a bad drug experience. For most people, that last joint or tablet is the last they will ever take, and many feel that the "one toke over the line" has taken them to a place from which they will never return.

My own experience, echoed by many others, consisted of an initial terrifying panic attack, followed by a day of complete normalcy, followed by repeated, unprovoked attacks for many evenings to follow. After that, the panic subsided, but long-lasting chronic depersonalization, with its most insidious symptoms, set in. For others, the last bad trip takes the form of depersonalization itself, which may subside, then return finally for good.

How can the triggering episode repeat itself out of the blue? Some people report an initial panic attack or bad trip after taking drugs followed by a period of recovery and normalcy. Then, from nowhere, a duplicate of the original triggering experience emerges for seemingly no reason. Even though cannabis remains in the system until it is excreted (within a few weeks) the triggering traumatic event may repeat itself long afterward.

The best explanation offered to date stems from the familiar concept of "flashbacks."

Initial theories of drug-induced flashbacks favored the late release of tissue-stored drug molecules. But Mauricio Sierra points out that there has never been any evidence to support this idea. More likely, some authors have suggested that flashbacks are manifestations of a "state-dependent" learning process. They might, in fact, correspond to sensory, implicit memories whose retrieval takes the form of an actual re-experiencing of the original altered state of consciousness, "not unlike the way in which amputees with phantom pains often re-experience the exact quality of previously experienced pains before the amputation."[18] It is just one of the topics that reminds us that the more we know, the more we realize how much remains to be studied.

Is Depersonalization from Drugs Different?

If the precise mechanisms of DPD were known and understood,

it would be easier to understand how THC can trigger it. Likewise, if THC were the only substance that triggered Depersonalization, it might be easier to determine its mechanisms. But pot is not the only catalyst involved. Ecstasy (MDMA), Ketamine, LSD and other hallucinogens such as psilocybin (found in "magic mushrooms") trigger DPD in certain people. Pot, Ecstasy and LSD have profound effects on serotonin's function in the brain. Ketamine is glutamate or NMDA antagonist, which is something we'll look at in Chapter 9. The fact that very different drugs, and very individualized stressful circumstances can trigger DPD, fuels the idea that depersonalization is a thing unto itself. It is something that is set in motion by certain circumstances or substances, not something inherent to any one situation or substance.

Many of us, for whom pot was decidedly the trigger, have long wondered whether we would have been the same if we had never smoked. And, just as often, we have wondered if what has come to be called Depersonalization Disorder is the same for people who can trace their onset to some form of neglect, abuse, or relatively minor traumas. How could smoking pot (in some cases only one time) bring on the same horrible disorder as years of early life incidents at the hands of uncaring parents or abusive siblings or friends?

Experts tend to agree that in certain people, if pot does not awaken a predisposition to Depersonalization Disorder, something else likely will. Not all of us are 100 percent convinced, however. Harris Goldberg and I may have endured mild childhood neuroses, but they were fleeting. It is hard to imagine that any of the life stresses we have known since could ever have been as devastating as the result of our smoking pot. Still, for the time being, the evidence does seem to support this viewpoint.

To further explore any differences between marijuana-triggered DPD and drug-free onsets, Daphne Simeon and colleagues looked closely at the experiences of 196 drug-induced chronic depersonalization cases, compared to 198 non-drug induced cases. Subjects were screened from online interviews posted on the website of National Organization for Drug-Induced Disorders from September

2005 to January 2006.

The consensus, published in 2009, was what might be expected. There were no significant differences regarding phenomenology, course of illness, levels of impairment, suicidal tendencies, or response to treatment.[19] As in some earlier studies, the most common problem drugs were cannabis and hallucinogens, followed by Ecstasy and ketamine.

One interesting finding that provides a ray of hope for people who can trace their DPD to drugs is the fact that the drug-induced group showed more rapid improvement over time, not necessarily linked to treatment.

"If a substance is responsible for the manifestations of an underlying diathesis, future abstinence may increase the likelihood of remission. On the other hand psychological stressors can be chronic and less controllable and, even if no longer present, their impact on the psyche may persist," Simeon stated.

Ketamine and salvia were seen as triggers less often but they are also less commonly ingested. Interestingly, opioids, cocaine, and stimulants have never been reported as triggers, the report states.

The vast majority (87%) of the drug-induced group cited a "bad trip" and Simeon feels that this suggests that the subjective quality of the intoxication experience may also contribute to triggering dissociation, especially if the "bad trip" was perceived as terrifying or life threatening. The survey revealed that the majority of individuals don't touch the drug in question again, for obvious reasons. If the drug was tried again, the survey showed that a negative impact on the depersonalization was predictable and likely. Also, prior lifetime drug use was limited; for example, almost 40% of the pot-triggered cases reported having smoked fewer than 10 times.

The precipitation of chronic depersonalization through salvia in a few individuals was a novel finding in Dr. Simeon's study because little has been published about salvia to date. Salvia is known to induce acute depersonalization in some individuals, and it is becoming an increasingly popular recreational drug.

Comparison of the participants in the study indicates a preponderance of younger and male participants in the drug group, attributable to the demographics of substance use. The non-drug group reported earlier onset by about two years, which could be attributed to psychological stressors occurring in childhood and adolescence. The longer syndrome duration in the non-drug group may just reflect the earlier onset combined with older age at participation.

If the results of this study are in fact accurate, it does make a strong argument for the idea that certain people are indeed predisposed to DPD and all it takes is a trigger of drugs, stress, or something that forever remains illusive to set it off. On one hand, this may come as a relief to people who had always assumed they had "fried" their brains. But on the other hand, if they had never done that drug, would it have appeared at all? If so, when and why? These questions torment many people who can trace their onset to drugs simply because the other triggers are often unlike anything they ever encountered, especially if they considered themselves reasonably happy and well-adjusted until the DPD came along. But it is also likely that on some level, people who considered themselves normal until they became depersonalized through drug use don't like being categorized with "victims" of life experiences that resulted in the same disorder any more than they like being "mentally ill."

Still, differences between the drug and non-drug groups cannot be ignored. For instance, there appeared to be a greater prevalence of emotional "numbing" in the non-drug group (which, Simeon et al state, was no longer present when controlling for gender.) One possible explanation for this finding could be the greater proportion of female subjects in the non-drug group, with possibly greater traumatic stress histories or depression and associated numbness. However, this could actually represent a "true" difference between the two groups, with greater numbing being an integral part of a chronic depersonalization syndrome related to psychological stressors. (The personal stories posted on *depersonalization.info* reflect a greater degree of panic and anxiety in the drug-triggered accounts and more deadness and numbing when DPD appeared early, and often for no apparent reason.) This difference between the groups in this study, may in time prove to be an important difference. Emotional "deadness" may likely be the least disturbing path depersonalization takes and, in my opinion, being "numb" alone does not adequately reflect the rich perversity of the condition overall.

Importantly, this study did put some speculative topics to rest. It has often been suggested by patients and clinicians alike that drug-induced DPD may involve more perceptual symptoms, especially visual, and more derealization than depersonalization. It has also been suggested, using common-sense reasoning, that because drug-induced cases may be less "psychologically" driven and more "chemically" driven, they may be less likely to impair the core sense of selfhood and its associated symptomatic manifestations (e.g. unreality of self). This study employed detailed symptom assessment and clearly showed no differences in phenomenology between the two groups in any domain, strongly supporting the unity of the syndrome.

Finally, the nature of cannabinoid receptors themselves have been under investigation in recent years as well. Are these receptors in individuals with a predisposition toward depersonalization disorder different than they are in other people? If so, will scientists be able to predict who will experience a negative drug experience leading to DPD and who won't? While current investigations have proven inconclusive, this prospect may become a reality in the not-too-distant future.

All of the research and the findings presented here bring home a number of points. First, DPD is not being ignored, though its enigmatic nature continues to challenge some of the finest minds in medicine. Secondly, the biology underlying depersonalization is extremely complex, often leading researchers down several different paths at once. In an age when anything and everything seems technologically possible, DPD not only humbles those who suffer from it, but those trying so hard to understand it. Is it something so unique that it is beyond understanding? Perhaps. But it is not beyond being treated successfully, and the next chapter explores the many options available, thanks to the persistence of devoted doctors, clinicians, and patients.

REFERENCES

1. Hunter, E.C. , Phillips, M.L., Chalder, T., Sierra, M., David, A.S. (2003) Depersonalization disorder: a cognitive behavioral conceptualization. *Behaviour Research and Therapy*, **41**, 1451-1467

2. Mayer-Gross, W. (1935). On depersonalization. *British Journal of Medicine and Psychology, 15,* 103–126

3. James, W. (1902/1961). *The varieties of religious experience.* New York: MacMillan, p. 138.

4. James, William (1950) *Psychology*, Vol. 1, Dover Publications Inc., NY, p. 377-378.

5. Meuret, A.E., White, K.S., Ritz, W.T. Roth, Hofmann, S.G., & Brown, T.A. (2006). Panic attack symptom dimensions and their relationship to illness characteristics in panic disorder. *Journal of Psychiatric Research*, **40**, 520–527.

6. Ibid.

7. Segui, J., Marquez, M., Garcia, L., Canet, J., Salvador-Carulla, L., & Ortiz, M. (2000). Depersonalization in Panic Disorder: A Clinical Study. *Comprehensive Psychiatry*, **41**, 172–178.

8. Restak, R., (2004) Poe's Heart and the Mountain Climber: Exploring the effects of anxiety on our brains and culture. Nw York. Three Rivers Press. p 36.

9. National Survey on Drug Use and Health (Substance Abuse and Mental Health Administration.

10. Steinherz, K., Vissing, T., (1997) The Medical Effects of Marijuana on the Brain,. 21st Century Science and Technology, Vol 10, No.4.

11. Simeon, D., Kozin, D., Segal, K., Lerch, B. (2008) Is Depersonalization Disorder Initiated by Illicit Drug Use Any Different? A Survey of 394 Adults. *J Clinical Psychiatry* **70:** 1358-1364

12. D'Souza DC, Abi-Saab WM, Madonick S, et al. Delta-9-tetrahydrocannabinol effects in schizophrenia: implications for cognition, psychosis, and addiction. *Biol Psychiatry.* 2005;**57**(6):594–608.

13. Feigenbaum JJ, Bergmann F, Richmond SA, et al. Nonpsychotropic cannabinoid acts as a functional N-methyl-d-aspartate receptor blocker. *Proc Natl Acad Sci USA.* 1989;**86**:9584–9587.

14. Simeon D, Hollander E, Stein DJ, et al. Induction of depersonalization by the serotonin agonist meta-chlorophenylpiperazine. Psychiatry Res. 1995;58(2):161–164.

15. Southwick SM, Krystal JH, Bremner JD, et al. Noradrenergic and serotonergic function in posttraumatic stress disorder. Arch Gen Psychiatry. 1997;54:749–758.

16. D'Souza DC, Gil RB, Zuzarte E, et al. Gamma-aminobutyric acid-serotonin interactions in healthy men: implications for network models of psychosis and dissociation. *Biol Psychiatry.* 2006;59(2):128–137.

17. Simeon, D. (no 11)

18. Sierra, M. (2009) Depersonalization: A New Look at a Neglected Syndrome, Cambridge University Press. p. 64

19. Simeon, D. (no 11)

9 Living Unreal: Chemical Readjustment

Life begins on the other side of despair.

—Jean-Paul Sartre

How do you deal with a changed sense of self, altered perceptions, or a complete shift in consciousness? Is it something that can be treated? Or must it be accepted?

There are no magic bullets to "cure" depersonalization. In fact, unlike the many other slings and arrows that can afflict the body, depersonalization requires a large degree of understanding and patience on the part of its victim. You don't need to read books about infections to be cured by penicillin. But DPD, which seems to take so much from you, demands some intellectual investment before it will give something back.

Ultimately, how you deal with depersonalization depends largely on how you interpret it. Though often described as Hell itself, DPD is more accurately depicted as a kind of purgatory—an uncomfortable middle ground between the old self and the new. Most often, people simply want to return to being their old selves but have difficulty facing the fact that this is neither likely nor necessarily desirable. DPD is a life-changing experience comparable to the death of a parent or spouse, or even winning the lottery. The goal is to reclaim the good feelings of being human that were possible before its onset and incorporate them into a new and better self that has been shaped, not by living with DPD but by going *through* it, emerging whole with a clear sense of the true self, less the fragile illusions that previously held the constructed ego in tact.

Many people visiting the depersonalization-related websites today reflect an unfortunate trend—something that was not quite so apparent a decade ago. They are increasingly younger and have encountered DPD, or think they have, quickly, often as the result of some illicit drug. Most of them are looking for a fast fix, a way to get well so they can get back to their old lives without losing any time.

Fortunately, for many of them DPD does sometimes lift on its own if they stay away from the triggers that precipitated it. Unfortunately, if it does not go away, it requires time and thought that they are simply not willing to invest. Choosing the path of least resistance, these people grow into adulthood feeling lost, often resorting to whatever substances help to get them through each day.

DPD has been been trivialized by various websites and media outlets which tend to view it exclusively as a subcategory of dissociation, or a variation of Posttraumatic Stress Disorder (PTSD). People find it difficult to believe that DPD has been around for so long and remained unrecognized as a thing unto itself. It seems that severe traumas such as rape or war wounds, and resulting dissociative reactions such as out of body experiences or fugues, are more comprehensible than a disorder triggered by lesser traumas or drugs that brings the very nature of perception and existence to the forefront.

DPD is neither a stop on the way to insanity, nor a death sentence. The depersonalization websites are replete with personal accounts of sources of onset and subsequent suffering. But stories about improvement or cures are rare. Why?

Unfortunately, DPD has proven to be an every-man-for-himself phenomenon. People interact on the websites, but when life improves, most choose to place as much distance between themselves and the depersonalization community as possible. Mental illness is as difficult to confess as it is to endure. Often people request that their personal stories be removed once they are better and they resume normal lives out in the "real" world.

My own story is perhaps an aberration, not only because DPD lapsed into various levels of anxiety and clinical depression at different times, but because I found myself jumping back into the waters of depersonalization intentionally, to learn about the condition, and myself. Studying it can mire you in it, cloud your opinions about it, and create biases not based in science. The fact that most researchers do not live in a constant state of depersonalization may prove to be a benefit, as their objectivity remains unscathed. The very symptoms of the condition confuse the patient, and confound his or her doctor, especially when sensations of detachment resist description. The high incidence of co-morbidity with other disorders, and the prevalence of one symptom over another at different times makes DPD extremely difficult to diagnose unless its long-term manifestations are discussed in detail with a knowledgeable psychiatrist. In my own case, other than being chronically *not right*, I had no idea what was wrong with me nor what kind of damage I had inflicted on my brain. But the knowledge that I had done it to myself was at times unbearable.

After eleven years in and out of the Nine Circles I was weary of its unpredictability and realized that I could never ever really trust my mind to entail a consistent sense of self. Despite being able to work, travel, and function on a high level for years, a wide assortment of drawn-out stresses finally converged in the early 1980s to trigger the "triple whammy" in me—depersonalization, anxiety, and that curious kind of depression not marked by sadness—just what William Styron called the "shipwreck of the mind." As the anxiety, fragmented thinking, and sense of strangeness built toward an unbearable denouement, I tried to subdue it with a standby that had helped considerably a few years earlier, the tricyclic antidepressant/ tranquilizer combo called Triavil. When that failed, I tried Valium, Ativan, and Adapin, all to no avail. For the first time in my life I began to consider suicide, not because I was unhappy, but because I could feel my mind breaking up into shards of broken mirrors of a self. Consciousness itself was unbearable, existence was nothing but an unendurable pain tinged with fear and mental confusion. I remember riding up a small hill in Manhattan Beach in my little Fiat convertible when the idea of ending it all emerged for the first time. The day was perfect, sunny with low humidity. The sound of the waves hitting the shore rose up from the bottom of the hill where fisherman impatiently tugged at their lines on the pier. Everything was perfect, pregnant with life and potential and hope. But all that existed was the desire to end this horrible consciousness that held no memories, no hopes, no prospects, nothing. Nothing but pain and the desperate need to end it.

Situations like this often foretell a coming change, for better or worse. It is easy to attribute good fortune, luck, or the interceding hand of something larger to magical thinking. Whatever the reason, my life was indeed about to change.

I knew that a good friend had been seeing a noted psychiatrist for several years. I was leery of mental health professionals. Years of analysis were not going to help me. But when she assured me that this doctor's expertise lie in the chemistry of the brain, rather than in unraveling psychological cobwebs, I agreed to make an appointment with Dr. Oscar Janiger.

Janiger was well known in Los Angeles in the 1950s and 60s as the "psychiatrist to the stars." While his list of patients was a Who's Who of Hollywood celebrities, he was best known for his groundbreaking research into LSD and creativity, conducted long before acid became a pariah and ultimately banned. The combination of LSD and psychotherapy had in fact helped a number of stars, notably Cary Grant, in personal development and insight into their own psyches. Lenny Bruce, Jack Kerouac, a young Jack Nicholson were also among his patients, some referred by Janiger's famous cousin, the beat poet Allen Ginsberg. Anais Nin even wrote about Janiger and her LSD experience in her Diaries.

Yet despite this close alliance with both the genius and the foibles of the famous, Janiger did not discriminate when it came to seeing people needing help. I was a twenty-something nobody, present by referral. The fact that I was desperate was all that mattered. Janiger was a fatherly figure that everyone knew as "Oz," long before others wanting to project some suggestion of wizardly science grabbed the moniker. "Oz" reflected his broad experience with psychedelics to some, but for most it was simply short for "Oscar," nothing more.

As I sat anxiously in the small waiting room outside Janiger's Beverly Hills office, a famous middle-age actress was scheduling her next appointment at the secretary's glass partition. I knew who she was immediately. I had seen her in a popular movie a few months earlier. She eyed me with a slight smile as if I were part of some inner circle unified not by fame, but by pain. She seemed somehow to be saying, "You've come to the right place. It will be okay now."

For a moment, I thought of Hermann Hesse's novel Demien, and its characters who quietly recognized those who were different, those who, like themselves, bore what Hesse alluded to as "the mark of Cain."

My friend had told me nothing about Janiger's notoriety or reputation. I expected an encounter with my preconceived notion of a shrink—bearded, scholarly, perhaps pompous and entombed by walls of books written by predecessors of the same schools of thought. The man I met taught me never to jump to conclusions again. Janiger was much shorter than I but visually impressive, elderly but robust, a cross between a wild-eyed scientist and Picasso in his later years. His broad smile exuded warmth and humanity, and a raspy voice that bore traces of a New York accent, which sounded pleasantly familiar. His office hardly resembled any kind of medical facility. A wall of glass looked out to a window well of subterranean plants, books of all types, and scattered objets d'art. Most noticeable, and most imposing, a large ancient Kachina doll stood protected within a glass case on a table. It would somehow be centerpiece, not only of the office, but also of every memory captured that day. This was my last stop, the last oasis for hope; it was *meant* to be remembered.

After exchanging pleasantries about the friend who had referred me, I sat in a chair directly across from the doctor with nothing between us. After a short pause he asked quietly:

"So tell me. What is it at this point of your life that would bring you to a psychiatrist."

Slowly, deliberately, clearly, I told him everything about the night in the dormitory eleven years earlier, the Nine Circles, the fleeting periods of "normalcy," the descents into depression or anxiety, the existential rumination, the strangeness of everything without and within—as if finally encountering my creator I told him everything that I had endured for more than a decade."

Through much of my testimony, Janiger's eyes were closed as he

sometimes rubbed his forehead. Was I boring him? Was he asleep?
No, because moments later he would squint as if enduring my pain,
or shake his head slightly as if to answer me with some compassion,
some understanding.

I thought for a moment, and after spilling my guts, quietly
concluded: "Even he can't help me."

Then Janiger began to speak animatedly, as if awakened with a
start.

"You know, I have heard every single thing you described a
hundred times," he said. "And it absolutely amazes me that in every
case it is *exactly* the same. I knew what you were going to say before
you even said it. It never ceases to amaze me how similar these
descriptions are.

"You have what is known as Depersonalization Syndrome,"
Janiger continued. "And you know what? It *was* the pot,"

The conversation continued for some time. He spoke about neurotransmitters, about drugs, and about sensitivities in certain people.
Depersonalization was like the ocean he said, an amazing and won-
drous phenomenon. But not if you were drowning, as I was. All
the ramifications of depersonalization could be discussed later, if I
cared to. The first step was to get me out of the frightening waters,
back into the boat.

Dr. Janiger gave me a prescription for a medicine that had
succeeded for some of his patients in the past. If it didn't, there were
other options.

For the moment, the specifics are unimportant. Dozens of effective medicines available today did not even exist at the time.
What *is* important is that the feelings, thereafter, and throughout the
days and weeks that followed, closely paralleled those for whom
acknowledgement of a true disorder and the appropriate medicine
bring substantial, even rapid improvement.

The change in how you feel as the medicine takes hold by pen-
etrating the so-called blood-brain barrier can be subtle. Over a period of days, then weeks you begin to somehow feel more integrated
mentally. The knowledge that a medicine is working against the hor-

rible sensations you have known for so long seem to bolster that action. You begin to feel hope in a way you had not felt for a long time. You may find that memories and emotions begin to recapture some of their old vividness and color. Feelings of nostalgia or sentiment reappear as may an interest in sexuality and grooming. In time you find that you need less sleep and awaken in the morning without trepidation of the day ahead. When all of this happens, you know that the medicine or medicines are working. The danger lies in self-monitoring so much that you are not satisfied with gradual, minor degrees of improvement. Wanting to be exactly as you were before the onset of any mental illness is unreasonable and unrealistic, much like a butterfly wanting to return to the security of the cocoon.

Whether your psychiatrist is fully familiar with DPD, or incorrectly attributes your descriptions to atypical depression, Bipolar Disorder, Panic Disorder or something else, the tools at his or her disposal are the same. Some patients do respond to the most frequently prescribed antidepressants such as certain SSRIs. Other patients require a "cocktail" that may include an SSRI or a tricyclic antidepressant coupled with benzodiazepines such as Xanax (alprazolam). Some new and interesting treatment possibilities have come to the fore as well. Let's examine the various classes of medicines available for treatment.

Selective Serotonin Reuptake Inhibitors

These medications were created in the 1980s as a safe, specific alternative to the older tricyclic antidepressants and monoamine oxidase inhibitors (MAOIs). They were tagged as "designer" drugs early on, not because they rapidly came into vogue, but because they were designed specifically to act on serotonin. SSRIs such as Prozac, Celexa, Zoloft, Luvox, and others work by increasing the level of serotonin at the junction between nerve cells by preventing its reuptake, or re-absorption, into the releasing nerve cell, as well at is subsequent breakdown. The increased amount of serotonin between nerve cells in turn influences the activity of brain neurons.

From the outset, SSRIs were marketed as an anti-depressant and they proved to be effective against Obsessive-Compulsive Disorders (OCD). Since obsessive thinking so often appeared in the constellation of Depersonalization Disorder complaints, Eric Hollander, MD, chair of psychiatry at Mount Sinai Medical Center in New York, felt that they might prove effective against DPD. Daphne Simeon, MD, subsequently headed up the center's Depersonalization Research Unit and serious clinical research into depersonalization began in this country for the first time.

Initially, SSRIs looked promising in combating DPD based on minimal trials with placebos used for comparison. In 2004, however, a definitive study published in the *British Journal of Psychiatry* failed to show benefit with fluoxetine (Prozac).[1]

In this study, 25 individuals with DPD were randomly assigned to fluoxetine treatment and 25 to placebo treatment. The patients were not allowed to take any other medication. The treatment lasted 10 weeks, and participants built up to a rather high dose of fluoxetine, almost 50 milligrams per day. The study found that the people taking fluoxetine showed significant *overall* improvement in their depersonalization, as opposed to those taking placebo. However, when this improvement was "corrected" for changes in anxiety and depression, fluoxetine no longer appeared better than placebo. Furthermore, the overall improvement of depersonalization on fluoxetine was on average rated as "minimal," indicating that the effect was not potent enough to be considered clinically worthwhile by usual research standards for treatment symptom response. Finally, the actual depersonalization symptoms of participants in the two groups were rated both by a clinician-administered and by a self-report scale, and neither scale showed any differences between fluoxetine and placebo.

Within the fluoxetine-treated group, the DPD participants who experienced some benefit were more likely to have also shown improvement in concurrent anxiety disorder, in addition to their DPD. So it seems plausible that patients with major anxiety that respond to fluoxetine can also show some degree of improvement in their particular depersonalization experiences.

Since SSRIs act as *weak* inhibitors in the reuptake of non-serotonergic neurotransmitters such as norepinephrine, but act as *strong* inhibitors in the reuptake of serotonin, they are considered more "selective." This explains why they are usually less effective against symptoms that are not simply serotonin related. Selectivity also accounts for fewer side effects.

Serotonin–norepinephrine reuptake inhibitors (SNRIs) are another class of antidepressant drugs used for mood disorders. They are sometimes also used to treat anxiety disorders, obsessive-compulsive disorder (OCD), attention deficit hyperactivity disorder (ADHD) and even fibromyalgia syndrome (FMS). SNRIs act upon and increase the levels of two neurotransmitters in the brain that are known to play an important part in mood— serotonin and norepinephrine. Anecdotally, SNRIs reflect the track record of SSRIs, with Effexor often cited as providing some relief when anxiety and obsessiveness are involved. Theoretically, since the specifics of DPD remain relatively unknown, any medicine that affects additional neurotransmitter systems in a positive way increases that possibility of affecting those that may play some hidden role in DPD.

Benzodiazepines

Often prescribed as a first line of defense against what appears to be an anxiety disorder, benzodiazepines, colloquialized as benzos, are a considerable improvement over their tranquilizing predecessors, barbiturates. Benzos have become a favorite for people suffering from anxiety and panic attacks and, for many patients, they have made depersonalization more tolerable. They also can be used in combination with many other antidepressants and frequently become part of the cocktail psychiatrists prescribe in attempts to combat all of DPD's diverse symptoms. Their names are familiar: Alprazolam (Xanax), Clonazepam (Klonopin, Rivotril), Diazepam (Valium), Lorazepam (Atavin), Triazolam (Halcion) as well as dozens of others.

Benzodiazepines enhance the effect of the neurotransmitter gamma-aminobutyric acid (GABA) which results in sedative, hypnotic (sleep-inducing), anxiolytic (anti-anxiety), anticonvulsant, and muscle relaxing actions. Benzodiazepines are categorized as either short-, intermediate- or long-acting. Short- and intermediate-acting benzodiazepines are preferred for the treatment of insomnia; longer-acting benzodiazepines are recommended for the treatment of anxiety.

In general, benzodiazepines are safe and effective in the short term, but you can build up a tolerance to them and you may need an increased dosage to achieve the same effect. They can be difficult to withdraw from if you've taken them for a long time.

The other problem with benzos is that they are the perfect example of a band-aid, a temporary fix, when a condition needs to be dealt with in a more permanent way. You may find yourself "chasing" your anxiety, as the medicine's effects wear off. In contrast, today's antidepressants remain in your system longer and do more to build a lasting "floor" of mental stability. You still have to take them at regular intervals, but the ride is less bumpy with a substance that is rearranging your neurotransmission rather than zapping them with temporary fixes.

Tricyclic Antidepressants

Tricyclic antidepressants (TCAs) were first developed in the early 1950s and subsequently introduced later in the decade. They are named after their chemical structure, which contains three rings of atoms. The tetracyclic antidepressants (TeCAs), which contain four rings of atoms, are a closely related group of antidepressant compounds.

TCAs are not as popular as they once were, simply because most doctors prefer to prescribe SSRIs. The reasons for this do not seem to be justifiable through anything other than the fact that SSRIs appear to be more widely tolerated by people with minor depression or anxiety issues, create less problems if an overdose occurs, and the simple fact that "newer" is often misinterpreted as "better."

Tricyclic antidepressants work to raise the levels of the neurotransmitters serotonin and norepinephrine in the brain by slowing the rate of reuptake (reabsorption) by nerve cells. TCAs act as strong inhibitors in the reuptake of both norepinephrine and serotonin. The TCAs also block certain other receptor sites that can result in unwanted side effects such as weight gain, dry mouth, constipation, drowsiness, and dizziness, all of which mean very little to a patient in mental turmoil. Names of many of the tricylics are well known — clomipramine (Anafranil), amitriptyline (Elavil), and imipramine (Tofranil).

A small, early study by Dr. Simeon at Mount Sinai showed a glimpse of promise for clomipramine, which in contrast to most tricyclics, also acts as a potent serotonin reuptake inhibitor. In the late 1990s, Simeon and colleagues conducted a small study evaluating clomipramine versus desipramine treatment of DPD (desipramine is another tricyclic antidepressant that does not have strong serotonergic properties).[2] The small number of subjects in the study did not allow statistical comparison of the two medications, but the study did find that of the four subjects treated with clomipramine, two showed significant improvement of DPD. One of these two patients showed almost complete remission for years afterward while still taking clomipramine, yet suffered setbacks whenever she stopped taking it, or switched over to other medications like SSRIs.

Interestingly, medications designed to help depression also address the hypothalamic-pituitary-adrenal axis, which we looked at in Chapter 7. The HPA axis is often hyperactive in depressed patients, but it appears that antidepressant-induced increases in the cellular corticosteroid receptors render the HPA system more susceptible to feedback inhibition* by cortisol. That's a good thing. And the point is that this re-regulation of the HPA axis may in fact be one of the reasons why antidepressants work, in addition to their increasing the levels of various neurotransmitters.

---

* A cellular control mechanism in which an enzyme that catalyzes the production of a particular substance in the cell is inhibited when that substance has accumulated to a certain level, thereby balancing the amount provided with the amount needed.

Monoamine Oxidase Inhibitors (MAOIs)

The acronym MAOI has very likely reached your field of vision or your ears many times without earning your attention. Many over-the-counter medicines state in the fine print: *Do Not Use If You Are Taking an MAOI.* You'll hear the same warning in virtually every television commercial pushing new antidepressants (along with warnings ad nauseum). What are these things called MAOIs?

Monoamine oxidase inhibitors (MAOIs) are one of the oldest and most powerful antidepressants available. Most younger doctors do not even consider prescribing them. Why? Because there are many newer meds, specifically the SSRIs, which are reputedly safer, though few have ever claimed that they are more effective. And, perhaps more realistically, doctors smell a malpractice suit written somewhere in the fine print of an MAOI's extensive warning labels. There were cases, early in its history, when MAOIs caused blood pressure to soar, raising the possibility of a stroke or death. This deadly reaction can occur if you take certain other medicines while you are using an MAOI, or from eating certain foods containing tyramine. Still, MAOIs have been prescribed for decades, often and safely.

The MAOIs are a classic case of science stumbling across uses for a new medicine originally intended for something else. Iproni-azid, the first MAOI, was initially created to treat tuberculosis. But when patients' moods and activity levels improved dramatically, it was clear that science had inadvertently given birth to something unforeseen—an effective antidepressant.

An enzyme called monoamine oxidase breaks down the neu-rotransmitters norepinephrine, serotonin, and dopamine in the brain. MAOIs inhibit the actions of monoamine oxidase, making more of these neurotransmitters available. Like most anti-depressants, they take a few weeks to work effectively, but some people do notice im-provement in a matter of days. In addition, it may well be that many antidepressants, noticeably the MAOIs, go beyond addressing the specific neurotransmitters mentioned above. Their overall effects on other brain systems remain somewhat mysterious, yet may also positively impact the degree of improvement in many patients.

From their inception, MAOIs have proven themselves to be effective against depression, panic attacks, anxiety, "atypical depression" (resistant to treatment through other medications), agoraphobia, and for some people, Depersonalization Disorder.

Since their invention, MAOIs have gone in and out of vogue and until very recently were thought to be obsolete by many doctors sold on the virtues of the new designer drugs. The dietary restrictions always made some doctors and patients nervous, so the drug was easy to dismiss as old hat. People taking MAOIs should avoid foods containing the naturally occurring monoamine compound known as tyramine. These include aged cheeses and wines, broad (fava) beans, and something I personally can live without, pickled herring. These foods have been known to cause hypertensive crises in rare instances. (Remember Hannibal Lecter's taunting remarks about eating liver, fava beans, and a nice Chianti? Some say it was an intentional inside joke about a psychiatrist violating every MAOI dietary rule.)

St. John's Wort, one of the "natural" supplements people often take for depression appears to function in a way similar to the MAOIs. For this reason, it, too, is on the MAOI list of strictly taboo substances.

The Institute of Psychiatry's Maurico Sierra wrote recently that while there have been no systematic studies on the effects of MAOIs on Depersonalization Disorder, they have been found useful "in the treatment of a type of depression characterized by depersonalization and anxiety."[3]

Interestingly, Sierra adds that this effect might have something to so with serotonin since it had been observed that "pretreatment with MAOIs can attenuate [weaken] or abolish the effects of LSD. The latter is known to act mainly on the serotonin system and to induce depersonalization symptoms."[4]

If people experienced dissociation and depersonalization-like sensations while tripping, perhaps the MAOIs could reverse these sensations when they lingered way beyond the time of LSD intoxication. (This kind of logic would later be applied to numerous medications experimentally used to treat depersonalization.)

Dr. Janiger was one of the world's few experts on LSD. He knew these things long before they ever hit the medical journals. So the medicine he prescribed for me was an MAOI bearing the impressive name Isocarboxazid, and the brand name Marplan.

Other patients, I learned later, responded well to a different MAOI called Parnate (Tranylcypromine) and a few achieved some success with the best known MAOI called Nardil (phenelzine).

Many years later, I learned that there were other reasons why Dr. Janiger prescribed what he did. He shared with me his own experiences with depersonalization, which emerged decades earlier through an explosive shift in consciousness while he was giving a lecture before a large gathering of his peers. Chronic, relentless depersonalization persisted for months thereafter. Recognizing the symptoms, he contacted Sir Martin Roth in England, who was already well known in the psychiatric world for his anxiety-depersonalization-syndrome paper.

Oz Janiger visited Roth in England. The result of their talks was a prescription for something new at the time, something that seemed to hold tremendous potential for treating atypical depression, panic, and strange feelings of unreality experienced by a variety of patients. Roth prescribed an MAOI.

Janiger revealed to me that through the years, about half of his depersonalized patients responded to MAOIs. Since founding the website *depersonalization.info* in 2000, I have communicated with hundreds of people suffering from depersonalization. On occasion I have gently suggested specific MAOIs as a possible treatment. In most instances, their physicians have complied. In most cases, they had tried every other antidepressant without success. (For some time, advertisements for products like Abilify have played on the fact that many antidepressants don't help patients enough, or simply don't work at all.) Unfortunately, the majority of people to whom I have recommended MAOIs have not enjoyed positive results. In many instances they have sensed no difference in how they feel at all.

Admittedly this has puzzled me. How could something work so well for me, and fail so miserably for others?

The problem is that depersonalization is unique. Although the symptoms remain consistent, and have throughout a century of medical documentation, and are presumably caused by identifiable dysfunctions in several brain regions, the individual's DPD experience can prove to be as unique as a fingerprint. Depersonalization attacks the individual self, and while we are all human, made of the same materials, the manifestations of depersonalization can include subtle differences that may be addressed by equally subtle differences in medications. Research has shown that MAOIs are best against a kind of depression that is marked by anxiety, panic, fragmented thinking, and depersonalization. More often than not, the people to whom I have suggested MAOIs have been locked in the "pure" DP experience of dissociation and physical/mental detachment; these other symptoms were secondary if present at all.

The scant trials of MAOIs among other meds concluded that they were ineffective in treating DPD.[5] As a result, they may have been written off prematurely, and unfairly. The chemical compositions of each of the MAOIs differ slightly. This explains why Parnate or Marplan may work for one person while another fails miserably. The clinical tests at Mount Sinai, however, only included one MAOI. From personal experience I can state that each MAOI can render very different results. (Marplan worked subtly, quietly for me, while Nardil made things seem too bright, too real, too sharp, too fast). But an entire class of medicines was eliminated as treatment options based on the failure of just one product with minimal trials. These variations also exist among the tricyclics and the SS-RIs, which it why people often have to try numerous meds before hitting on the one that offers the most improvement.

Ultimately, I cannot recommend an MAOI over any other available medicine. I can only relay my personal experience and anecdotes of others. Still, psychiatry's honeymoon with Prozac and the other SSRIs may be coming to an end. MAOIs and other time-honored medicines are enjoying a revival in more knowledgeable

circles, and variations are beginning to emerge free of dietary restrictions altogether. Perhaps more promising is that other drugs affecting different brain-body systems entirely are beginning to show
viability as treatment for DPD.

Lamotrigine

In earlier chapters we looked at the possible links between depersonalization and the neurotransmitter glutamate. One medicine
that has shown promise in treating DPD in some patients is the anticonvulsant drug known as Lamotrigine (Lamictal), which inhibits
the release of glutamate. This possibility arose once again through a
back-door approach. Lamotrigine was created to treat certain forms
of epilepsy, and the depersonalization-like sensations that can accompany temporal lobe epilepsy are well documented. The fact that
Lamotrigine could block the actions of the known dissociative an-
esthetic Ketamine also came into play. So just as the MAOIs could
block the effects of LSD, and theoretically help reverse the chemistry involved in depersonalization, logic followed that Lamotrigine,
because of its effects on Ketamine might do the same. Studies conducted in England have shown Lamotrigine to benefit about half
of the DPD patients treated with it.[6] This figure rises to 70 percent,
however, when lamotrigine is combined with an antidepressant such
as citalopram, an SSRI known as Celexa. Still, the verdict remains
out when it comes to Lamotrigine as the primary line of defense
against DPD. Many experts suggest that it is a good possible addition to one of the effective antidepressants rather than vice versa.

Sometimes, the many allusions to sleep and dreaming have
prompted psychiatrists to consider that DP patients somehow need to
be "awakened," especially when the symptoms lean predominantly
toward lack of emotion and lifelessness. The prospect of prescribing
an amphetamine-type med has not gone unexplored. Atlanta psychiatrist Evan Torch, whose well-known papers focus on the obsessive
aspects of the disorder, uses a combination of an SSRI and modafinil
(Provigil) a mild stimulant sometimes used to treat narcolepsy. Some
medications such as the MAOIs may also instigate increased alert-

ness in patients who ultimately find themselves sleeping less and, on occasion, leaning towards manic behavior if they take too much.

Depersonalization and the opioid system

Any of the natural substances, such as an endorphin, released in the body in response to pain is called an opioid. The term stems from the word opium, which in Latin variations of the Greek means "poppy juice." Synthetic compounds that exhibit similarities to the opium alkaloids that occur in nature also fall into this group.

Years of research have pretty clearly indicated that our endogenous opioid system is involved in the regulation of emotional and behavioral responses to stress.

Activation of this system has been shown to lead to a higher pain threshold, suppressed emotional experiencing and repression of negative affective states, notes Mauricio Sierra of London's Institute of Psychiatry.[7]

Stress-driven activation of the opioid system helps people deal with adverse situations through the blunting of their emotions, particularly fear. In the interests of self-preservation, this enables them to tackle a negative situation with greater calm and clarity.

In addition, there is also evidence that chronic conditions such as depression and anxiety disorders may involve a dysregulation in the opioid system. For example, patients with panic disorder show abnormally high levels of endogenous opioids in cerebrospinal fluid,[8] and the opioid concentration increases after panic attacks are induced with lactate.* This panic-induced release of endoge-

---

* Several studies have examined the relationship between panic and lactate. In a 1988 study by McGrath et al, 47 depressed outpatients were infused with sodium lactate to explore the relationship between history of panic attacks and lactate-induced panic. Lactate panic was rated without knowledge of history of panic. Fifteen of 29 patients (52%) with a history of spontaneous panic experienced panic attacks in response to lactate. Only 1 of 18 patients (6%) without a history of spontaneous panic experienced a lactate-induced panic attack—a highly significant difference. The likelihood of lactate panic was related to frequency of spontaneous panic attacks.

nous opioids is potentially relevant to depersonalization, since the latter is a frequent symptom of panic attacks.[9] Moreover, recent findings suggest that the experience of panic is indeed a mediating mechanism capable of triggering dissociative responses during acute trauma.

Effects of Opioid Antagonists on Depersonalization

One feature of depersonalization, which may indicate an overactive opioid system, is the fact that patients with chronic depersonalization appear to show higher thresholds for pain detection.[10] The endogenous opioid system suppresses both emotional and physiological pain in stress-related situations. So it seems possible that it relates to such "numbing" in depersonalization. In 2001, Russian researchers tested the hypothesis that long-lasting depersonalization stems from a dysregulation in the opioid system.[11] They carried out a single blind, placebo-controlled trial with Naloxone on 14 patients suffering with long-lasting depersonalization of one to 16 years duration. Six of their patients met DSM-IV criteria for Depersonalization Disorder with no comorbid conditions, while, in eight patients depersonalization existed alongside depression.

Naloxone is a drug used to counter the effects of opioid overdose. Familiar opioids like morphine or heroin can dangerously depress the central nervous system or the respiratory system, often resulting in death. Naloxone counters this negative reaction.

In this trial, Naloxone was administered intravenously as a single dose of 1.6-4 mg in 11 patients. Three patients who failed to show any initial response were administered subsequent doses up to a maximum of 10 mg. The authors reported that three patients had a complete and lasting remission of depersonalization, while seven experienced significant improvement (a 50% symptom reduction on a depersonalization scale). Only one patient showed moderate improvement, while in two of them improvement was minimal and short lasting. Only one patient failed to experience any kind of symptom amelioration. In summary, 71% of their patients experienced a significant reduction in the intensity of depersonalization.

Surprisingly, in most cases, symptom improvement was reported to occur within the first 20-40 minutes following Naloxone administration. In keeping with the hypothesis that depersonalization represents an opioid-driven suppressive effect on the stress response, patients were found to have low basal plasma cortisol levels, which subsequently increased after Naloxone administration.

To further examine any relationship between opioids and depersonalization, Drs. Simeon and Knutelska[12] carried out an open-label trial with Naltrexone on 14 subjects with DPD. While seven subjects received a maximum dose of 100 mg/day for 6 weeks, the other seven went on to receive 250 mg/day for 10 weeks. Three patients reported a marked improvement, with a more than 70% reduction in symptoms. The mean intensity reduction for the whole sample was 30% (as measured by three dissociation scales). Although these results are far less dramatic than those reported by the Russian study by Nuller et al, the very way in which Naltrexone works certainly affected the results. Naltrexone is twice as potent as Naloxone and has a considerably longer half-life, but its "bioavailability" is more unreliable. In other words only five to 12 percent of a dose reaches the target of systemic circulation.[13]

It is curious that as of this writing there have not been any published follow-up studies of Naloxone's use in treating DPD. There have been anecdotal reports of individuals who have been able to induce their doctors to prescribe it. These patients have self-injected Naloxone in the same dosage as the Russian study, they claim, with little or no effect. Others have tried Naltrexone with equally discouraging results. This pattern of success in a clinical setting and failure in the trenches is not uncommon. The issue of whether the individuals taking the suggested medication truly suffered from DPD remains open. So is whether or not the medicine was administered properly. (One woman repeatedly injected Naloxone into her leg, despite instructions specifying intravenous injection). Ultimately this is one area of exploration that needs to be examined more closely.

The Cocktail Cure

To date, some patients have not found relief through a single medicine, but rather a combination of meds tailored to their symptoms. In recent years, Abilify, promoted as the antidepressant that may work when others do not, has joined the possible mix. A 2010 article in *Current Psychiatry* reported on a case study in which Abilify was used with other medications to treat depersonalization specifically.[14]

The patient in question reflected a history of anxiety, panic attacks, as well as the trauma of a sexual assault at age 18. According to her doctors, her symptoms, which included persistent feelings of detachment and emotional numbness, met the criteria for DPD outlined in the DSM-IV, as well the depersonalization rating scales.

Various SSRIs and SNRIs proved to be ineffective as treatment, although Luvox (fluvoxamine) did relieve her anxiety. The psychiatrists augmented the Luvox with 2.5 mg of Ability (aripiprazole) per day. After five weeks, her depersonalization symptoms lessened from 10 to 6 on a 10-point self-report scale.

Seeking further improvement, the psychiatrists discontinued Luvox but added amantadine (a drug used to treat Parkinson's disease) in an attempt to raise dopamine levels. After a period of improvement, the patient's depersonalization symptoms worsened. After further experimentation, a regimen of 50 mg of clomipramine (Anafranil) at bedtime, 10 mg of diazepam (Valium) at bedtime, and 2/5 mg of Abilify per day resulted in complete remission of depersonalization symptoms after four months time.

Is this "cocktail" the cure for DPD? Perhaps for some people, as it was for this single patient. But the authors of the article admit: "We are not certain whether her response was caused by aripiprazole, a delayed reaction of clomipramine, or a spontaneous remission." However, the addition of Abilify at the beginning of treatment, and at the end, did seem to have the most positive effects for this particular patient. Only further clinical testing will reveal Abilify's effects on large numbers of DPD patients. But a small number of visitors to *depersonalization.info* and other websites have reported little success with Abilify, just as they have with Naloxone and Naltrexone.

In the last analysis, the variety of medicines covered herein can and do control the varied symptoms of DPD. Time and again people report improvement to websites like *depersonalization.info* and others. Individual ratings of degrees of improvement run from 15 to 20 percent to 80 to 85 percent. But to date, unless DPD simply leaves on its own, no one can lay claim to a true pharmaceutical cure, either through a single medicine or a self-tailored cocktail of several. Fortunately, DPD can disappear on its own, but no one can predict when, or why. In addition to the medicines that can be quite helpful, new therapies are doing much to speed the process of living with DPD, or even conquering it completely. Next we'll look at the types of therapy that have been particularly effective.

REFERENCES

1. Simeon, D., Guralnik, 0., Schmeidler, J., Knutelska, M. (2004). Fluoxetine therapy in depersonalisation disorder: randomised controlled trial. *The British Journal of Psychiatry*, **185**, p 31-36.

2. Simeon, D., Stein, D, clomipramine. *Biological Psychiatry*, **44**, p 302-303.

3. Davidson, J.R, Woodbury, M.A., Zisook, S., Giller, E.R Jr. (1989). Classification of depression by grade of membership: a confirmation study. *Psychological Medicine*, **19**, p 987-998.

4. Sierra, M. (2009). Depersonalization: A New Look at a Neglected Syndrome. Cambridge: Cambridge University Press, p 143

5. Simeon, D., Abugel, J. (2006) Feeling Unreal: Depersonalization Disorder and the Loss of the Self. Oxford: Oxford U Press, p 160.

6. Sierra, M. (no 4) p 116.

7. Ibid. p 117.

8. Eriksson, E., Westberg, P., Thuresson, K, Modigh, K, Ekman, R, Widerliiv, E. (1989). IIncreased cerebrospinal fluid of endorphin immunoreactivity in panic disorder. *Neuropsychopharmacology*, **2**, p 225-228.

9. Ball, S., Robinson, A., Shekhar, A., Walsh, K (1997). Dissociative symptoms in panic disorder. *Journal of Nervous and Mental Disease*, **185,** 755-760.

10. Ibid. p 118.

11. Nuller, Y. L., Morozova, M. G., Kushnir, O. N., Hamper, N. (2001). Effect of Naloxone therapy on depersonalization: a pilot study. *Journal of Psychopharmacology*, **15**, p 93-95.

12. Simeon, D., Knutelska, M. (2005). An open trial of Naltrexone in the treatment of depersonalization disorder. *Clinical Journal of Psychopharmacology*, **25**, p 267-270.

13. Sierra, M. (no 4) p 119.

14. Janjua, A., Rapport, D., Ferrara, G. (2010). *The woman who wasn't there*. Current Psychiatry, **4**, 10.

10 Effective Therapies

Writing is a form of therapy; sometimes I wonder how all those who do not write, compose or paint can manage to escape the madness, melancholia, the panic and fear which is inherent in a human situation.

—Graham Greene

When I first attempted to explore treatment for my problem, which was clearly a mental one, the prospects were discouraging. A doctor at a psychiatric clinic recommended psychoanalysis, which would take years, and neither he nor I had a clue as to what we were treating. I knew that my problems were physiologically based, and after eleven years, a proper diagnosis, an appropriate medicine, and an understanding of what had occurred finally brought resolution and sanity.

Today, treatments not only involve a variety of helpful medicines, but new forms of therapy that bypass lengthy, interesting, but seemingly antiquated psychoanalysis. You can endure depersonalization, and transcend it, without ever studying the theories of Freud, Jung, or Adler.

Many people who suffer from depression, anxiety or depersonalization are initially resistant to "talk" therapy, with good reason. If you were once "normal" and now feel mentally fragmented, empty, anxious, and afraid of going crazy, you know that *something* has changed. Something inside is *not right*. The damage done by a drug or event that triggered it all somehow needs to be reversed. Pharmaceutical intervention can go a long way toward readjusting the chemistry that is out of whack, especially in the early stages. But Depersonalization Disorder goes through different stages with different, though consistent symptom clusters. When panic and anxiety subside (assuming they are present to begin with), and endless rumination, lack of emotion, or other chronic discomfort such as feeling detached from your body or living in a bubble take hold, therapies that help you "ground" yourself, control worry, and change your thinking patterns also can assure a faster recovery or, at least, a comfortable adjustment to a different way of perceiving life.

Two types of therapy are currently being used with varying degrees of success in treating DPD. To resort to well-worn clichés, one, Cognitive Behavioral Therapy (CBT) broadly involves the concept of "mind over matter," while the other, Acceptance and Commitment Therapy (ACT) is a newer spin on the "go with the flow" philosophy.

Cognitive Behavioral Therapy (CBT)

This type of therapy has been effectively used to help people cope with anxiety disorders and panic. Developed by psychiatrist Aaron T. Beck in the 1960s, CBT is based on the premise that specific thoughts, or thinking patterns influence our behavior, mood, and reactions to the outside world. If you can control and guide your thoughts away from catastrophic assumptions, negativity about your self, and generalizations and exaggerations, you can ultimately change your outlook as well as the brain chemistry behind it. Because of the frequent connections between anxiety and panic and depersonalization, the leading researchers at London's Institute of Psychiatry, including Drs. Hunter, Sierra, and Phillips proposed CBT as a possible treatment for depersonalization in a 2005 article in *Behaviour Research and Therapy*.[1] Since then, Cognitive Behavioral Therapies or variations of its basic tenets have been employed effectively by hundreds of doctors and therapists worldwide.

At the heart of the argument for using CBT lies the idea that we have alluded to in Chapter 6. Except for being dissociative in the sense that the mind and body may feel separate or detached, depersonalization holds little in common with the other known dissociative disorders. Its frequent appearance alongside panic attacks has fueled the assumption that such therapies might positively affect the thoughts and attitudes of people with depersonalization.

A key element to the application of CBT to depersonalization involves knowing the condition itself—what it is and what it is not. Unfortunately, many people never even arrive at this starting point.

Transient symptoms of depersonalization/derealization are not uncommon in the general population. Neither is anxiety. But interpretations of these sensations are what can drag them out unnecessarily, causing them to become chronic. "It is the catastrophic misinterpretation of these symptoms as indicating threat that leads to a vicious cycle of increasing symptoms, since the secondary anxiety about the meaning of the symptoms adds to the initial anxiety," note Dr. Hunter and colleagues.

Finding the right medicine is important because many can assist in recreating mood, reintegrating thinking, and providing a sense of calm in order to deal with the condition's psychological aspects.

Cognitive Behavioral Therapy begins with clarifying what DPD is, its specific symptoms, how common they are, as well as all the terrible things that will *not* happen, namely losing control, or going insane. This so-called psycho-education phase brings tremendous relief to people. Knowing you actually suffer from something with a name goes a long way towards getting better. There is little doubt that dealing with the unknown fueled my Nine Circles far longer than necessary.

Other key techniques include:

- *Diary keeping.* Therapists suggest that keeping a diary is helpful. It can help establish any existing symptom patterns or triggering circumstances. It can help to identify factors that make things worse. If writing is your passion, you will have already noticed that tapping into this creative outlet somehow puts your mind in another place. Your stream of consciousness at times will actually become whatever project you are working on, and any time spent creating thoughts on paper or computer screen is time not spent in fruitless worry.

- *Reducing Avoidance.* If you suffer from DPD you know which situations you avoid—the ones that increase anxiety such as social gatherings, crowded public places, driving, flying, or any number of scenarios typical of people who develop phobias. Therapies in this case may involve those frequently used to treat these phobias. Facing situations head on, in gradual, limited doses goes a long way toward conquering them. In social situations, "safety behaviors" might include retaining a fixed expression, keeping very still, making minimal eye contact, always forcing out the right thing to say—all of which leaves you feeling as if you are just going through the motions of social interaction. "Role playing, with and without, the use of safety behaviors, will allow the patient to see for themselves whether their safety behavior serves to help or hinder their performance," Dr. Phillips and colleagues suggest.

- *Reducing self-focused attention.* Attention training and task concentration training have proven helpful in getting patients to stop obsessing about DPD or other things, and veer away from hypochondriachal tendencies. If you spend too much time focusing on yourself, you'll neglect focusing on the people, places, and things around you. This makes you feel even more detached and alienated. Get "out of yourself" by engaging in life and occupying your mind with activities other than worry. Attention training enhances one's ability to control sustained attention, attention shifting, and divided attention through a series of exercises. This can be as simple as focusing in on different sounds in your house or backyard, then consciously shifting your attention from one to the other. Similarly, task concentration training helps you gain insight into the proportion of your attention focused on (1) internal stimuli; (2) external, irrelevant stimuli; or (3) external, task-related stimuli. Exercises help you increase the degree of externally focused, task-related attention, initially in non-threatening situations and subsequently in threatening situations.

- *Challenging catastrophic assumptions.* Cognitive interventions such as thought records can be used to identify specific

negative automatic thoughts which occur in anxiety producing situations, or when the symptoms of DPD increase.
These negative cognitions can then be recognized as such,
and replaced with balanced, logical thoughts. When anxiety
arises from intense focus on the self, or the frightening nature of existence itself, it is eased by the knowledge that you
are not going insane. As moments pass, existence continues,
thoughts continue, even a song running through one's head
will proceed as if nothing was wrong through the moments of
anxiety or panic. The stream of consciousness continues no
matter what surge of momentary panic presents itself. Once
you realize this you are better equipped to just go *through*
these incidents and come out of them feeling more relaxed.
You endured intense fear and the momentary thoughts that
you were losing your mind, but you didn't. Nor will you if
it happens again.These catastrophic misinterpretations can
be gradually challenged through education, experimentation
and evidence gathering. For example, Hunter et al suggest,
"if a patient fears that an increase in their DPD would result
in them losing control, a detailed list of what this would entail
should be constructed. The patient is then encouraged to test
this hypothesis by carrying out behaviors that have previously increased the DPD severity to discover if their predictions
are realized." Or, the therapist and patient can examine the
patient's worst episodes to determine why the feared conse-
quences were not realized. "Obtaining belief ratings for each
feared consequence at regular intervals through therapy will
monitor the success of these interventions."

Finally, physiological interventions also can be incorporated into
the treatment of patients with DPD, such as applied relaxation training and education regarding the role of hyperventilation in anxiety
and panic, with training in diaphragmatic breathing. However, over-
reliance on relaxation techniques may exacerbate DPD symptoms in
some cases, Hunter notes.

On the surface, some cognitive therapies may seem self-evident, even simplistic. They may parallel techniques people have stumbled across, or invented on their own in their attempts to deal with chronic depersonalization. But they have shown that they can be effective for many people, with or without the continual guidance of a therapist.

Acceptance and Commitment Therapy: A Case History

Through the years, thousands of people have visited *depersonalization.info* looking for help or advice. The number of visits is closing in on the 200,000 mark. Most of these people come and go, never to be heard from again. Sometimes individuals exhibit a relentless determination to make things right. Often a parent or significant other is involved in the process.

Sarah, a young Australian woman, and her mother, serve as a good example. For years, both have kept me abreast of Sarah's progress as she walked a road to recovery that included misdiagnoses, personal confusion, assorted medications, and several hospitalizations. At last, Sarah enjoyed a breakthrough by closely working with clinical psychologist Kristy Attwooll of New South Wales.

Some types of therapy are designed to help you avoid or stop certain thought patterns. Others, specifically Acceptance and Commitment Therapy (ACT), are designed to help you go *through* those thought patterns, just as the word "acceptance" implies.

Like Cognitive Behavioral Therapy, Acceptance and Commitment Therapy (ACT), developed by Hayes, Strosahl, and Wilson in 1999[2], recognizes that psychological distress is often caused by "experiential avoidance" that is, efforts by an individual to escape, avoid, or remove unpleasant thoughts, feelings, body sensations, urges, images or memories. Often avoidance can work in the short-term resulting in some relief; in the long term such avoidance usually fails and thereby contributes to further psychological distress. Moreover, the preoccupation with escaping or removing unwanted private experiences can be extremely time-consuming, and prevent a person from identifying and engaging in actions consistent with their "deepest values".

As we look at some of the philosophical aspects of depersonalization in the next chapter, comparisons between unwanted DPD and *desired* Buddhist states inevitably come into play. It is no wonder, then, that Steven C. Hayes, one of the developers of Acceptance and Commitment Therapy has also written about the parallels between ACT and Buddhist teachings that include "the ubiquity of human suffering, the role of attachment in suffering, mindfulness, wholesome actions, and self."[3]

This doesn't mean that ACT requires that you become a Buddhist. Rather, certain Buddhist teaching and practices seem to be more grounded in science than the dogma of other purely faith-based philosophies, Hayes contends.

In Sarah's case, Dr. Attwooll felt that ACT might be worth trying, given that everything else had failed.

"I was upfront about the approach and the fact that the empirical data was limited with regard to the use of ACT with depersonalization disorder. However, given that Sarah was also reporting some anxiety, it did not seem an irresponsible choice of treatment to pursue," Attwooll states. (Her instincts proved correct. Not long after beginning Sarah's treatment the book *Overcoming Depersonalization Disorder*, by Fugen Neziroglu and Katherine Donnelly[4] specifically addressed using ACT to treat depersonalization).

Attwooll's approach paralleled what is now recommended for many DPD patients. In Sarah's case, therapy employed "metaphor, paradox, mindfulness, and experiential exercises" to:

1. Accept unwanted private experiences and let go of struggling with them.
2. Be more "present," which refers to paying ongoing attention to, and making non-judgmental contact with, private experiences (e.g., thoughts, feelings, and body sensations) and one's external environment (e.g., sights, smells and sounds).
3. Disentangle from unwanted private experiences.
4. Acknowledge an observer part of oneself that is always constant and thus can watch the coming and going of private ex-

periences.

5. Identify what is most important for an individual (i.e., what they want their life to stand for).

6. Make a commitment to act on goals that relate to the person's own values, while at times anticipating and making room for unwanted private experiences that may visit when a person is choosing to behave in accordance with their values. Accordingly, ACT aims to help individuals live a more satisfying and meaningful life.

"ACT differs from other evidence-based psychological interventions such as Cognitive Behavioral Therapy (CBT)," Attwooll explains. "In a very simplistic comparison, CBT focuses upon teaching a person to change or modify cognitions to improve the person's emotional state (i.e., reduce anxiety or depression). The goal is to eliminate and control thoughts in order to eliminate or control feelings. ACT, in contrast, does not focus on elimination or control but rather acceptance, without judgment, of all private experiences including highly unpleasant thoughts and feelings. Further, CBT encourages behavior that will minimize uncomfortable or distressing emotional states, while ACT encourages behavior that is consistent with an individual's values.

Research evaluating the effectiveness of ACT interventions with clinical populations has shown promising results, with improvements in psychological functioning of people with depression, anxiety, psychosis, and substance abuse, even after only a few treatment sessions, Attwooll points out.

In Sarah's case of chronic, long-term depersonalization, ACT was near to being her last resort. There was nothing left to lose by trying it.

"Within an ACT framework one might consider dissociative states as an experiential avoidance," Attwooll says. "While functional during a trauma or extreme stress, dissociation can be highly dysfunctional when it persists under non-traumatic circumstances." An approach that discourages experiential avoidance and is more accepting of all private unwanted experiences while safely observing such experiences seems to be clinically beneficial. "Further, acknowledging a set of values that are constant and permanent to the individual could be extremely reassuring and provide direction to individuals who (potentially as a result of prolonged states of depersonalization) are unclear of who they are and what preferences they might have in any given situation. The degree to which ACT helped Sarah is best illustrated by her personal story, told in her own words:

"This is the story of how DP has become a guest in my life—a visitor who may show up again but doesn't make me who I am. I can't pinpoint when the depersonalization started, I just knew this indescribable blankness and silence of not having thoughts. I could write English essays, speak in front of the school and maintain a large group of friends—all the time thinking that there was something very different and exhausting about the way that I related.

"As my parents separated and divorced, this DP took on a life of its own and devastated mine. Severe episodes lasted for months and it visited me three or four more times over the next ten years, all at significant crisis points in my own relationships. Not many knew about it, however, as I somehow found the resilience to continue to work at university.

"On a long road that involved many incorrect diagnoses and several hospital admissions, I was diagnosed with 'a type of dissociation which was triggered by anxiety.' Anti-depressants would only reduce the fear and alleviate some of the distress. Leading psychiatrists searched for signs that might provide answers as to why the depersonalization was so prominent. But they finally agreed that Depersonalization was my *primary* condition. All the while, I felt like a cheating ghost making herself who she was through every planned movement and decision. As I sat reading descriptions of Depersonalization Disorder one day, the relief that came with the knowledge that I could know the world differently than I did was beautifully overwhelming.

"I was in a vicious cycle of DP, anxiety, avoidance, DP and anxiety about the DP. A psychiatrist drew this cycle for me and it started to make sense that maybe I was using the DP to avoid anxiety and other feelings that I was too vulnerable to deal with. Until I could somehow recognize the way I was reacting to the DP, it wouldn't loosen its grip.

"In hospital I was introduced to Acceptance and Commitment Therapy (ACT). We were shown some bamboo finger traps commonly used as party tricks. The more you pulled your fingers apart the tighter the trap became, giving rise to fear and anxiety. Your immediate reaction was to pull more, but this was useless. When you relaxed your fingers and even pushed into the trap there was room to move and wiggle. The trap was still there but there was room. The idea behind it all was to relax and accept, not fight. Afterward, I wrestled with the frightening thought of letting the depersonalization be there exactly as it was, without fighting.

"My psychologist in the hospital suggested I accept this intruder and treat it like a guest instead of engaging in a futile battle. What an outrageous suggestion! To me, it was like finding a spider resting on your back and being told to stay calm. It's the last thing you want to hear, but the panic only adds confusion and greater distress. I knew that desperate attempts to get rid of my experience were based in fear.

"I learned to name the internal stories and sensations, and when they came I would now say to my Self 'Here is the 'I've got nothing to say' story again', or 'Here comes the agitation again', or 'Here is the 'I must be stupid' story again.' I began to imagine myself finding that place which is the eye of the storm—the place that is still as the storm swirls around you. My 'self' and the depersonalization symptoms had become intertwined. When I could see that I was the quiet observer of these experiences there wasn't as much of my self at stake.

"I began to notice patterns in my thoughts. There were prejudgments about how the symptoms of depersonalization and panic could impact the rest of my life. I now see this very attitude in the desperate pleas in various online Depersonalization Forums. All these people want to hear is that someone else knows their experiences. They want to know that it might change, that they aren't crazy.

"The 'Commitment' part of the therapy focused on identifying what is important to me, and how to make choices consistent with my own dreams and values. With a weak sense of self, it was hard to determine what *was* important to me. I committed to making room for the feelings I had always sought to avoid, even making room for the DP. Time and time again I would sit in a draining and exhausting social situation and waver between simply observing my experiences and being completely choked by the anxiety they created. I went away on family trips, played volleyball, and sewed little treats for friends (even if every last movement was painfully planned). Being an 'observer' meant that the sensations weren't me and I could stay with my choices.

"One week short of a year ago, I went away for Easter to a family event. By going I knew that I would have to face the DP as it took hold. I talked with loved ones, and laughed and shared food and family—all things that were so valuable to me. Then for one instant I felt the sun like never before and I was lost in the moment. I caught a glimpse of being lost in time. The analysis, comparisons with others, the distraction of judging the blankness and lack of sense of self faded into the background. All of the long painful minutes that weren't connected started to fit into a bigger picture. My mind was full with my preferences, joys, curiosity about the conversations I took part in, the temperature in the air, and warm spots of sun on my face. It didn't last, and I had to be prepared to lose this feeling over and over again. But each time, a little less fearful that it would never return.

"I continued to take part in activities that held value for me, each time writing down what I was willing to experience to follow through with my goals. When I chose to talk with my friends, put on my favorite clothes, or study a topic I was interested in, the DP and panic came along for the ride but didn't determine the direction I would take. Like a scientist, I described the shape and color of my sensations as they expanded in my body. This helped me remain grounded.

"I discovered this extraordinary new way to see the world without the cloud of judgment, and I didn't want to live life any other way. Some compare it with a religious conversion. As I recovered, I fought hard against the natural doubts, questions and insecurities that reminded me of the DP. Struggling to try and get rid of them was exhausting, and took my focus off listening, feeling, and re-learning my likes and dislikes. These insecurities had to come along for the ride. As I learned that feelings do change and grow and fade and don't make you who you are, I learned to let them be, just as they are.

"I can say that I have recovered from DPD. I may still experience the distraction of the stories that our minds tell us, but that's normal. I am prepared to let this visitor come and go if it shows up. Now, instead of blocking out certain feelings and depersonalization, I am learning they have a purpose. They show us what we like and don't like, they warn us against danger and they are what make us feel connected. I have learned that we all try to fix or change a situation by shifting it to our heads. I now notice it when I send a feeling to my head to change it, or to my gut to feel the weight of it. The quality of life I know now is richer and clearer, truer and finer than most people, perhaps, because I have learned that I am not my thoughts, feelings and sensations. I no longer have to face my experience with fear. Discomfort sometimes, yes, but that's okay."

During the therapy, Dr. Attwooll observed: "Sarah benefited considerably from adopting a posture of acceptance and willingness to embrace *all* her psychological experiences, even the psychological experience of numbness and disconnection with the world, which had dominated her entire existence for some time." Interestingly, Attwooll says, "Sarah found that the more she let go of her struggle to control and eliminate depersonalization, the more she actually realized that this experience in itself could be tolerated and would pass in time (given, of course, enough time). This allowed her to be curious, and open to the emergence of other experiences, including various emotional states (even pleasant feelings and sensations) that began to be experienced more often as she let go of her individual struggle."

Sarah also benefited from awareness of the fact that she does have values that can guide her actions in the moment, even when feeling numb and disconnected from the world and others. This helped her to reestablish a sense of self that was not solely defined by her Depersonalization Disorder.

As treatment progressed, Sarah became more aware of emotional states (such as anxiety) that tended, at times, to precipitate her depersonalization. Again, her willingness to experience, accept, and tolerate this anxiety allowed her to endure the temporary visit of this emotion and yet still, in these moments, engage in behavior that she finds purposeful and satisfying, Attwooll notes. Accordingly, Sarah was no longer avoiding various situations but instead, she was free to experience life as she had always hoped she could. Experiences, that during her darkest moments, she did not think possible again.

"I think the story of Sarah demonstrates that ACT intervention could have a strong place in the treatment of Depersonalization Disorder, not to mention existing alone as a wonderful story of hope for other sufferers of DPD. It cannot go unsaid that in my opinion, Sarah's recovery and ongoing clinical improvement is a testament to the dedication, courage and commitment of Sarah herself," Attwooll concludes.

Stories of hope such as Sarah's are beginning to emerge with greater regularity. Her account is particularly important because it illustrates how the professional instincts of a good therapist can head a patient in the right direction. Dr. Attwooll held little information about the use of ACT in treating Depersonalization Disorder, even though studies were already underway at the time she began treating Sarah. Her instincts and experience, not the track records of others, ultimately guided her toward the best therapy for her patient.

People contact *depersonalization.info* regularly looking for the name of a doctor or therapist specializing in DPD in their locale. Unfortunately there are very few experts to recommend. All psychi-

atrists have the tools to deal with depersonalization on a individualized basis at their disposal. They also have access to, and should
be familiar with, the most recent research published in the medical
journals. This applies to psychologists as well. You don't need an
expert in DPD, per se, just a committed, caring professional willing
to try new things and learn new things. As in any profession, the
ones who claim to know it all are probably the least likely to help
you. The best doctors continue to learn and grow, as we all do. Mauricio Sierra, arguably Europe's leading expert on Depersonalization
Disorder reflected this trait when he told me, "I have to say that the
more I study DP, the less I understand it." Anyone claiming the opposite simply doesn't know the complexity of the condition.

Other Stories of Success

Different people respond to different therapies. The fact that Acceptance and Commitment Therapy at times seems as much like a
philosophical way of dealing with depersonalization as a therapy
should not go unnoticed. In the next chapter we'll look at ways of
adapting to, or altering, the depersonalization experience to fit into
a new, perhaps "enlightened" way of thinking and living. Others
have visited *depersonalization.info* with greater frequency in recent
years, wishing to leave messages of hope for those who currently
live without it.

One of these was Jamie, who had contacted me during the time
I was working on *Feeling Unreal*. She was suffering from what
sounded like depersonalization, but also visual abnormalities that
she could not explain. We made arrangements to meet and discuss
her situation while I was visiting with Dr. Simeon in New York. She
never appeared, however, and I did not hear from her again until I
began working on this book. She surfaced, older and wiser, and happier as she now gives visitors to the *dpselfhelp.com* website these
words of encouragement:

"I was planning to return to my old forums (they were many) to
offer genuine words of hope and support to those still in the midst
of this 'abstract veil.' In fact, there were many words I used to de-

scribe my severe Derealization— Sub reality. I got so desperate for answers or an explanation that I once decided I was 'chosen' to see the world from a different angle, to see stuff others around me could not. The constant abstract questioning.... what are people, what is a chair, what is language, why do we look so 'perfect' as beings and yet we are stuck on this rock in the middle of space/nothingness? These questions would torture me. They were no longer fun to ponder. *Everything* freaked me out. I found solace in sleeping. And I pretty much slept my seven years of DP/DR away. I still managed to hold a part time job and finish college (looking back, I have no idea how I did it but my parents were in denial of my illness and would not accept dropping out as an option.) Speaking of parents, I grew up in a highly anxious, loud, and abusive environment. Dad had a short temper and was a total narcissist and mom was an enabler who was passive/aggressive. We didn't have much family time, unless we were bickering with each other. I think my DP/DR started from dropping Ecstasy pills every day for a month, and maybe smoking pot that was laced with something. No one knows for sure. I was told it could have stemmed from my household and that the DPD was acting as a 'defense mechanism.' Despite the suffering, it was designed to protect me from my anxious surroundings (hence the 'living in a bubble feeling'). I read that people with this illness are usually *very* introspective, analytical, and have a high IQ. For me, it was total Hell for seven years. As an anxious person, the DP/ DR made my anxiety hit the roof. Walking outside scared me. I felt the earth was too round and that our atmosphere was a bio-dome. Everything felt altered.

But it began to decrease in its strength. The sheer fear of the illness itself began to fade as I researched more, took my SSRI, and avoided any illegal drugs, of course. Time is what healed me. I always believed the SSRI helped to alleviate the anxiety, but time is what truly got me over this. It was an extremely slow process...as if someone took the recovery remote control and hit 'Slow'. And as I was shifting slowly back to myself, I was no longer the little teenager that it began with. I was a grown young lady now. Along with my slow recovery process, I learned the virtue of patience, the precious opportunity I am given to live my life, my talents, the goodness in people around me, being responsible for MY mental health, and some nifty research skills to boot. I realized how relentless and resourceful I can be, and that I was brave. I also realized human beings are really amazingly resilient when faced with adversity. In a way, I'm thankful for the experience (when I'm not pissed at the amount of years I wasted). Well, not all was lost. I spent my entire seven years researching my illness and also learned I had Hallucinogenic Persisting Perception Disorder (HPPD) from the Ecstasy and weed, which caused the visual distortions (that too gets better only with time!)

The good news is, once you feel this veil lifting, you are so overjoyed that you forget how bad you felt. Life just falls back into place. You pick up the pieces and continue on. I made it a priority to find the best therapies and meds for me. I would never sit back and deal with it. I was a fighter. You must be, too.

To feel like myself and even better than before, unfortunately, took some time. For some it takes months, for others, years. Time is against everyone individually, but we all will experience our outcome one way or another. I made many friends on the forums and even was sent a gift from New Zealand from someone's mother. You don't forget the journey, but when you do recover, you will find it extremely hard to recall this awful feeling of DP/DR. It's as if it truly was all but a dream. You will all overcome this. I am proof."

Another contributor to *depersonalization.info* had this to say:

"I have been DP free for years. Depersonalization does go away. Mine started with an intense one-time experience with weed. For me, the feeling of unreality lasted for five years. No medications helped. What did? Time, and distraction. The less I focused on it and tried to lead a normal life, the more normalcy returned.

Three or four years into it, I no longer even thought about it. Someone asked shortly afterward about the DP, and I responded, 'Oh that, I don't have it anymore.' It was that simple. It was a gradual tapering off to where it just disappeared without me acknowledging it. There was no 'Oh, it's gone!' moment.

When the time came, it felt so casual to say I didn't have it. I know the hellish experience it can be.

Some people will take less time, some more. Just know it WILL go away!

I just wanted to stop by these forums after all these years and contribute. Keep in mind, most of us that do overcome this, don't come back. This is why you'll hear more negative stories than positive ones. Why revisit the past if you're free?"

There are many success stories just like these. But it's understandable that when people improve, either on their own or with the assistance of a professional, medications, or therapies, they simply want to live again, sometimes in a new way that can be as incomprehensible to "normals" as the disorder that defied explanation. Why try to explain the cure to someone who never understood what was wrong to begin with? Conquering, or adapting to depersonalization is as private as the suffering it can present. Yet this strange state of mind is nothing new. Literature, philosophy, and religion have addressed it for centuries. Now it's time to dive deeper into that mysterious ocean.

REFERENCES

1. Hunter, E.C. M., Phillips, M., Chalder, T., Sierra, M., David, A.S., (2003) Depersonalisation Disorder: a cognitive behavioural conceptualisation. *Behaviour Research and Therapy.* **41**, p 1451-1467.

2. Hayes, S.C., Strosahl, K.D., Wilson, K.G., (1999) Acceptance and Commitment Therapy: An Experiential Approach to Behavior Change, Guilford Press, New York.

3. Hayes, S.C., (2002) Buddhism and Acceptance and commitment therapy. *Cognitive and Behavioral Practice.* **9**, p 58-66.

4. Neziroglu, F., Donnelly, K., (2010) Overcoming Depersonalization Disorder: a mindfulness & acceptance guide to conquering feelings of numbness & unreality. Oakland, CA. New Harbinger Publications.

11 The Veil of Maya

Who looks outside, dreams; who looks inside, awakes.

—Carl Gustav Jung

The Boston Museum of Fine Arts' permanent collection includes a large and famous painting by Paul Gauguin, perhaps his masterpiece. Typical of the artist, the highly decorative work depicts native Tahitians in a variety of poses and activities. A closer look reveals that each figure suggests some part of life's universal processes — birth, experience, wonder, and contemplation of impending death. Assorted animals share this scene and its symbolism amidst a tropical paradise. The title of the painting illuminates the imagery through the questions: *Where Do We Come From? What Are We? Where Are We Going?*

What puzzled the Tahitians, and an ailing Gauguin, is no closer to resolution today than it was when the work was completed in 1897, despite technology that would seem to provide answers for everything. For most people, the "great mysteries of life" are accepted as such, and gladly. People live their lives as if death, or realities of the infinite in time or space, does not exist. But as we have seen, depersonalization changes that perspective. When the self that is normally entrenched in daily life, rooted in a predicable continuity of thoughts, memory, and planning is shattered, the mind inevitably veers towards the unknowable, the abstract. As a tiny, breathing being on a spinning ball in the midst of endless night, why wouldn't it? "Where Do I Come From? What Am I? Where Am I Going?," suddenly seems to demand an answer.

As Blaise Pascal observed in the 1600s:

"When I consider the short duration of my life, swallowed up in the eternity before and after, the little space which I fill, and even can see — engulfed in an infinite immensity of spaces of which I am ignorant and which know me not, I am frightened, and am aston-

*ished at being here rather than there, for there is no reason why here
rather than there, why now rather than then. The eternal silence of
these infinite spaces frightens me."*[1]

Pascal's observations relay the essence of existential angst. Insomniacs may find themselves pondering these realizations, and for most people, a trip to the refrigerator or turning on the television alleviates what proves to be no more disconcerting than a bad dream. Depersonalization can bring such existential ruminations to the forefront. It can also manifest itself in sensations so anomalous as to defy explanation entirely.

So far we've looked at how researchers have attempted to nail down the brain chemistry behind Depersonalization Disorder. We also have looked at a variety of psychological explanations. Yet after a century of observation, analysis, and treatment, the condition remains elusive, intractable, and largely unknown in popular culture. Why?

One answer emerged in 1970 from a professor of psychiatry named T. E. Weckowicz:

"Depersonalization and derealization phenomena are of great theoretical interest since they are concerned with the core of personal experience. They are linked up with the sense of ultimate reality of the external world and the self and, therefore, they are of great importance for epistemology, ontology, and other problems of philosophy of mind. Because of the metaphorical language in which they are described, and because they belong to a field in which the physical world and the world of symbols overlap, and where mythical thinking interpenetrates reality thinking (Mayer-Gross), depersonalization phenomena offer great difficulty to an experimental attack. For this reason they have been largely ignored by experimentally oriented psychologists."[2]

Whether the exploration of depersonalization involves PET scans and pictures of cockroaches, or pinpointing a "vestigial" defense mechanism, there seems to be more to the phenomena than dreamt of in any medical researcher's lab. Though it is hardly pleasant, depersonalization is a distinct human experience. As such it has appeared in literature, philosophy, and spiritual practices for thousands of years, under different guises. One just has to know where to look. Gauguin's masterpiece elicits a "Now I get it" moment once you know its title. Depersonalization is often the same, once you have witnessed its presence beyond the realm of pathology.

Birth of a Syndrome

People familiar with DPD are by now well aware of the origins of the term *Depersonalization*. Ludovic Dugas has emerged from obscurity as the man who coined it after having read it in the *Journal Intime* of French diarist Frederic Amiel. The latter's published confession, which contains some 17,000 entries written between 1848 and 1881, is rich with passages alluding to feelings of depersonalization. Some experts see these as merely philosophical meanderings, but I disagree. Having assigned myself the grueling task of reading each and every entry, I not only recognize that Amiel suffered from depersonalization but I believe that he exhibited lifelong behavior patterns that appear in most people with the long-term syndrome.

Amiel's diary reveals more than a thinker contemplating the nature of the self. He is a dreamer who, for lack of a clear sense of identity, never acts upon nor achieves his worldly ambitions. As many individuals today wait to begin their lives "once the DPD has cleared up," Amiel waits because he lacks the self-confidence necessary to try. He spends his life as a provincial professor known only for dry lectures and a lackluster personality.

Interestingly, the journal reveals much more. Much like others discussed herein, Amiel concludes that True Reality, beyond the veil of the day-to-day world, consists of the eternal, the infinite, God. The more the self disappeared, the closer one came to the truth and to God, he felt.

His insights frequently echo the Buddha as well:

"Nothing is more hidden from us than the illusion which lives with us day by day, and our greatest illusion is to believe that we are what we think ourselves to be."[3]

Depersonalized individuals also may find themselves grappling with the same internal conflicts as Amiel. An enlightened worldview and a spiritual awakening seem to be waiting just around the bend. Some higher consciousness seems to be beckoning. Yet the rewards of selfhood, the joys of earthbound personhood beckon powerfully as well. Often such a conflict ends in neither self-fulfillment nor enlightenment.

"What is it which has always come between real life and me?" Amiel writes. "What glass screen has, as it were, interposed itself between me and the enjoyment, the possession, the contact of things, leaving me only the role of the looker-on? False shame, no doubt. I have been ashamed to desire. Fatal results of timidity, aggravated by intellectual delusion! Fear, too, has had a large share in it—*La peur de ce que j'aime est ma fatalite...*" [The fear of what I love is my fatality.][4]

While Amiel's term "depersonalized" was quickly recognized by Dugas as something that would resonate with both patients and the psychological community, Amiel's depersonalization was examined later by other experts on dissociation, notably John C. Nemiah, one of the few experts in clinical analysis to cross the line between science and art, and draw from the latter. Writing in the *Comprehensive Textbook of Psychiatry*, Nemiah drew directly from Amiel's diary to illustrate the DP patient's "capacity for insight." Wrote Amiel in 1880:

"Since the age of sixteen onwards I have been able to look at things with the eyes of a blind man recently operated upon—that is to say, I have been able to suppress in myself the results of the long education of sight, and to abolish distances; and now I find myself regarding existence as though from beyond the tomb, from another world; all is strange to me; I am, as it were, outside my own body and individuality; I am depersonalized, detached, cut adrift. Is this madness? No. Madness means the impossibility of recovering one's normal balance after the mind thus played truant among alien forms of being, and followed Dante to invisible worlds. Madness means incapacity for self-judgment and self-control."[5]

According to Nemiah, Amiel made numerous references in his

Journal Intime to states of estrangement such from which "it is clear that he frequently experienced attacks of depersonalization.

"What is of particular interest in the journal entry quoted here [*above*] is Amiel's awareness that his capacity for insight into his condition was maintained throughout all the alterations of his perceptions of himself and the world. He also recognized that no matter how bizarre his experiences were, the preservation of insight kept them clearly out of the realm of madness," Nemiah observed.[6]

Psychologist Elena Bezzubova notes: "Amiel's fear to begin, to accomplish, really a fear of being himself is a kernel of the self while at the same time the root of self decay. Without it, you're not completely human. With too much of it you cannot "grasp" reality and you continue to fluctuate in ever-changing arabesques. Reality's static, half-true nature is deathlike. But searching for reality as a permanent process can also kill, dissolving the self into particles of estrangement."

In this sense, Amiel is stuck in classic analysis paralysis common to so many who, while waiting for the depersonalization to lift, "practice scales," as he put it, without ever producing a symphony, preparing for the life that is just around the corner without ever living in the present.

Amiel ultimately is trapped in the Neverland inhabited by the chronically depersonalized, those who never truly recognize their plight, or their options. If he had known even some of what is known today, this sad, lonely, perfectionist of a man might have produced the fiction or philosophical work that never materialized instead of the diary that remains one of the great curiosities of literature today.

At about the time Amiel began his journal in 1845, another writer whose works periodically touched upon the themes of depersonalization was beginning to achieve a hard-earned degree of success in the United States. His name was Edgar Allan Poe.

Poe, arguably the most popular American storyteller, grew up under circumstances laden with triggers for DPD. His beautiful mother, a well-known actress, died when he was only two years of age. His father who had earlier abandoned the family was a less-ac-

complished actor, known primarily for his obvious stage fright and
excessive drinking. Poe was taken in, but never formally adopted by
a Scottish merchant of Richmond, Virginia, John Allan, known to
be cold, parsimonious, and pretentious. Allan's wife Frances, while
more affectionate toward young "Eddy," suffered from a variety of
real and imaginary illnesses. Hence, she was more likely focused on
her hypochondriasis than the needs of a young orphan.

The Allans afforded Edgar a good, if underfinanced education,
including five years spent in England. But strife between Poe and
his foster father, and the deaths of young friends sowed early seeds
of detachment, loneliness, and depression.

Contrary to popular opinion, Poe's imagination and sense of the
macabre was not fueled by opium or other drugs. Stories of debauch-
ery, drug addiction, and general bad behavior were in fact part of a
posthumous character assassination on the part of Rufus Griswald,
a contemporary whose work Poe had once given a negative review.
Obsessively vengeful, Griswold's scurrilous obituary of Poe was
later refuted vigorously by many who knew the author personally.
But the damage was done and much of it remains to this day.

Poe was neither a degenerate nor dope fiend, but he did in fact
drink too much and spent much of his time trying not to. He kept
no diary from which we can glean his inner thoughts, but themes of
dreams, reality, and unreality pervade his poetry and prose. Works
like *Annabelle Lee* and *The Raven* captured a wide audience, not
because of the macabre but rather the feelings of loss they painfully
emoted. Mortality rates were high in the early 19th century. People
lost spouses, lovers, and children with great regularity, and Poe's
poetic homages to loss itself stuck a universal chord in the reading
audience.

Unlike today's publishing world, saturated with memoirs and
autobiography, in Poe's time personal thoughts were usually limited
to words coming from characters in works of fiction, much as it was
when Shakespeare wrote. Poe's fascination with the transience and
dreamlike nature of life, and the nature of sanity itself, came through
often in his short fictions and poetry, in phrases such as:

- *All that we see or seem is but a dream within a dream.*
- *I became insane, with long intervals of horrible sanity.*
- *It is by no means an irrational fancy that, in a future existence, we shall look upon what we think our present existence, as a dream.*
- *Science has not yet taught us if madness is or is not the sublimity of the intelligence.*
- *The boundaries which divide Life from Death are at best shadowy and vague. Who shall say where the one ends, and where the other begins?*
- *They who dream by day are cognizant of many things which escape those who dream only by night.*
- *All Created things are but the thoughts of God.*

The last quote directly echoes Hinduism, the contemporary theosophies of people like Alan Watts and Ken Wilbur, and the so-called New Age movement. It reflects the hidden Poe, rarely discussed or written about. There is more than sufficient evidence to suggest that Poe's dark periods were marked by at least transient depersonalization, even if they lasted no longer than a bad hangover. The stage for dissociation and anxiety was set early in the form of loss, a loveless childhood, and the trauma of death of yet another loved one always lurking.

Neuroses, anxiety, dissociative fugues, and doppelgangers were portrayed in Poe's stories and poems; "The Tell-Tale Heart," "The Cask of Amontillado," "Berenice," and "William Wilson" are prime examples. Yet of all the works he created as a magazine editor, literary critic, poet and storyteller, the piece he was most proud of remains rather obscure. It was a lengthy essay entitled "Eureka."

Written in 1848, late in Poe's life, Eureka is "An Essay on the Material and Spiritual Universe." Poe prefaces the work by asking his readers that the piece be judged as a poem only, after his death, likely in the knowledge that many would think he had become either sacrilegious or had finally gone insane.

Eureka was based on a lecture Poe had given a year earlier to a confused and unreceptive audience. When it appeared in book version in 1848, most critics thought that his precarious mental condition had finally taken a turn for the worst. Others, who vaguely grasped his meaning, felt that it was either a transcendental work or one mocking the transcendentalists.* Poe was openly critical of transcendentalism, calling it "incoherent mysticism." The fact that Eureka was decidedly more mystical than the bulk of what the transcendental writers produced stymied many critics.

In the essay, without any hard scientific evidence, Poe proposes what we have now come to call the Big Bang Theory. He argues that the universe emerged from one "primordial particle" that God willed into being. He postulates that "space and duration {time} are one," and stresses that with light "there is a continuous outpouring of ray-streams, and with a force which we have at least no right to suppose varies at all." The language is different, but reflects Einstein's theories nearly three decades before the author of the Theory of Relativity was born.

Poe's distant cousin and biographer Harry Lee Poe also notes the author's observations on the true nature of the self:

"In the conclusion of Eureka, Poe drew another startling conclusion: that in creating the primordial particle and dividing it throughout what became the universe, God dispersed himself throughout the whole and that what we call his creatures are actually 'infinite individualizations of Himself. By multiplying himself through division, God maximized his experience of happiness, but also subjected himself to pain.

"In the end," Harry Poe writes, "Poe argued that the force of 'Attraction' will draw all the universe back into the 'One.' Poe reached a pantheistic conclusion in which all is God and all individual identity becomes lost in the One."

In recent years, Poe scholars have taken a closer look at some of the odd behavior the poet exhibited even during periods in which he never touched a drop of liquor. After the death of his young bride,

---

* Transcendentalists were a group of New England writers who believed in an ideal spiritual state that transcends the physical and empirical and is realized through an individual's intuitions, rather than doctrine.

Virginia Clemm, Poe experienced periods of delirium that could not be attributed to drink or drugs. He was never quite the same after her death; he was known to have a deteriorating heart, but it is likely that something that would have affected his personality, perceptions, and writing was at work—a brain tumor. When the author's gravesite was moved in 1875, part of the coffin fell off. Witnesses claim to have seen "Poe's brain." But forensic scientists have noted that the brain itself deteriorates rapidly; a calcified tumor would have remained, giving the appearance of a brain remnant.

If the tumor theory is true, changes in Poe's brain may account for his fits of incoherence. They may also explain his later thoughts about existence; views that are shared by many for whom loss of the self and Oneness with the universe emanate from changes in the brain.

Being and Nothingness

Perhaps the most chilling and accurate depiction of pure depersonalization is found in Jean Paul Sartre's first novel, *Nausea*. For many people in the DPD community it has become scriptural in importance. Sartre was greatly influenced by the German philosopher Martin Heidegger's works on being. This raises the question of whether *Nausea* is autobiographical, or a brilliant interpretation of Heidegger's "primordial dread" and "the Nothing nothings." Either way, *Nausea* is the most compelling confrontation with the Void in literature to date.

Princeton University lecturer Russell Nieli has written compellingly on the correlation between the works of William James, Heidegger, and Sartre and clinical Depersonalization Disorder. In his 1987 book on philosopher Ludwig Wittgenstein, he explores how Heidegger, in a famous lecture entitled "Was ist Metaphysik?," expresses the derealization-depersonalization experience in terms of "dread" and "the Nothing." Dread is the beginning of the alienation process, the attentional disengagement from both self and world (ego and environment), and the gradual slipping away of both self and world into an all-encompassing mood of anxious indifference.

Heidegger describes it as "unhomelike-and-uncanny" (*unheimlich*).

Heidegger's description of "The Nothing" becomes a little more obtuse to the layperson, particularly when translated literally from the German. Nieli's explanation is simpler, but still difficult to fully grasp:

"The radical alienation experience (derealization-depersonalization) involves "a drawing, sinking, and slipping away of the world (derealization) from psyche (*Dasein*), which, in its desperate efforts to re-engage reality, can find nothing to hold on to… Since the ego has been annihilated (nothinged), it makes no sense to speak of a 'you' or a 'me' to which all has become alien, for such would presuppose the self and self-consciousness, which no longer exists. As we ourselves slip away and the whole world becomes unhomelike-and-uncanny (derealized, alien, estranged), we attempt, in our forlornness and dread, to maintain contact with some kind of reality through compulsive, involuntary talk."

Part of the problem in completely understanding Heidegger's ideas, Nieli notes, lies in translation. Another problem stems from Heidegger's tendency to lump the milder forms of depersonalization experience, such as "indifference," (emotional numbing) with "primordial dread" (destruction of the Ego). "But that he is alluding in his treatment of the Nothing to the derealization-depersonalization-type of experience, there seems little cause for doubt," Nieli concludes. The topic itself, if not Heidegger's way of relaying it, so impressed Jean Paul Sartre that it served as the inspiration for the latter's *Being and Nothingness*, and his first and greatest novel, *Nausea*.

Unlike Amiel's *Journal Intime*, Sartre's 1935 novel is not a written recording of feelings and thoughts, but thoughts as they happen. It is not a clinical recollection, but the voice of depersonalization unfolding second by second in an individual's consciousness.

For *Nausea's* narrator, Antoine Roquentin, mundane daily life in a provincial town of Bouville (Mudville) seems unreal, or *too* real, and consequently, nauseating. Without medical terminology at hand, Roquentin describes his unpleasant sensations as nausea, or "the filth."

"Things are bad!" he writes at one juncture. "Things are very bad: I have it, the filth, the Nausea. And this time it is new: it caught me in a café. Until now, cafés were my only refuge because they were full of people and well lighted: now there won't even be that anymore"[7]

It is surprising that out of all the clinical case studies depicting first-person accounts of depersonalization and derealization, the articulation of Sartre's character Roquentin remains unnoticed. Perhaps *Nausea* has largely been ignored in medical literature because it is a work of fiction. Or maybe Sartre is perceived as purely philosophic, hence unscientific. Yet some philosophical writers have recognized "the filth" as *exactly* what it is.

In commenting on *Nausea*, Nieli again writes: "While a mood of estrangement—of aloneness in one's own private world, of being cut off from the surrounding social and physical work—permeates the whole novel, what is designated by the term Nausea (and what is easily recognizable as acute attacks of the derealization-depersonalization experience) occur at definite, peak instances. A gradual buildup in the feeling of estrangement precedes each attack[8]:

I must finally realize that I am subject to these sudden transformations. The thing is that I rarely think: a crowd of small metamorphoses accumulate in me without my noticing it, and then, one fine day, a veritable revolution takes place."[9]

Roquentin's detachment and depersonalization grows in intensity as the book builds to a climax. After suffering acute anxiety in a trolley, he finds himself in a park where his perceptions finally shift completely, in view of an ancient chestnut tree with enormous, gnarly roots:

I drop onto a bench between great black tree trunks, between the black, knotty hands reaching towards the sky. A tree scrapes at the earth under my feet with a black nail. I would so like to let myself go, forget myself, sleep. But I can't, I'm suffocating: existence penetrates me everywhere, through the eyes, the nose, the mouth...

And suddenly, suddenly, the view is torn away, I have understood,

I have seen.[9]

Analyzing what has happened, he writes:

I can't say I feel relieved or satisfied; just the opposite, I am crushed. Only my goal is reached: I know what I wanted to know; I have understood all that has happened to me since January. The Nausea has not left me and I don't believe it will leave me soon; but I no longer have to bear it, it is no longer an illness or a passing fit: it is I...

... in the park just now. The roots of the chestnut tree were sunk in the ground just under my bench. I couldn't remember it was a root any more. The words had vanished, and with them the significance of things... I was sitting, stooping forward, head bowed, alone in front of this black, knotty mass, entirely beastly, which frightened me. Then I had this vision.

It left me breathless. Never, until these last few days, had I understood the meaning of "existence..."

The ultimate realization that existence is only in the moment, that everything else past or present or connected to a name is an illusion. Things and names are "in the way."

For both Amiel and Roquentin, feeling unreal has become a glimpse into a different, and in their eyes, a *true* reality—timeless and free of our subjectivity—seen with the filter of the ego removed. Amiel's perception, and Poe's late in life, includes a sense of Oneness, spiritual awakening, Roquentin's does not. But unlike Amiel, Roquentin refuses to let this glimpse behind the façade of life lock him in limbo, stuck between two worlds. Instead, he sees complete freedom and a call to action. By the end of *Nausea,* his manner of action becomes clear. He decides to devote his life to writing. Clearly, Sartre himself followed that path, not by creating an introspective diary, but rather by giving voice to a philosophy.

Sartre determines that it is a conscious choice to live one's life "authentically" and in a unified fashion, or not—this is the fundamental freedom of our lives. Highly suggestive of today's Acceptance and Commitment Therapy, Roquentin decides to live *through* the filth, now having seen all it can show him. He could have interpreted it as a spiritual awakening, but he chose not too. It is something that simply *IS,* that's all. And writing becomes the one thing he knows he actually can take charge of—his conscious actions.

The Lost Samurai

Another 20th-century writer represents a curious anomaly from what usually plays out for people for whom depersonalization represents either a point of departure or a major life change.

On November 25, 1970, Yukio Mishima, the most famous writer of post-war Japan, took over an Army general's office with a small band of followers. After his cohorts tied the general to a chair, Mishima stepped outside to a balcony to present his demands. The soldiers were not receptive to his rants glorifying the emperor and calling on them to return to the ancient Samurai ways. They responded with obscenities and insults, laughing at this famous toy soldier who had finally gone insane.

Mishima cut short his speech, and returned inside. In classic samurai style, he disrobed, sat on the floor and began the ritual of seppuku. Using an ancient short sword, he proceeded to cut open his lower stomach. He had intended to write the traditional death poem, but the pain was too great. He cut across his gut, awaiting the moment when his *kaishakunin* (his second) would slice off his head. The young man assigned this task failed to complete the job cleanly. Another devotee took the sword and decapitated Mishima in one stroke. This, psychologists have said, was the ultimate narcissistic act. He had lived his entire life for this final moment. He was 45 years old.

Mishima was an enigmatic, master storyteller, whose existential novels captured the attention of the west, and fostered adulation in his native land, through what became known as the Cult of Mishima. He is noteworthy here because his early childhood may well have sewn the seeds of depersonalization, not unlike that portrayed by Jean Paul Sartre. The difference is, Sartre, or his character Roquentin, transcended "the Filth" by moving forward into a life of writing and creating a vast philosophical library initiated by his early feelings of non-existence. This was certainly Mishima's earliest objective, quickly achieved through his fiction and Noh plays. But for his complex personality, writing proved to be insufficient to satisfy a greater demand for self-realization. The evolution of Mishima's *self* proved to be rooted in self-deception and fantasy.

Born in 1925 with ties to an ancient Samurai family, Mishima was a sickly child who spent his early years held in virtual isolation by a domineering grandmother often sick with neuralgia. Her over-protectiveness and complete control over his life, often against his parents' better judgment, worked against his physical development and contributed to the creation of an imaginative, fantasy-driven mental life. She was, in essence, a chronically ill woman who kept the child as her personal pet.

From an early age Mishima exhibited exceptional intelligence and writing talent. But when he finally returned to his parents, his father forbade him to write so he did so in secret. The imaginary life he created while with his grandmother translated into forbidden written tales. He was a stranger to his own family, and his awakening homosexuality alienated him from the norms of traditional Japanese society.

As Mishima blossomed into a popular and acclaimed writer in both the east and west after World War II, he lived a conventional life on the surface by marrying and living in a handsome western style house in Tokyo. Like Andre Gide, to whom he was sometimes compared, Mishima lived a double life—one of conventional success and propriety, the other indulging a growing narcissism and sado-masochistic inclinations.

Like Poe and other writers, Mishima idealized beauty in all forms. He was disgusted by the sickliness of his grandmother, as well as the pale, slump-shouldered stereotype traditionally afforded intellectuals and writers. So he sought to create beauty on his own, not only in writing but also through a rigorous program of body-building and mastery of Kendo, the ancient Japanese martial art.

As his muscles developed, Mishima became more of a Renaissance man, writing plays, acting in gangster movies, and posing in semi-nude photo books such as *Torture by Roses.* In one photo he recreated the famous image of Saint Sebastian, bound to a tree and pieced by arrows. (As Mishima recounts in *Confessions of a Mask,* it was a picture of Guido Reni's original painting that inspired his first ejaculation.)

Mishima's exhibitionism puzzled many of his Japanese followers, but it did not diminish his popularity. Through it all, he maintained a steady obsession with the purity and beauty of the ancient samurai code. Ritual suicide was part of that code and so fascinated Mishima that he even starred in a film in which his role foreshadowed his own painful demise in chilling detail.

Ultimately, the duality of Mishima's life remains intriguing. He wrote every day and produced novels of sensitivity and insight that while distinctly Japanese, proved compelling and popular to a worldwide audience. He dressed like a banker, lectured around the world and lived with his wife in an elegant western-style house. At the same time, he became a narcissistic, yet disciplined body builder well known in the homosexual underground. He proudly displayed his physique, which he viewed as such an anomaly for an intellectual, in suggestive photo layouts and films.

Having predetermined his ultimate fate within his private fantasy world, Mishima formed a private Army with its own uniforms, field exercises, and ill-conceived plans of returning Japan to the old, purely Japanese way of life. Deep inside, he certainly knew it would never work. But it was the perfect device for achieving what he was destined to achieve, the thing he felt was most beautiful of all—a Samurai death.

Critic Hisaaki Yamanouchi of the University of Cambridge has speculated on the real reasons for Mishima's ritual suicide, and why such a gifted and logical intellect would follow a life path that seemed like nothing less than madness. In a review of John Nathan's 1974 biography, Yamanouchi writes:

"It is evident from Nathan's detailed analysis that Mishima suffered invariably from alienation from the external world. Partly, the external world was felt to be unreal and partly, he felt that his own existence was unreal. Mishima's strong personality enabled him to put up with life while denying its significance. Such a mode of life involved the ultimate paradox that one could attain the highest sense of being alive by replacing life with death. In modern psychological terms, the state that Mishima suffered was one of 'unreality' feeling, consisting of either 'derealization' or 'depersonalization.'"[10]

I find it interesting that a literary critic and academic like Yamanouchi can clearly identify depersonalization and its possible ramifications while so many doctors have hardly even recognized its existence. In Mishima's instance, I think his diagnosis is probably on track. Mishima endured his feelings of unreality through escape into his writing, his dual private lives, and ultimately into the Void itself. And yet, his fiction may well have been the one place in his life wherein "reality testing" remained in tact.

The final pages of his longest work, a four-volume tetralogy entitled *The Sea of Fertility*, were delivered to the publisher on the day of his death. Considered his masterpiece, the story follows the life of Shigekuni Honda from 1912 to 1975. Honda begins as a law student in the first book, *Spring Snow*, and winds up a wealthy, retired judge in the last, *The Decay of the Angel*. Each of the novels depicts what Honda comes to believe are successive reincarnations of his school friend Kiyoaki, introduced in the first book. At the end of the work, it all proves to have been an unfounded illusion. Honda questions not only reincarnation, but also whether or not his childhood friend ever existed, and ultimately, whether *he* exists.

According to biographer Henry Scott-Stokes: "Honda, it seems, has entered Nirvana, or extinction, in Buddhist terms—a cold and comfortless place "that had no memories," a place akin to the surface of the moon." This is the ironic ending of the ironically titled *Sea of Fertility...*"

It was not early depersonalization that killed Mishima. It merely demanded that he recreate himself. When he did, his personality took two paths, both of which were guided by fantasy. In fiction, the quest for beauty resulted in lasting works of art; in life it led to narcissism and self-destruction because of a mythology created in his own mind.

The Spiritual Perspective

Everyone is likely to encounter depersonalization at some point in life. In its chronic form, however, DPD surfaces as the Achilles heel of your existence as a human being, invalidating any previous contexts in which to ground yourself in the scheme of things. The eternal mysteries have always been there; how you perceive them, and worry about them is what makes the difference. It's not that your insignificance in the universe is anything new, it's the fact that it is so apparent and so frightening that it cuts you off from those around you. When the fear elicited by realizations such as these becomes intense or chronic, medicine offers a diagnosis of anxiety, or panic disorder. Philosophers refer to an existential crisis. The traditions of Yoga refer to it all as something else—Kundalini. According to Yogi Sanat Kumar:

"The Kundalini syndrome's main symptom is a progressive deconstruction of the mind in which the personality gets stripped in an extremely painful way over a number of months, or years in some cases. Sometimes the signs could be revealed to the subject in a tremendously forceful way in which the individual can suffer a very strong detonation at the foundations of being. Here, the ego could be painfully annihilated, bringing an instantaneous enlightenment experience that will end in pure and continuous bliss which comes after this cataclysm."[11]

Depersonalized westerners can concur with most of the description, *above*, but wonder, where is the bliss? Eastern tradition suggests that without a guide or guru leading one through this experience, the results can be anything but blissful.

One example often cited is that of the philosopher Friedrich Nietzsche. When he was 45 years of age, after years of prolific writing on the death of God, the "Ubermensch," "Will to Power" and other theories for which he is remembered, Nietzsche became seriously mentally ill. Doctors then, and most today, attributed his decline to tertiary syphilis. Others have more recently suggested frontal temporal dementia.

On the other hand, 20th-century philosophers René Girard and Georges Bataille both believed that the foundation of Nietzsche's breakdown had its roots in depersonalization, exhibited by his "modern way of thinking" and deep contemplative periods in which he looked absent minded.

Yogi Kumar, who has studied Yoga and meditation worldwide for more than 20 years, says this about Nietzsche: "What I believe by studying his symptoms and the way his writings evolved is that he had a blasting experience of Kundalini evolution in his body that caused an abrupt energy onset too early for his unprepared nervous system and brain to handle. This contributed to the development of a condition of ego and mental collapse, triggered by a major depersonalization experience."

"If you stare long enough into the abyss, the abyss stares back at you." Nietzsche said. Ultimately, the abyss swallowed him whole. But based on what is known today, it's safe to say that while he almost certainly experienced depersonalization, it was more than likely that the advanced syphilis took him into hellish realms beyond the subject at hand.

Different religions throughout time have fostered different attitudes toward the individual self. Eastern philosophies such as Buddhism have, contrary to popular opinion, not emphasized that there is no self, but rather that the elements that come together to form what we perceive as a self are in fact transient illusions. The very thing that depersonalization inflicts, the feeling that the self is an illusion, works to validate what Buddhism tries to impart to those who, through their egos, see themselves as real and impenetrable.

The Judeo-Christian tradition is today, largely based in the normal, expected self that makes decisions through free will. Despite many histories of mystical experiences in the early church, interpretation of the Bible from the pulpit is predicated on a sane and normal congregation. In this sense, intense no-self or mystical experiences are usually viewed as mental illnesses. Despite the advent of megachurches and the somewhat formulaic path to eternal salvation for both Catholics and Protestants, Christian mystics have written of depersonalization and the loss of the self since the earliest days of the church. In the 1860s, the writings of an obscure Jesuit priest, Jean-Pierre de Caussade were published, more than a century after they were written. (He would certainly have been tried for heresy during his lifetime.) Commenting on the no-self experience, he wrote in 1731: "Often indeed God places certain souls in this state, which is called emptiness of the spirit or of the intelligence; it is also called: being in nothingness (*etre dans le rien*). This annihilation of our own spirit disposes wonderfully to receive that of Jesus Christ. This mystical death of the operations of our own activity renders our soul apt for the reception of divine operations."[12]

More recently, Bernadette Roberts' *The Experience of No-Self* reflects this type of being, and hearkens to Amiel's desire to be an "empty vessel" filled with the presence of God. Roberts' writing describes her personal struggle with mysterious moments of deep, silent "stillness" that from early childhood she interpreted as the presence of God. To explore the source of this stillness, she entered a convent. But whenever she meditated in an effort to recapture it, she felt herself losing her identity, and suffered intense fear because of it. Ultimately her "self" completely disappeared.

The experiences described by Roberts and other "Christian Contemplatives" are akin to those recounted in many cultures throughout history. The problem is that the Christian tradition provides no systematized method for achieving this enlightened state. Often, it seems to appear spontaneously, and certainly could be interpreted as depersonalization and nothing more. Also, when a certain Oneness with God or the Cosmos has been achieved, the language with which to describe it is completely inaccessible. While many of Christ's more cryptic phrases, i.e. "Before Abraham was, I *am*," seem to hint at the more mystical aspects of Christianity, the church itself has evolved through dogma aimed at the individual thinking, decision-making heart.

Buddhism, however, provides an organized road map to "enlightenment," with depersonalization serving as one of the first steps of the journey. This first stage, called Sotāpanna, involves the freeing of certain of the mind's "fetters," namely one's view of identity, skepticism, and clinging to rites and rituals. Of these, the first involves the realization that the self exists only through the five aggregates or *skandas*—form, feelings, perceptions, thoughts, and consciousness. Their interaction creates the *illusion* of self. They do not actually make up the self, Buddhism teaches. In the second stage, one has eliminated the three fetters of Sotāpanna and works towards the elimination of sensuous craving and ill will. The process continues through additional stages with the goal of reaching Nirvana, or freedom from suffering (dukkha). In Hindu philosophy, this is a union with the Supreme Being through *Moksha*—liberation from the suffering inherent to the cycle of birth, life, and death.

There are other viewpoints, however, in terms of depersonalization and reincarnation. Some visitors to the depersonalization websites have referenced a "karmic dictionary" and a website *healpastlives.com* which echoes the beliefs of holistic counselor Ellen Mogensen:

"In Depersonalization Disorder, an advanced soul incarnates into physical body where the mental component of the inner energy bodies is 'detached' from all the other bodies. This enables the advanced soul to break down disempowering thought patterns 'inherited' from many past lifetimes.

Those who contract Depersonalization Disorder are very old souls with strong mental energies, Mogensen writes. These energies are resistant to the normal evolutionary processes of karma and reincarnation. As a result, these souls will reincarnate time and again only to run into the same blocks to their spiritual progress thrown up by their powerful minds. Contracting this disorder becomes a last ditch effort by the old souls to overcome their mental blocks. So they agree to being largely detached from their mental body in the lifetime of depersonalization to effect real spiritual change and growth. The major spiritual problem of most who are afflicted with Depersonalization Disorder is a lack of patience with the process and flow of life. This impatience arises from many past incarnations where they were extremely successful at manipulating the universe with the power of their minds.

"Depersonalization Disorder is usually a life sentence," Mogensen adds. "The older the soul, the stronger their mind, the more they cling to their 'identity' of the 'mind as Self,' the longer it will take to overcome the mental/body imbalance that this disorder was designed to correct. Often it will take several lifetimes to get the mind to accept its proper role in the individual's spiritual development. Once the mind is realigned with the rest of the body in a future incarnation, the individual will emerge stronger for the experience — their heart and their intuition will have finally 'caught up' to where their mind has already evolved.

"As it says in the Kabala: 'I have a body and I am more than my body. I have emotions and I am more than my emotions. I have a mind and I am more than my mind. I am a center of pure consciousness and energy.' Until those with Depersonalization Disorder learn to move past their minds, they will never be free of this disease. This is extremely difficult for the depersonalized individual to do because their personal sense of identity is so deeply ingrained with their mind that their own internal resistance to this process is tremendous and overwhelming," Mogensen says. But old souls are usually exceptionally good at developing solutions to their problems. They must 'feel' their way through their healing process by relying more on heart-centered feelings, inner knowingness, and spiritual guidance. "The depersonalized individual must trust that they can find what they need without relying on their strong mind."

A Western Perspective

People with Depersonalization Disorder usually know little about eastern religions and are likely to have little use for "old soul" theories of reincarnation. Still, if their private investigations take them beyond psychology and brain chemistry, they often try to learn what they can about Buddhism or Hinduism. This sometimes leads to further confusion and an increased desire to get back to whatever western beliefs they leaned toward earlier. Sometimes, however, even a person well-versed in eastern philosophy may find themselves depersonalized in a way that seems to be anything but part of the road to enlightenment. Such a case was well documented by Suzanne Segal in her book *Collision with the Infinite,* published in 1996.

As a young girl, Segal sometimes would repeat her own name in her head over and over. Eventually, "a threshold was crossed and the identity, as that name, broke like a ship released suddenly from its mooring to float untethered on the ocean waves," she writes. "Vastness appeared...There was no person to whom that name referred, no identity as that name. No one." Then came fear, eventually followed by a return to normalcy. But the compulsion to do the same thing once again always returned.

Many people with DPD have cited similar early life incidents. They may involve repeating words until they lose their meaning, or looking intently in the mirror until an overwhelming sense of strangeness emerges. Usually these episodes pass, are forgotten, and remain in the realm of youthful mind games.

Perhaps because she was a product of her time (the 1960s and 70s), the young Suzanne Segal, along with several of her closest friends, developed an interest in Transcendental Meditation (TM). After several months of regular meditation at a retreat she found herself awed by "profound" experiences:

"The experience of transcending had been explained to me variously as a gap in thoughts where time seems to be suspended; a time of quietness when the mantra disappears; and the "source of thought," whatever that might mean. Never had I heard a description that matched what occurred in my delighted mind as I was gripped by a tremendous power, like a huge magnet, that pulled me into a tunnel of light at infinite speed. At the same time, the tunnel itself expanded outwards at infinite speed with a tumultuous roar that rose to an ear-splitting crescendo as the infinity exploded in light. The moment of explosion marked the crossing of a threshold. In an increment of time too small to be measured, the blaze of some

invisible inferno engulfed everything, turning all phenomena inside out, exposing the underside of all creation—emptiness.

"Nearly three hours after I had begun meditating the first morning of the retreat, I opened my eyes and rose from my cushion as if I were drunk, walking without the sensation of possessing a body. The world no longer looked the same; solid matter had been transformed into the luminous transparency of silence."[13]

Clearly parallels can be drawn between Segal's experience in deep meditation and Dostoyevsky's auras, which preceded his seizures. One major difference is that hers was followed by exhaustion and fear, while his led up to an anticipated attack.

Wondering if all of this was normal in meditation, Segal approached one of the retreat leaders who told her to simply "Enjoy the bliss."

Segal's gurus told her that true enlightenment would come after six to eight years of meditation. Her plans to follow that path were thwarted, however, when, while continuing her TM studies in Europe, she became disillusioned with the organization's autocratic rule and inflexibility. Blissful leaders did not make for an enterprise free of conflict or politics, it seemed.

She moved to northern California, which somehow seems appropriate, and studied at the University of California-Berkeley. After two years she gained a degree in English literature. Then she moved to Paris where she married and gave birth to a daughter. Seemingly from nowhere, the event that would forever change her life took place.

As she waited in line to get on a bus, she suddenly felt her ears pop and was at once "enclosed in a kind of bubble" which cut her off from the rest of the scene and left her acting and moving in the most mechanical way. In *Collision*, she describes that moment in detail:

"I lifted my right foot to step up into the bus and collided head-on with an invisible force that entered my awareness like a silently exploding stick of dynamite, blowing the door of my usual consciousness open and off its hinges, splitting me in two. In the gaping space that appeared, what I had previously called "me" was forcefully pushed out of its usual location inside me into a new location that was approximately a foot behind and to the left of my head. 'I' was now behind my body looking out at the world without using the body's eyes."

Walking home from that bus ride, she felt like a "cloud of awareness" was following her body. The cloud was a "witness" located behind her and completely separate from body, mind, and emotions. The witness was constant and so was fear, the fear of complete physical dissolution. The next morning, when nothing had changed, she wondered if she was going insane, and if she would ever be herself again.

What Segal refers to as the "witnessing" continued for months, and her only relief came in sleep into which she "plunged for as long and as often as possible." She explains, "In sleep, the mind finally stopped pumping out its unceasing litany of terror, and the witness was left to witness an unconscious mind."

It occurred to her that this might be some kind of "cosmic consciousness," something her guru had described to her as the first stage of "awakened awareness." But it seemed impossible to her that this hellish realm could have anything to do with the enlightenment she had been seeking.

After months of the presence of this mystifying witness, it disappeared, Segal writes, leaving her in a new state that was far more baffling, and consequently more terrifying, than the experience of the preceding months. "The disappearance of the witness meant the disappearance of the last vestiges of the experience of personal identity. The witness had at least held a location for a 'me,' albeit a distant one. In the dissolution of the witness, there was literally no more experience of a 'me' at all. The experience of personal identity switched off and was never to appear again."

Although internally Segal knew that she had changed radically, no one else noticed. She functioned as smoothly as ever, "as if there were an unseen doer who acted perfectly." She even managed to earn a doctorate in psychology in the years to follow. And yet, she writes, "The oddest moments occurred when any reference was made to my name. If I had to write it on a check or sign it on a letter, I would stare at the letters on the paper and the mind would drown in perplexity. The name referred to no one. There was no Suzanne Segal anymore; perhaps there never had been."

She consulted psychiatrists in an attempt to understand what had happened to her. Some diagnosed her with Depersonalization Disorder. Others had no clear explanation. As she lived in this mysterious state day after day, she became increasingly filled with fear. "Everything seemed to be dissolving right in front of my eyes, constantly. Emptiness was everywhere, seeping through the pores of every face I gazed upon, flowing through the crevices of seemingly solid objects. The body, mind, speech, thoughts, and emotions were all empty; they had no ownership, no person behind them. I was utterly bereft of all my previous notions of reality."

In time, Segal recalls episodes of derealization. "Everything seemed more fluid," she writes. "The mountains, trees, rocks, birds, sky, were all losing their differences. As I gazed about, what I saw first was how they were one; then, as a second wave of perception, I saw the distinctions. From that day forth I have had the constant experience of both moving through and being made of the 'substance' of everything."

After Segal's *Collision with the Infinite* was published, she received numerous congratulations from spiritual teachers around the world. The medical community paid little attention to the book or the phenomena she so eloquently described.

It was, for a time, a unique Western account of what could either be interpreted as depersonalization with a happy ending, or one of those rare instances wherein a person with a predisposition to depersonalization or enlightenment actually achieves the latter. But Suzanne's Segal's story did not end with her book, and what followed is rarely commented upon.

As noted, during her early investigations into her strange sensations, Segal had been diagnosed with Depersonalization Disorder. But there were no clear treatments, and few answers.

The enlightened state of mind did not last. The fear and anxiety she thought she had left behind reappeared with renewed intensity. She continued meeting with fellow therapists and, in time, revealed that she had suffered from a long history of migraine headaches. She also began to recover memories of abuse during her childhood. As a psychologist, she was well tutored in a possible ramification of childhood abuse—dissociation. Once again, Segal began to perceive things differently, this time from the psychological viewpoint rather than that of transcendent spirituality. In the end, there was not much time left to debate the matter. As her physical and mental capabilities began to decline rather mysteriously and rapidly, doctors found that she was suffering from a malignant brain tumor. She was also experiencing repeats of the initial "bus hit" as she called it, chronic depersonalization, and fear.

In an almost prophetic introduction to her book, knowing the way psychologists think, she issued a caveat that seems to validate the spiritual nature of her experience, despite the things that were uncovered near the end:

"Do not make the mistake of reading the story of Suzanne Segal searching for the childhood events that "caused" the subsequent dropping away of self. There is no linear causality here. The powerful influences of Western psychology in our culture have led many to believe that the roots of all human experience lie in early childhood and that psychological theories can account for any point on the continuum. The events of our past tell us about the personal, not the impersonal; about the individual self, not the Universal Self. It is essential that this story be read with a spacious awareness that eschews reductionist categorization or the psychological tendency to pathologize."[14]

She died in the spring of 1998 as a result of the tumor.

God in the Brain

Recent brain research has shed some light on the mechanisms involved in depersonalization. At the same time, a dedicated group of scientists have been exploring the internal mechanics of spirituality and "enlightenment." Interestingly, the areas of the brain involved are quite often the same.

For centuries people around the world have ingested peyote, mushrooms, or other substances for the purpose of gaining spiritual enlightenment, if only for a while. The substances often are part of religious rites that require a "cleansing of the doors of perception," in the words of William Blake. In doing so, "all things appear as they are, infinite."

This gives credence to the thought that our brains are somehow designed to keep out spiritual mysteries, and require some cleansing agent to open the pathways to a higher consciousness. Writer Aldous Huxley, whose *Brave New World* and *Island* played upon such themes, explored the concept of a reductive mind in his works on psychedelics: *The Doors of Perception* (1954), *Heaven and Hell* (1956), and *Moksha* (1962). Huxley rekindles a theory that the functions of the brain, nervous system, and sense organs are primarily eliminative, rather than productive. In other words, instead of absorbing all information like a sponge, they are designed to keep information that is not of practical use *out*, for the sake of survival.

In a way, this is merely a form of sensory gating—information comes in from the senses and is tagged against a template of stored memories. When this gating is disrupted or slowed down, familiar things may seem foreign or strange. But Huxley goes further, contending that each person is at each moment capable of remembering all that has ever happened to him and of perceiving everything that is happening everywhere in the universe. The function of the brain and nervous system is to protect us from being overwhelmed and confused by this mass of largely useless and irrelevant knowledge. According to such a theory, each one of us is potentially what Huxley calls "Mind at Large."

However, to make biological survival possible, "mind at large" has to be funneled through the reducing valve of the brain and nervous system. "What comes out the other end is a measly trickle of the kind of consciousness which will help us to stay alive on the surface of this particular planet." Huxley's means of opening the doors of perception was first mescaline, then LSD. For him, these substances led to dissolution of the self, Oneness, and a kind of enlightenment reserved for those devoting decades to meditative practices.

"I was seeing what Adam had seen on the morning of his creation—the miracle, moment by moment of naked existence," he writes. "Reality was being experienced moment to moment by a blessed 'not-I.'"[15]

These experiences, highly spiritual in nature, correlated with chemical changes in Huxley's brain brought on by taking mescaline. Huxley's death, on November 22, 1963, was overshadowed by the assassination of John F. Kennedy. On his deathbed he asked his wife Laura to give him LSD, which she did. Apparently Huxley wanted to get a head start in his transition to the infinite with a substance he surely believed had already given him fleeting glimpses of it.

Huxley's interest in psychedelics raises questions about the areas of the brain that may serve as the receptors for spiritual experience. In recent years, a number of scientists have been able to provide some compelling insights.

In looking at the brain centers of spiritual activity, scientists are finding themselves going over some of the same territory their predecessors covered when investigating depersonalization, epilepsy, or memory functions decades earlier. Wilder Penfield, for example, wrote about epileptic patients experiencing strong feelings of depersonalization. The relationship between Temporal Lobe Epilepsy and DPD has long been established, and epileptic auras and "spiritual" sensations have been well documented.

Michael Persinger, a neuroscientist at Laurentian University in Sudbury, Ontario, has created a modified motorcycle helmet which he calls the "God helmet." It is designed to stimulate the right temporal lobe with weak magnetic fields, and create the illusion of God, or at least a sensed presence—a feeling that another being is in the room. Sometimes it works, sometimes it doesn't.

A more impressive account comes from Andrew Newberg, a neuroscientist at the University of Pennsylvania and author of several books, including *How God Changes Your Brain*. Newberg has been scanning the brains of spiritually minded people for more than a decade with fascinating results.

Newberg ran scans of a subject who is a medical doctor and Tibetan Buddhist who has meditated at least an hour a day for the past 40 years.

During a peak meditative experience marked by feelings of oneness with the universe and the elimination of time, the subject's frontal lobes lit up on the screen. This would happen during intense concentration, which, after all, is part of what's involved in meditation. What fascinated Newberg was that the subject's parietal lobes went dark.

"This is an area that normally takes our sensory information, tries to create for us a sense of ourselves and orient that self in the world," he explains. "When people lose their sense of self, feel a sense of oneness, a blurring of the boundary between self and other, we have found decreases in activity in that area."

The results were the same when Newberg scanned the brains of Buddhist monks, Franciscan nuns praying, and Sikhs chanting. They all felt the same oneness with the universe.

When it comes to the brain, Newberg says, spiritual experience is spiritual experience. "There is no Christian, there is no Jewish, there is no Muslim, it's just all one."[16]

Near Death Experiences (NDEs), which have made their way into the popular consciousness considerably more than Depersonalization Disorder, have also been the subject of laboratory experiments and skepticism. Such experiences can be replicated when test pilots are subjected to extreme G-forces in experimental settings. The test subjects mentally experience the bright lights at the end of the tunnel and many of the other phenomena recounted by people who claim to have been clinically dead for short periods. Some psychologists have cited these experiments as proof that NDEs are strictly a physiological phenomenon triggered by a diminished flow of oxygen to the brain. But the fact that an experience can be replicated, or that certain physiological changes correlate with such experiences, does not diminish their validity, in my opinion.

Say, for example, a mother is feeding her newborn for the first time. She feels love in a way she has never experienced. Nothing on earth can separate her from her child, physically or emotionally. These intense feelings correlate with specific activity in the brain. It is possible through probes, wires, and chemicals to replicate similar feelings. But try telling that to the mother. Tell her that her feelings don't mean anything because they can be duplicated in someone without a child, or erased from her brain completely through the right manipulations. If you are able to leave her hospital room without having your eyes ripped out, you have learned that there is considerably more to being human, more to love, and more to spirituality than can be discovered in the laboratory.

Ultimately, the Diagnostic and Statistical Manual of Mental Disorders (DSM-IV) has wisely, to resort to a colloquialism, "covered its ass," by clearly drawing the line between depersonalization disorder and "certain meditative states:"

Voluntarily induced experiences of depersonalization or derealization form part of the meditative and trance practices that are prevalent in many religions and cultures and should not be confused with Depersonalization Disorder.[17]

But is this accurate? Is Depersonalization a disorder that is purely Western in origins? Some would argue that a wild rose growing between the cracks in a sidewalk is somehow different than one sprayed, pruned, and cultivated in a horticulturist's yard. They are still both roses. And the experience of the vanished self is certainly analogous to this. Whatever its source—hours of meditation, smoking pot, or sitting by the fireplace—the terror, the emptiness, the Blow of the Void is essentially the same experience.

One visitor to *depersonalization.info* explained the difference in the simplest terms:

Depersonalization: No self, but self-perspective.

Buddha: No self-perspective.

Culture and Depersonalization

As early as the 1970s, psychologists James and Jane Cattell began to thoroughly examine modern society's effects on individual personality. Compared to today, and our ever-changing technologies, the 70s can often seem relatively quaint. But certain observations hold true.

"People working under centralized bureaucracies are routinized, humiliated, and thereby, dehumanized. The economic system prevents involvement and fosters detachment. It generates competition, creates feelings of inadequacy and fear of human obsolescence. It creates hostility and suspiciousness."[18]

Quoting the French writer Simone de Beauvoir, the Cattells agreed that the basic characteristic of the American value orientation is that the source of one's value and truth is perceived in things and not in oneself. Consequently, material comfort has a high place in the value hierarchy. Success puts its emphasis on rewards. "The success system, which William James has colorfully described as 'the bitch Goddess success,' is comprised of money, prestige, power, and security."[17]

Despite the relative truth in these statements, dehumanization by society or corporations, or selling one's soul by linking identity solely to a career does not necessarily lead to depersonalization. But what is noted in these observations has led us to where we are today. And where we are may prove to be fertile ground for increasing numbers of people to *feel* depersonalized, if not afflicted with the clinical disorder.

Let's say a visitor from an advanced civilization on Mars dropped in to observe American culture for a while, relying primarily on our media and mass communications for information. It wouldn't take long to surmise that our civilization is comprised of two classes — those who are celebrities and those who are not. One class lives in wealth, privilege, and self-indulgence; the other does society's work while vicariously living through the celebrity class — a class comprised, to some degree, of humans who play act at being someone that they are not.

I would point out to the Martians, however, that this is characteristic of humanity throughout its history. The Ancient Romans were held at bay with bread and circuses; gladiators were often the superstars of the day. Royal families ruled for centuries, inspiring both awe and contempt from more common people. Celebrity based on accomplishment, or nothing at all, is not new to our species, nor is it novel to our time. And, to our credit, our entertainments may be shallow, but they are not cruel, as they often were in antiquity. What is characteristic of the 21st century, however, is the exponentially expanding universe of technology and communications. Images, conversations, entertainment, practical and useless information bombards us nonstop from little machines that we cling to like newly evolved appendages. In time, computer chips will enter our heads to download languages, books, directions, or even in some way treat mental disorders. Our very speculations about the future of technology will be antiquated by newer technologies more advanced than what we had imagined. And there is the chance that somewhere along the line we will forget that we are born of this earth, and return to it. Somewhere, sometime we may forget what it was like to simply be human.

Curiously, one message sent to *depersonalization.info* from a "fully-wired" young person expressed concerns about these very issues:

"I just feel like I've lost my ego, or my idea of 'self.' It is hard for me to focus on tasks because nothing feels real anymore. I have no solid ground on which to base my life.

"I think this modern life is to blame. I feel detached from both the past, which seems distant and prehistoric in comparison to modern day life, and a future which is so tumultuous and unpredictable. The explosion of technology and the depersonalization that modern life brings makes me feel like a spectre floating over this world and not actively participating in it. Right now, I'm typing on a computer and interacting with millions of faceless, disembodied people. There is no precedent for this in human history. We exist in both a physical world and an electronic world and that juxtaposition creates such a disconnect with who we are as a person.

"We act differently around different groups of people, online, or over the phone. All of these mediums of communication and the personalities we adopt during our use of each one, cause division of our ego nature. This, in my opinion, is having profound implications for the human race. I think most of our psychological disorders arise because of our technology. Television, internet, music: they all lead to reinventing and dividing of the ego. This is continuously occurring, again and again and again. It will only increase as new technologies are introduced and we are further depersonalized, or should I say de-humanized?"

This one young woman's capacity for insight fills me with hope for the future. But how many are there like her? In the future, will such observations come only from the alienated, the depersonalized, while their peers gorge themselves on technology and electronic socializing?

Variations in Prevalence

Depersonalization, particularly when it relates to panic disorder, is largely a disorder of western culture in societies where "individualism" takes cultural precedence over "collectivism," according to Mauricio Sierra. The data backing up this statement was gathered through a systematic review of more than 350 published studies on panic disorder in which the frequency of depersonalization-derealization during panic attacks was reported.[19]

The study found that the prevalence of "depersonalization" was significantly lower in Asian and South American countries as compared with North America, Western Europe, Australia, and New Zealand. The frequency of "fear of losing control" was also significantly lower in non-Western countries.

According to Sierra, people from individualistic societies are more "self-absorbed" and more sensitive to threat, to feelings of alienation, and of not being in control. "In contrast, it would seem that a sense of belonging and shared values in relation to a cultural group provide individuals from collectivistic societies with a sense of 'implicit social support' whose protective effect to threat has been shown in the form of attenuated psychological and biological responses (blood pressure, heart rate, cortisol levels) to experimental stressful conditions."

On the surface, this study seems to make sense. Western culture is replete with people who are disenchanted, alienated, and dissatisfied because no one has noticed their individual worth or rewarded their accomplishments. But the matter of interpretation enters the picture as well. I suspect many people interviewed in the non-Western countries also experienced depersonalization and panic but simply interpreted it differently. In some cases, no doubt, they did not view it as pathological, but rather as just something inherent to their religious or cultural traditions. Time will tell whether a homogenization of world cultures contributes to a universal interpretation of similar experiences.

Still, all the *Facebook* friends on earth are not going to supply the 'implicit social support' of a flesh and blood community. Within western culture, studies have found the incidence of panic and depersonalization to be lower among church attendees. Perhaps surprisingly, the data indicates that this reduced vulnerability to panic or DPD stems not from the actual religious beliefs of the church, but rather the sense of community and support that it affords each individual within it.[23]

In the last analysis, no man or woman is an island. We are products of our respective cultures and we are social beings.

Some time ago, a young graduate student from the University of California at Riverside sent me a paper he had written about Depersonalization in Contemporary Culture. He systematically reviewed the thoughts of psychologists and philosophers who had given names to the various ages through which modern society has evolved. These included the "Age of Freud," the "Age of Anxiety," the "Age of Narcissism" and others leading up today. We are living in the "Age of Depersonalization," he suggests, based largely on the factors discussed above. He may be right. Others have suggested to me that depersonalization is the next and final stage of human evolution. The individual mind has nowhere else to go in the evolutionary process.

All of this may be prophetic, or sheer conjecture. I honestly don't know. What I do know is that depersonalization exists and it can be interpreted or dealt with any number of ways. How that is done may prove to be the most pivotal decision in any individual's life.

REFERENCES

1. Pascal, Blaise, (1995*) Pensees*, N.Y., Penguin Books, p 19
2. Weckowicz, T., (1970) John Wiley & Sons, Inc. N.Y., *Depersonalization, in Symptoms of Psycopathology, A Handbook.* p 151-163
3. Amiel, Frederic, (1906) *The Journal Intime of Henri-Frederic Amiel*, Macmillan Co., New York, p 84
4. Ibid. p 304
5. Ibid.
6. Nemiah, J.C., (1984) Dissociative disorders (hysterical neurosis, dissociative type). In *Comprehensive Textbook of Psychiatry*, ed 4, Kaplan, H.,I., Sadock, B., J., editors, Williams & Wilkins, Baltimore. **20**, p 1042.
7. Sartre, J.P., *Nausea*. (1964) New Directions Publishing Corp. N.Y. p 18
8. Nieli, Russell (1987) Wittgenstein: from mysticism to ordinary language. SUNY Press, Albany, N.Y. p 30
9. no.7. p 126
10. Yamanouchi, Hisaaki (1976) Cambridge University Press. *Modern Asian Studies*, 10, 5, p 632-637
11. website: yoganirvana.com
12. de Caussade, J.P. (1751) Excerpt from a letter to Sister Mary-Antoinnette de Mauhet.
13. Segal, S. (1996) *Collision With the Infinite*, San Diego, CA. Blue Dove Press, p. 12.
14. Ibid, p. xv
15. Huxley, Aldous, (1954) *The Doors of Perception*. N.Y. Harper and Row. P 23

16. Hagerty, Barbara Bradley (2019) Fingerprints of God. N.Y. Riverhead Books Div of Penguin Group (USA)
17. Simeon, D., Abugel, J. (2006) Feeling Unreal: Depersonalization Disorder and the Loss of the Self, Oxford U Press, N.Y. p 63-64
18. Ibid.
19. Sierra, M. (2009) Cambridge: Cambridge University Press. *Depersonalization: A New Look at a Neglected Syndrome*, p 108

Epilogue

Invisible things are the only realities.

—Edgar Allan Poe

When I was ten or eleven years old, I rode in the back seat of my parents' car on a Sunday night. As we drove over the Whitestone Bridge in New York, I stretched out on the slippery vinyl seat cover and looked at the back of my parents' heads. The street lamps raced by in succession, each lighting the car's blue interior for a moment until the next one followed. Midway across the bridge, something happened.

Everything I had ever known, or thought, or felt, or knew existed, completely disappeared with a single pure realization:

"There is no God."

I was immediately emptied and then filled by something that was a fear *beyond* fear. There was no God. And there was no "I."

I tried to pray for forgiveness for even imagining such a thought, but the prayer was not a prayer anymore than the thought was a thought. I became nothing *within* Nothing. Nothing that could ever be expressed or explained.

It only lasted a few minutes. And as I regained some small sense of being, I wanted to be at school taking a test, I wanted to confront some situation that formerly incurred dread, a test, or a bully, because that dread was part of the life I knew. And it was nothing compared to what I had just experienced.

Time passed, life resumed, and the incident was erased from my young mind. I didn't know what had happened, only that I never wanted it to happen again. And it didn't.

Then, one Friday evening when I was twelve years old, my father came home to our second-level apartment with tickets to a New York Mets game. I was an avid Mets fan. Like many New Yorkers, I respected the history of the Yankees, but preferred going to Shea

Stadium. The Mets' home park was new and modern and colorful, and it was adjacent to the New York World's Fair. It did not happen often, but whenever my father came home with those yellow or orange tickets sticking out of his shirt pocket it felt very much like Christmas. No single thing made me happier than going to a Mets game. And there could be no greater dream, no greater thrill in all of life than to one day actually catch a foul ball.

That night I laid down to sleep in my small room. In the darkness I debated whether or not I should do something. It was a selfish thing, a stupid thing, like asking someone else for their lunch simply because it looks more appetizing than your own.

Deciding that it was perhaps not a stupid or selfish thing, I began to pray in my mind. I quietly asked that if it were not too stupid or selfish, might I catch a foul ball at the game the next day. It was childish to ask for such a thing in a world such as ours beset by suffering and loss and heartache and hunger. But there was more. With a sincerity that is natural to a child but rarely accessible to adults I added that this request could be withdrawn if there was someone poorer in the stands, someone sadder, someone who really needed the ball more than I did. Let that person have the ball, I thought.

Through the years I have attempted to recapture the essence of this prayer, without much success. Our rituals and repetitions and anthropomorphication of the Infinite have cheapened the word *prayer*, rendering it meaningless, like all words, and most prayers:

My words fly up, my thoughts remain below: words without thoughts never to heaven go.

But on that particular summer night, the innocence and authenticity of childhood reconnected with something of which we are all part, something *right*.

The following day was perfect for baseball—sunny and warm, and my *ancient olfactory lobe* delighted in the stadium's aromas of hot dogs and popcorn, eliciting pure joy.

At 2:15 in the afternoon, in the third inning, Mets' shortstop Roy

McMillan hit a foul ball into the air. It quickly soared above my father and I, and began to descend in our direction. As always, I had brought my glove. I stood up as tall as I could stretch and stuck my gloved hand into the air as far as it would reach. When I brought it down, the ball was in it.

I looked in my glove and shook my head in amazement. My father's tanned and handsome face burst into a broad smile of excitement as he tousled my hair and shook my shoulders and emoted animated delight in a way I had never seen. A month doesn't pass without my thinking about that day in the sun.

Was it sheer coincidence? Perhaps. Was it the power of desire and will? Successful visualization? Or, as psychologists would likely suggest, was it merely an instance of magical thinking? I really don't know. Nor do I care what others might make of it.

Depersonalization has been called a dysfunction of the ego. Hence, many of us have lived, often for years, with a dysfunction of something that doesn't really exist. This realization is what makes it painful, even unbearable. It is an awakening, to another way of being, a true Self.

The writings of Luis Borges often relay the simple message that Everything and Nothing are but one and the same. I tend to agree. True reality reveals itself to us is many forms, often when least expected. Sometimes it is terrifying. Sometimes the forever *rightness* of it all is crystal clear. All one needs to do is recognize it when it comes, as a chestnut tree, a step onto a Paris bus, or, in my case, from the sky, not as a ball of fire, but a ball of cork and cowhide.

Index

CPSIA information can be obtained at www.ICGtesting.com
Printed in the USA
BVOW010807140911

271223BV00002B/13/P